Out of the Pits

OUT OF THE PITS

Traders and Technology
from Chicago to London

Caitlin Zaloom

The University of Chicago Press * Chicago and London

The University of Chicago Press, Chicago 60637
The University of Chicago Press, Ltd., London
© 2006 by The University of Chicago
All rights reserved. Published 2006
Paperback edition 2010
Printed in the United States of America

19 18 17 16 15 14 13 12 11 10   2 3 4 5 6

ISBN-13: 978-0-226-97813-0 (cloth)
ISBN-13: 978-0-226-97814-7 (paper)
ISBN-10: 0-226-97813-3 (cloth)
ISBN-10: 0-226-97814-1 (paper)

Figures 1.1, 1.3, and 1.4 are reprinted from the Chicago Board of Trade Records (CBOT neg. 111, 75-68 [1-1], 75-68 [1-9], Special Collections Department, University Library, University of Illinois at Chicago. Photos of the Chicago Board of Trade taken by permission of the Board of Trade of the City of Chicago, Inc. This publication has not been reviewed by the Board of Trade, and the Board of Trade makes no representation regarding the accuracy of this publication.

Portions of chapter 4 were previously published in "The Productive Life of Risk," *Cultural Anthropology* 19, no. 3 (2004): 365–91. Copyright © 2004 by the American Anthropological Association. Portions of chapter 6 were previously published in "The Discipline of Speculators" in Aihwa Ong and Stephen Collier, eds., *Global Assemblages: Technology, Politics, and Ethics as Anthropological Problems* (Oxford: Blackwell, 2005), 253–69. Portions of chapter 7 were previously published in "Ambiguous Numbers: Trading Technologies and Interpretation in Global Financial Markets," *American Ethnologist* 30, no. 2 (2003): 258–72. Copyright © 2003 by the American Anthropology Association.

Library of Congress Cataloging-in-Publication Data

Zaloom, Caitlin.
    Out of the pits : traders and technology from Chicago to London / Caitlin Zaloom.
        p.   cm.
    Includes bibliographical references and index.
    ISBN 0-226-97813-3 (cloth : alk. paper)
    1. Stockbrokers. 2. Stock exchanges. 3. Electronic trading of securities.
4. Finance — Social aspects. 5. Business anthropology. I. Title.

  HG4621.Z35 2006
  332.6'2 — dc22

                                                              2006002490

✳ CONTENTS

The brassy shouts, ringing bells, and thrashing arms of the floor traders are the most recognizable sounds and sights of Wall Street. On the trading floor of the New York Stock Exchange (NYSE), the fevered pitch of buying and selling stock certificates sets the tone for global finance at its most clamorous. The business media offer a daily dose of trading images—heads in hands amid the debris of discarded tickets when the market is down, arms raised in frenzied activity when the market is rising—as they diagnose ever-changing economic conditions.

Despite its centrality to the image of American economic dominance, this iconic place is under threat. In April 2005, the NYSE announced that it would merge with Archipelago, an all-electronic stock exchange based in Chicago. Archipelago's trading system would replace the tumult of the trading floor with the hum of online circuits, ushering the recalcitrant NYSE into the electronic era. Speculators enthusiastic about the union between the two exchanges propelled the price of a membership on the NYSE to $2.6 million. Yet players on both sides of the merger debate noted that the transition to electronic trading would come at a high cost, one that could not be measured in dollar terms.

Digital dealing on the Big Board would effectively end floor trading at the exchange, transforming the way traders had conducted business for more than two hundred years. Many NYSE floor dealers lamented this change, resisting the new technologies. Many others considered electronic trading inevitable and worked to define the terms on which the NYSE would go digital, seeking to secure the future of their institution and, at the same time, a handsome profit for themselves. On both sides of the divide, generations of traders have made the NYSE a crucible of capitalism that electronic trading is poised to smash. For them, the exchange is a place where financial firms built on family connections, personal trading skills, and local control of a key global market come together in one famous building. As brokers traffic in stocks, slivers of ownership in the world's most prestigious companies, they embody American economic mastery. Foreign officials and American celebrities acknowledge this as they accept prized invitations to ring the opening bell. The platform set above the floor provides a perfect vantage point for viewing the imposing sight of thousands of individuals united in the struggle for profit.

Electronic trading is designed to splinter this flesh and bone market into separate parts. Traders in the new digital dealing rooms sit within the walls of private trading spaces—whether banks, small firms, or their own homes. They surround themselves with the tools of online exchange: computer monitors displaying stock and commodity prices, news wires, and predictive charts. These instruments objectify information, facilitate calculations, and enable autonomous actors to buy and sell instantly with the touch of a finger. They offer access to the full ensemble of the market directly through the screen. Digital dealers are exquisitely connected, yet they act alone.

The editorial page of the *Wall Street Journal* (April 22, 2005) noted the demise of the trading floor as it lauded the deal: "While humans may continue to play a role in large or complex orders for stocks that don't trade often, the majority of trading will probably go electronic." The fate of trading floors in Chicago, London, Paris, Montreal, Tokyo, Sydney, and Singapore has confirmed this prediction. Scenes of traders sitting quietly behind computer screens quickly replaced the action of hangar-sized trading floors where men—and it was mostly men—competed for profitable deals, bringing the market to life with their bodies and voices. During the 1990s and early 2000s, financial exchanges across the globe underwent contentious transitions similar to the one taking place in New York, putting an end to forms of trading and institutional arrangements that were often, as with the NYSE, more than one hundred years old.

: : :

Nowhere were these battles fiercer than in Chicago, where the futures exchanges, the Chicago Board of Trade (CBOT) and Chicago Mercantile Exchange (the Merc), had helped the city become a hub of global capitalism. During the 1990s, these long-standing membership organizations wrestled with electronic trading and its proponents' promises that new technology would help them achieve the dream of truly global markets. The Merc adopted electronic trading quickly after its leaders convinced members that the new technologies would give them a competitive advantage over other exchanges. The directors also dissolved its membership system in order to become more flexible, reasoning that a conventional corporate structure would allow the organization to maneuver at digital speed. It even went public, so that floor traders at the NYSE could buy and sell stock in the cutting-edge Chicago market.

At the CBOT, however, digital dealing was far more controversial, and the struggle over the future of the exchange lasted a decade. The struggles at the CBOT over how to respond to the new possibilities of electronic trading allow us to see what is at stake not only for the Chicago floor traders, but also for markets more generally. Like their counterparts at the NYSE, CBOT members had money on the line. Electronic trading devalued access to the trading floor and dragged down the value of their seats. Like the NYSE floor traders, the Chicago dealers had built a living around the skills of buying and selling hand-to-hand. Most of Chicago's floor traders lacked the Ivy League pedigrees and MBAs that had become prerequisites for jobs in finance, and few could be confident that they would survive in a marketplace that no longer valued their abilities to make deals face-to-face.

As the world's exchanges went electronic, many of the CBOT's established leaders fought to preserve the pits, the open outcry trading, the membership structure, and the distinctive cultural environment of trading that had evolved in the city. Their opponents ridiculed them for old-fashioned sentimentalism, insisting that the transition was inevitable and warning that the delay would not only cost members dearly, but also render the entire CBOT expendable and obsolete.

The Chicago traders became more anxious when they looked across the Atlantic. In London, electronic exchanges had already driven futures traders off the floor, marking the demise of open outcry. The exchanges in Chicago and London had close ties, since the Chicago exchanges were the model for the London International Financial Futures Exchange (LIFFE), the British financial futures exchange. In London, some of the traders pushed off the floor had sought work as taxi drivers, others painted houses. The lucky ones got jobs in banks trading online. For some enterprising Chicago traders, however, the omen was an opportunity. They crossed the Atlantic with aspirations to remake the new market, opening boutique firms that would export Chicago trading styles—built on aggressive action, bravado, and bold risk-taking behavior—and distinctively American beliefs about economy and culture to London's exchange.

: : :

What was so compelling about electronic markets? Proponents of the new, digital dealing systems argued that trading through an electronic network would be fast, efficient, and transparent, displacing the antiquated system of person-to-person exchange. Separating individuals by fiber-optic cable and isolating them behind private terminals would allow a purer market to emerge, with anonymous, autonomous individuals replacing the trading "neighborhoods" and tight in-groups that evolved on the trading floor. The new electronic systems would offer pure individual competition: only the fittest would flourish, and those unfit for market competition would wither away.

At their inception in the mid-1800s the trading pits themselves seemed a novel and efficient technology for cleaving insular trading cliques and making the trading floor into a place where men could conduct business entirely on their own. Electronic technologies have made them seem insufficient. The advent of online markets created a new opening to use technological and human elements of the market—computer screens, techniques of trading, and the composition of trading rooms—to push even closer to economic ideals of autonomy for individuals and competition among them.

Yet there is no technologically determined script for changing the constitution of the marketplace. Shifting economic activity from the trading floor to the dealing screen requires many projects that I call "practical experiments" in market building. These experiments—in architecture and technological design, recruitment, self-discipline, and even the aesthetics of trading spaces—aim to bring economic ideals to life, and no ideal is more important than the competitive individual. The modern individual is often described as endowed with the properties of economic reason and competitiveness. But these are not innate predispositions that need only to be set loose. Even in the peak places of the quest for pure profit, individuals and environments must be shaped, managed, honed, and reconstructed to create the competitive situations that anchor capitalist practice. How market managers, technology designers, and traders attempt to equip men with market reason is the subject of this book.

* ACKNOWLEDGMENTS

Tracing the transformations of financial trading required many kinds of travel. But wherever I went I benefited from the guidance and support of a broad constellation of financial professionals, academic colleagues, friends, and family. My first debt is to the traders, managers, designers, and exchange officials in Chicago and London who gave their time to this project. Their generosity and cooperation are the foundation of this research. I would particularly like to thank the owners and managers of Perkins Silver and the trader known here as David for the crucial help and access they provided me.

As is conventional in ethnographic writing, I have created pseudonyms for people who offered their private reflections and experiences, many of whom shared with me a trading desk, cups of tea, and all the daily activity of traders' working lives that I write about here. Although I have renamed the trading firm that appears here as Perkins Silver, I would not try to hide the identity of the Chicago Board of Trade, one of the biggest players in global futures markets, or the other financial exchanges. The executives who directed the CBOT during my research are the public representatives of the exchange, and so I use their real names.

This book took shape amidst the intellectual guidance I received as a graduate student in anthropology at the University of California, Berkeley. Its trajectory began with the support of my advisor, Paul Rabinow, who recognized an anthropological project in the economic rationality of futures market and then guided me as I conceived, conducted, and committed an analysis to paper. Aihwa Ong constantly reminded me that a combination of human practices and technological materials lay behind the transnational phenomena that I was witnessing, and then challenged me to find them. Manuel Castells focused my attention on the urban nodes that organized financial markets and dared me to investigate the connections between the institutions and actors that shape the space of flows. Berkeley also provided the foundation for absorbing intellectual exchanges and enduring friendships with fellow graduate students, even as we scattered around the globe for research and jobs. I was privileged to get both careful criticism and steady support from Arianne Chernock, Stephen Collier, Jeff Juris, Nalini Kotamraju, Andrew Lakoff, Elizabeth F.S. Roberts, Natasha Schull, and Rachel Sherman. It's hard to imagine writing this book without them.

Beyond the Bay Area, I benefited from the generosity of Saskia Sassen and Richard Sennett, who provided scholarly inspiration and warm friendship in Chicago, London, and New York. Thanks to Stephen Barley, Greg Downey, Karin Knorr Cetina, Harris Kim, George Marcus, Bill Maurer, Ajay Mehrotra, Yuval Millo, Alex Preda, Kris Olds, David Stark, Nigel Thrift, and Marc Ventresca, each of whom has read, listened, and provided valuable feedback. And to my temporary hosts: the Kellogg School of Management, where the languages of both social theory and futures trading are spoken fluently; the American Bar Foundation, where I wrote much of my dissertation; and the Cities Program at the London School of Economics, which gave me a place to think after the trading day closed.

The soul of this book is in Chicago. Doug Mitchell, at the University of Chicago Press, lived up to his billing as the most effusively encouraging editor in the business, and Tim McGovern was equally helpful. I am grateful to them, and to their colleagues at the press, for their confidence in the book. Owen Gregory, the archivist of the Chicago Board of Trade, guided me through the more dusty stretches of CBOT history. The Special Collections Department of the University Library, University of Illinois at Chicago, kindly provided images from the Chicago Board of Trade Records (CBOT neg. 111, 75-68[1-1], 75-68[1-9]). The wonderful photographer Bob Davis captured the action of the trading floor in many of the images that enliven these pages. The Chicago Board of Trade gave permission to take these photos, but has not reviewed the book, and makes no representation regarding the accuracy of the content of the publication. Such responsibility clearly lies with the author.

It was fitting to finish writing this book in the financial capital of New York City. My colleagues at New York University—Tom Bender, Neil Brenner, Doug Guthrie, Phil Harper, Walter Johnson, Tim Mitchell, Harvey Molotch, Kim Philips-Fein, Mary Poovey, Mary Louise Pratt, Andrew Ross, and Daniel Walkowitz—welcomed me with both insightful commentary and true support. I am looking forward to all the exchanges to come.

Any book on markets should acknowledge where the money came from. Financial resources for research and writing came from the Social Science Research Council Program on the Corporation as a Social Institution (with funds provided by the Alfred P. Sloan foundation), the University of California Institute on Global Conflict and Cooperation, and the Center for German and European Studies at the University of California. In 2004–2005, I had the good fortune to spend the year at NYU's International Center for Advanced Study, where I completed the manuscript.

The support of close friends and family has been essential at every stage of crafting this book. Rona Talcott and Herb Davis welcomed me into their home when I did fieldwork in Chicago and helped to teach me about both the city and the small world of global traders. Over the course of this research they became great friends. Then they became my in-laws. I wish that Herb and I could share this one final book.

During my stay in London I lived with Priscilla Roth and Nick Garland. I didn't believe my friend Gabe when he told me that his mother would invite me to stay for the duration of my research. I was astonished when she did. Since that time Priscilla and Nick have become like family, and their kitchen table is my favorite seminar room. Many long-standing friendships have sustained me through the peaks and valleys of my writing process. Thanks to Mia Baricini, Matt Brown, Debi Cornwall, Jacob Gersen, Sarah Goodman, Adam Gross, Julia Gwynne, Heather Johnston, Valerie Reiss, and Megan Stephan. I am thankful to have them in my life.

Carolyn and Alan Grey, my mother and stepfather, gave me a model for adventures, both intellectual and otherwise. From my father, J. Gordon Zaloom, I inherited both a healthy skepticism and the strength and verve to pursue my own answers—the best legacy a parent could leave. Although he claims to not understand what I've been up to these past several years, my uncle, Roy Zaloom, never wavered in his support of my pursuits.

My deepest thanks are reserved for Eric Klinenberg. Our relationship and this book began together and he has supported me at every stage along the way with love, optimism, and an unflagging willingness to edit my prose. I am lucky that completing this project is only the beginning of our life adventures. I dedicate this book to him.

A photograph of the Chicago Board of Trade hangs in a crowded, central passageway of London's Tate Modern gallery. Every inch of its six-foot length vibrates with financial frenzy and spins with the disorder of time and space. The picture induces the vertigo of the contemporary world, and the frame spills over with traders, clerks, brokers, computer terminals, and telephones. The acid colors of trading coats swirl in and around the dealing pits. Hands and faces blur as they work to buy and sell financial commodities. The motion is not all in the present, though. Andreas Gursky, the artist, digitally layered the image to show traders who were once there and have now gone. Trading cards, bits of newspaper, and financial statements shine through spectral bodies. The camera can record only their traces as they hurtle headlong into the future. Just as past, present, and future blur together, space is also unstable. The trading area collapses inward as the plane of the floor tilts forward into the frame. The composition lacks a distinct center. The viewer is off balance—neither directly in the melee nor hanging above it.

This picture of a turbulent economy contains a few orienting markers—the rings of the trading pits, the padded railings that contain them, the rows of telephone booths that angle stadium-style, and the stairs and hallways leading in and out of the marketplace. The instruments of financial technology suggest that informational orderliness might be found on the trading floor, but instead they too are part of the din. A stack of price screens and monitors rises at the front of the frame. Electronic order books, telephones, paper trading cards, and time and sales sheets are scattered about the floor. The technologies of financial knowledge suggest quick access to concrete data that link the outside world to the trading floor. But even these informational objects cannot cut through the swirl of the market. There are simply too many of them, an excessive proliferation of the technologies of reason. Instead of imposing order, they provide conduits for the frenzied

Intro.1 Andreas Gursky, *Chicago Board of Trade II* (1999). Copyright © 2005, Andreas Gursky/ Artists Rights Society (ARS), New York/ VG Bild-Kunst, Bonn.

currents of money running through this trading floor. Both the equipment and the bodies of the traders are channels of a massive force.

The photograph is not a portrait of the particular character of the Chicago Board of Trade trading floor. As the curator and art critic Peter Galassi has written, the piece is a portrait of this financial market, "as a global institution and as a model of contemporary behavior."[1] Gursky's image has its place at the Tate Modern precisely because the Chicago Board of Trade (CBOT) is an exemplary site of modernity, a place that offers a refined case of financial speculation and the circulation of money. In this location, everyday relationships to the potential of money and the necessity of trade become extreme. Financial professionals bring together flow, speed, and technology in the pursuit of profits, and when thousands of them gather every day, they help create something larger—the market.

Gursky's image sends a clear message about the velocity of money and its disordering effects in the global economy. The market takes in vast waves of capital and spews them out again in a logic all its own. Yet for the crowd of spectators around the photograph, the commotion and disarray are entrancing. It is unsettling to examine the picture closely, especially because a literal understanding of the physical place, or of the traders' labor, is impossible. Instead, it is easier to step back from the photograph and absorb the overall impression of the global financial beehive.

Gursky captures the unease and amazement of economic life in an age of global markets. The postindustrial logic of speculation is partly responsible for this disquiet. In financial markets like the CBOT, there are no goods to trade. No grain or currency changes hands. There is only the accounting of gains and losses tabulated against traders' accounts at the end of the day. Here, capitalism is a pure search for profit, without any clear connection to commodities that people make or use. Unencumbered, the whirling of capital is alluring, and Gursky is not alone in his fascination. Observers from anthropology and the social sciences, the humanities, and the popular press have focused on the growth and speed of finance. Like Gursky, many of these cultural critics strive to understand global markets as a whole, both as a set of economic arrangements and as a reflection of the ways people live and work today. Much of this writing examines the effects of the market's financial velocity and its mercurial nature.

In much contemporary cultural commentary, the economic order of factories and nations is swept away by the digital symbols of financial deals. These descriptions have a metaphorical flair. For instance, David Harvey famously claimed that new financial regimes produce "flux, instability, and gyration."[2] He infused the financial market with its own volition and manic logic, claiming that capital does not keep its shifting ways isolated in the market. The constant search for new territory and the proclivity for taking a quick profit reproduce themselves in culture and individual affect.[3] The triumph of capitalism and its market-based reason is matched by new kinds of enchantments. Jean and John Comaroff direct us to the ironies of the parallel rise of hyper-rationalization in financial and legal regimes and the spread of occult practices. Their analysis of the "conditions-of-being under millennial capitalism" points to salvation and magic as much as to market logic.[4] Above all, the image of flow runs through the writing of both social and cultural observers, capturing the movement between places, adding to the mystical image of the market, and focusing our eyes on rivers of trade whose currents have the urgency of a natural force. The metaphor appears so often that it has lost its novelty. Flow is global common sense. But the image has an unfortunate side effect, encouraging analysts to position themselves as observers, standing at the river's edge rather than jumping in to understand the human actions and technological materials that make global exchange happen. Even when it is carefully defined and contextualized, as in Manuel Castells's account of the network architecture that structures informational economies and the space of flows, the powerful image of rapid flow draws attention away from the social processes that bring flows to life.

Many anthropologists, from Bronislaw Malinowski and Marcel Mauss to Claude Lévi-Strauss, Arjun Appadurai, and Karin Knorr Cetina, have shown how exchange stitches together collectivities separated in time and space. The same is true for global financial markets—they are engines of exchange frequently conceived of in metaphors of flow. They link individuals, cities, and collectivities through the process of trade. Gursky, Harvey, the Comaroffs, and Castells are showing something important. Contemporary markets are mesmerizing and immense. They are both a symptom and a cause of a changing world where trading links cities, organizations, and individuals. Financial exchange brings together some of the most powerful elements of the contemporary economy: calculative wizardry, information technologies, and the sharp wit of individuals drawing profit from the endless circulation of money. Markets are intimidating and confusing, and, above all, they have important consequences, enriching the fortunate or wiping out vast assets in an instant. Yet there is another equally powerful and far more prevalent image of markets, one that is difficult to reconcile with the confusion that global markets inspire. This other image portrays markets as zones of rational action, engines of risk management, places to profit and to protect wealth. Markets organize and filter information, matching supply and demand. Markets are separate spheres, apart from the social and cultural world, ordered by principles of self-interested action.

We need to take a closer look at markets if we want to transcend the idea that they are rational economic tools or, alternatively, that they are engines of chaos. In recent years social scientists from different fields have reinvigorated this field of research, drawing out the architecture of markets, as Harrison White, Neil Fligstein, and Mark Granovetter have done, and investigating the human action and technical scaffolding that make economic calculation possible, as Mitchell Abolafia, Michel Callon, and Donald MacKenzie have done.[5] At a still finer resolution, we begin to see that markets pose a particular set of problems, especially for the people who work to shape them and seek to draw their livelihoods from them. Financial markets are objects for inquiry into the culture and economy of contemporary capitalism. They are particular spaces of economic practice. In these markets, traders, managers, and designers constantly define for themselves, and for the markets as a whole, what constitutes principled economic action. They also debate how to create conditions that will make principled action possible. This means that market-makers work with the existing materials of the market—technologies, architecture, habits, and routines—to create what they would consider to be a better market, one where individuals can draw profit from their own financial acumen more than from their connections to others. They also reflect on how to make themselves into ethical actors and apply disciplined techniques that allow them to draw profit from the market.

Managers, designers, and speculators labor with and in these markets every day. Each of these positions—manager, designer, speculator—is defined by a relationship to the market and not simply by the individuals who occupy them. Individuals move in and out of these positions, bringing their experiences on trading floors with them to management offices and design firms. However, each position forces them to confront a slightly different set of problems. For designers, the key problem is how to think about the market—What is it? Where is it? Who acts in it? Most important, how can they bring the market more into line with a particular vision of how it *should* work? They analyze the technological and human components of the market with the goal of shaping an impersonal system that provides information to each participant equally, so that the most successful traders are the fastest and most agile *individuals*, regardless of their connections or social characteristics.

Managers have a different set of problems. Like designers, they face the question of what the best market might look like, but they are also concerned with how to implement these ideas, given the already existing marketplace. The managers of the CBOT organization had to contend with the physical structure of the market—the buildings of the CBOT and the technologies, like telephones and hand signals, that shape traders' actions in the market. Managers of trading rooms must work with the existing habits of traders that they want to shape or to reform. Their question is, What is the proper relationship of the individual to the market? Of course, their primary job is to organize profit-making activity for their firms. But profit is conceived as an end. Managers approach this problem by organizing the social composition of a trading room and shaping the conduct of others.

Speculators face a similar problem that challenges them to think about the means of profit-making. Speculators ask themselves, How can I conduct myself in a market to draw profit? This requires that they consider the trader's relationship to the market, to others inside the market, and to themselves as confronted by the market. In other words, the problems I consider here are problems of ethics: What is the proper relationship between thinking and acting in the market? What is the relationship between the norms of economic action and the material and human form of the market?

While I was doing research, a particular event was underway, a realignment of the technological and human materials of the market. A transition from face-to-face dealing to online trading was changing the market in two key ways. First, it changed where the market was. It was no longer located in the rings of trading pits and in the bodies and voices of traders gathered there. Now, the market was an entity beyond location that traders tapped into through computer terminals. This change also challenged the human foundation of the market. The market was not made up of individuals who thought and felt the markets through their bodies and connections to others.

The designers of the computer interfaces and dealing rooms were promoting a relationship to the market based on observation and more explicit analysis. Traders were now expected to watch the market and act on it, rather than being the market and acting in it. The technological possibilities of digital systems raised the interconnected problems of how the material form of the market and the human form of market reason should be related.

: : :

As a graduate student in anthropology at the University of California, Berkeley, I encountered a wide and contradictory set of views about financial markets. First there was the analysis of the external effects of the market versus the technical study of the market's interior workings. On a more public stage, market celebration raised another contradiction. In the late 1990s the Bay Area was the epicenter of a stock market craze fueled by information technology and speculative logic. My twenty-something friends monitored the value of their stock options from their desks at dot.com firms, watching their paper gains grow and grow as the stock in their companies changed hands again and again. Many more waited for Wall Street to take their companies public, making their shares tradable on the NASDAQ. Each time I drove across the Bay Bridge to San Francisco, a billboard reminded me that E*trade could help me turn the bud of my graduate stipend into a blossoming balance if only I would sign up for one of their active trader accounts. A sign designed to look like an old motel advertisement displayed both the wit and wealth of Yahoo! At the same time, news media like CNNfn and MSNBC kept us all abreast of the smallest shifts in stock-fueled fortunes. The sheer energy of the market was palpable, but as a graduate student I was looking in from the outside.

The vigor that markets were bringing to the streets and upscale restaurants of San Francisco collided with the more skeptical depictions of markets I gleaned from reading anthropologists, sociologists, and geographers. There celebration clashed with anxiety about the market's effects. First, I learned that the market in technology stocks was only a tiny fraction of the world of professional financial management and trading.[6] The swift trading in bonds and specialized products known as derivatives contracts were changing the landscape not only of finance, but also of politics and culture. In print, financial markets and the information technologies that supported them were credited with the breakdown of nation states, the rise of global production, the abandonment of the welfare state, and the rise of a global business class whose wealth grew larger as the wages of working-class people diminished.

Yet most of the authors I read approached these markets from the abstract perspective of political economy. I learned about the economic changes that financial markets brought and their effects on the cities of the world, but I did not see the interiors of these markets, where finance defined a way of life and labor. People did not make appearances in most of these accounts. I began to read business publications like *Business Week* and the *Economist*, which profiled practitioners of finance and the issues they faced in the day-to-day business dealings. From the pages of these journals emerged a world beyond Internet madness and theoretical abstraction. Cities, organizations, and individuals were all hard at work securing their places in global finance networks, trading financial instruments, forging alliances, and adapting organizations to new technologies. Even though globalization was often discussed as a *fait accompli*, the pages of the business media showed how firms and traders were bringing it into being as they tried to catch up with the idea. In other words, these actors were identifying problems and defining solutions to create greater profit from a constantly changing geography. This was not chaos, or the greater abstraction of market efficiency. Reading the critiques and praise of those in finance and business on their own practices led me to ask questions about the theories I was reading. But the business press and the economics journals did not answer them either. I set out to analyze global finance as a series of practical problems that the executives of financial exchanges, technology designers, and traders were working out themselves in their everyday labor.

I left Berkeley and headed for Chicago. Chicago is not the first city that comes to mind for most people when they think of finance. Wall Street towers and the imposing columns of the New York Stock Exchange are the market's global symbols. Chicago, however, has a special place in this universe. It is the capital of derivatives markets. Derivatives contracts are a special kind of financial product whose value is linked to another financial commodity, like bonds, or a "physical" commodity, like wheat. Futures and options are the two most common derivatives, and these are the staples of the Chicago marketplace. The city's derivatives exchanges run centralized markets for trading in these contracts. Derivatives have a dual life. They are tools of hedging, or risk management, and they are also tools of speculation. The Chicago exchanges bring together thousands of traders who work the derivatives markets for second-by-second profit. The work of these speculators ensures the market's liquidity. They are available in the market throughout their work days. The willingness to trade at all times allows banks outside the exchange to complete their deals whatever the amount and whenever their strategists choose. Traders are at the heart of derivatives markets and their culture of circulation, and Chicago is famous for its traders.[7] Global players bring their business to the shores of Lake Michigan for their skill and for the experience of the Chicago exchanges in derivatives dealing.

No longer "hog butcher to the world," Chicago now labors to create a global bazaar in these specialized financial goods.

I arrived in Chicago in the summer of 1998 and moved into a basement apartment about two miles from the financial district. The family friends who owned the house provided more than shelter. Their son, David, was a futures trader at the CBOT and had agreed to help me with my research. I called his house in the North Shore suburbs and began by asking if I could talk to him about trading. He cut me short. "I can't tell you anything. It is just something that you have to see for yourself. What did you say you're doing this summer?" I said that I was planning on researching the exchanges and doing some preparatory interviews. "Forget that," he instructed. "Can you be at work on Monday?" With one phone call to the firm's owner, he convinced the firm to hire me as a runner at the Chicago Board of Trade.

The CBOT looms over the city's main financial artery, LaSalle Street. But, like most other workers at the exchange, I approached from the rear. The elevated trains of the Chicago Transit Authority stop just behind the building, and my first morning the train was packed with traders and clerks on their way to work. I followed the mob down the stairs and underneath the enormous structure that connected the office building with the brand new trading facility. The offices of Perkins Silver looked down on an open courtyard that brought light and air into the executive offices. The secretary behind the elegant maple desk sent me to find Jim Alba, who ran the floor operations for the firm. After a gruff introduction, he sat me down with a stack of documents that outlined the hand signals, products, and market terminology of futures trading. They also gave instruction on how to conduct oneself, which I had to master for the exchange's own test. To gain access to the floor, clerks were required to demonstrate a basic knowledge of the rules of market conduct—from prohibitions on verbal abuse and throwing objects to the basics of pit trading. In the exam room deep in the basement of the Exchange, the new clerks grumbled over this scholastic exercise. The proctor handed us our graded exams and our newly minted badges with the same hand.

My first job was on the grain trading floor, delivering orders from the clerks at the phone banks to the traders in the pits. The clerk would answer a customer's call, scribble down the order, and shove the sheet under a time stamp. At the thump of the stamp, I snatched the paper from the clerk's hand and dove into the tumult. Runners elbowed each other out of the way. Discarded paper scraps slicked the floor. The noise was often deafening. One of the phone clerks scribbled a cheat sheet for me on a trading card, but even with the guide in hand, I confused the wheat and soy pits and brokers, and found myself lost in the shouts of traders as the market slid and peaked throughout the day. After a couple of weeks I could leave the homemade map in my pocket. My sense of the trading floor fell into place. In the meantime, I leaned on the phone clerks and other runners for help interpreting what I saw. I learned that many of them were there to launch their trading careers, so they, too, were hard at work deciphering the financial melee around them. Working the phones and customer orders was commonly the first step in getting to know how futures markets worked. From there I could begin to learn about the labor of financial exchange, as many traders do themselves.

Although I began in the agricultural futures room, my firm soon moved me to the much larger financial room, the engine of the exchange. This shift took very little adjustment. The work of the financial floor and the grain floor was essentially the same. The difference lay in the enormity of the financial floor and the products in which the financial traders were dealing—futures based on the debt of the American Treasury and on the movement of the Dow Jones Industrial Average (DJIA), as well as several more arcane contracts. I worked at a "desk," a long table lined with phones dedicated to the swelling business of the DJIA pit. Standing behind the phones, the clerks flashed urgent deals to brokers with hand signals and shouts. Legless seats swung out from the desks, but as I quickly learned, there was little time to sit.

Each morning I arrived at the CBOT at 6:45 a.m. and proceeded through a network of corridors and elevators to the firm's office. In the coat room where the traders' garish clothes hung, I donned my own oversized trading jacket coordinated with the firm's colors. I placed my notebook in a pocket alongside a stack of trading cards and took the elevator down to the fourth floor, the level dedicated to the trading rooms and set apart from the governing structures and back offices of the exchange. Security is tight around its perimeter. Each employee swipes an identity card and presses through a turnstile as a guard looks on. Traders and clerks open their pockets and purses for scrutiny.

Each morning, the clerks prepared for the opening bell, compiling orders and making predictions about whether the market would be rising or falling. But we were not the first to arrive. On our way from security to the desks, we passed a buzzing room full of clerks who had been there since 5:00 a.m. correcting errors from the previous day's work. On the trading floor, the pit slowly filled with traders examining their charts, looking at overnight reports from other markets, and gossiping. As 7:20 approached, everyone got quiet and waited impatiently for the buzzer. At its electronic screech, business came flooding into the market, feeding the raucous energy of the trading floor. Thousands of excited traders and clerks packed together is an irresistible thrill. Each day, however, the market would die down to a steady hum, and I used the opportunity to talk to the traders who trickled out of the pits and set up interviews for after the trading day.

It did not take long to see that the traders were preoccupied with a single issue — electronic trading. They were right to be concerned. In the spring, the Paris exchange had opened electronic markets. Weeks later they closed their trading floor. Later that year, the CBOT traders watched another coup. The German exchange, then called the Deutsche Terminborse (DTB), launched an attack on London markets, where futures on German treasuries traded. Again, it did not take long for the London pits to fold. The CBOT and its traders set their jaws for a fight. They argued that the CBOT had developed pit trading, that the liquidity of the market was legendary, that the cold operators of computers could never provide the kinds of markets the devoted pit traders gave the world every day. To fend off competitors, the CBOT opened its own after-hours electronic market, called Project A. But that did not deter a challenger with offices inside the building. That summer, Cantor Fitzgerald, a bond-trading firm headed by the infamous Howard Lutnick, set up an electronic exchange to deal in CBOT products. The new exchange soon folded, but the writing was on the wall.

As rumors about electronic trading deluged the financial floor, the firm I worked for was making its own plans. They were setting up shops in London and New York that specialized in online futures trading. I asked the firm's owners to bring me along. With six months on the trading floor behind me, I headed off for London to work for Perkins Silver as a new recruit among ten new traders. Each morning before sunrise in the fall and winter of 2000, I arrived by tube in the heart of the City, London's financial district. Along with my fellow trainees, I studied formal trading techniques in a classroom and, on the trading floor, adjusted them to my own risk-taking appetites. After the training, I traded German Treasury bond futures on a Perkins Silver account. I interpreted the market according to my new skills and gained the direct experience of risking money that is central to traders' experience of their own work. I spent nine hours a day with eyes fixed on my screen and fingers lying lightly on the mouse, poised to click the second an opportunity for profit appeared.

In both cities, my base was the trading floor. But I wanted to gain a view of the market that went beyond the floor. After work and during subsequent visits, I delved into archives, interviewed officials at the exchanges and technology companies, attended meetings on the reorganization of the industry, and reviewed documents and media reports that discussed the changing composition of futures markets from Singapore to London. From the CBOT trading floor and my seat at Perkins Silver, I worked to map how the changing terrain of global futures trading was rearranging the problems of circulation.

From the field's earliest days, anthropologists have examined patterns of exchange in places far from the economic centers of North America and Europe. Today, the world's powerful financial centers are the ones that need explanation. The mysteries of markets touch our lives, but few outside the financial profession understand them. I realized that no field site would be more challenging, puzzling, and important than financial markets, especially the derivatives markets of Chicago and London. From these cities, where organized financial exchanges, banks, and traders arrange and propel capital flow, I could begin to answer questions that neither anthropology nor business texts were asking. What were the places, people, and technologies that generated the flow? How did men shape themselves into risk-takers? What were the codes of conduct, strategies, and responsibilities of actors inside these markets? And how did this personal labor draw on and, simultaneously shape, the focus on rationality, profit, and competition that we think of as market values? How did these markets come to have a cultural infrastructure that allowed them to operate as a single, global force? What binds markets in and across time and space? Ultimately, how is financial circulation managed, imagined, and produced?

The change from face-to-face to online markets is not only a story of a disjuncture; it is also the story of strong continuities in the forms of financial exchange, as well as in the modes of exchange and practical ethics of markets. Anthropology offers tools to trace both the changes and continuities. Ethnographic fieldwork and the blended approach of cultural economy draw together economic practices, forms of knowledge, and disciplines that shape individuals into economic subjects in a way that can deepen our understanding of the contemporary complexity of an economic ethos. Following a long history in anthropological approaches to the economy, economic geographers Ash Amin and Nigel Thrift point out that "the pursuit of prosperity must be seen as the pursuit of many goals at once, from the meeting of material needs and accumulating riches to seeking symbolic satisfaction and satisfying fleeting pleasure."[8] This is true even, as we will see, in places explicitly designed to purge any other values from the pursuit of profit.

The approach I take here traces back to the roots of modern social science. Max Weber developed an understanding of the connection between economic systems and ethical orders, and Georg Simmel described the power of money to connect socially distant individuals, to mute passions, and to ignite economic lust.[9] This heritage informs the contemporary work of anthropologists such as Stephen Gudeman, Bill Mauer, Daniel Miller, Hiro Miyazaki, and Annelise Riles, who are beginning to study the intersection of economic and legal domains as governing the economy and profiting from exchange increasingly become the province of legal specialists.[10] I also draw on themes from the anthropology of exchange, the anthropology of reason, and the social studies of science and technology in order to make sense of the creation and destruction of the technologies in the Chicago futures markets, to analyze traders' ways of thinking, working, and living in the market, and to chart the extension of Chicago-style trading and forms of conduct to the City of London.

Anthropologists have long contested accepted ideas about the economy based in ideas about the nature of "economic man," drawing lessons about the competition for information that makes up economic exchange, arguing that economy is a category of culture, and, most recently, pointing to the ways that contemporary economic systems are built on revision and adjustment. Each of these arguments contests the idea that a unified core of economic impulses underlies human action. Fieldwork and the anthropology of exchange came together in Bronislaw Malinowski's *The Argonauts of the Western Pacific*. The father of ethnographic research devoted two years to documenting the *kula*, a type of trade practiced in the Trobriand Islands and arrived at his key conclusion that the *kula* was far from a pure economic system, arguing directly against explanations that reduced human economic action to a search for utility. In fact, trading in objects like necklaces, he contended, was more important than bartering in utilitarian goods like food and tools. His argument flew in the face of the "dismal fiction" of a "primitive economic man" driven by the satisfaction of basic need and the principle of least effort.[11]

Following his lead, work on exchange and economy has had a long and productive history in anthropology. Marcel Mauss continued Malinowski's project to engage arguments about the economy at home in France. In his classic work, *The Gift*, Mauss used the transactions of the *kula* ring to fight the oversimplified utilitarianism that dominated French universities. Mauss did not share the view that simple desire for useful goods was not the complete picture of an economy. He set out to show that the obligations of *social* credit and debt could not be separated from the exchange of commodities and that paths of trade bound together groups widely dispersed geographically and kept them together over time. Mauss was explicitly challenging the widely held view that market economies work by bringing together self-interested individuals aiming to satisfy narrowly defined needs. His approach struck a balance between the person who was always interested in calculating and manipulating her own social standing and the collective ideas about value, spirit, and status that hold the *kula* together.

Later both Clifford Geertz and Marshall Sahlins wrote against strictly economic visions of exchange and wealth. Geertz's essay on the bazaar economy of Morocco showed that the search for information, the manipulation of uncertainty, and client networks among vendors were integral parts of the economic picture. At the same time, Geertz sought a "reciprocally seditious" dialogue with economics that would allow for a more subtle understanding of the sociocultural nature of exchange.[12] Marshall Sahlins's essays in *Stone Age Economics* returned to Mauss's engagement with classical economists, aiming to "definitively abandon this entrepreneurial and individualist conception of the economic object." He claimed that "[e]conomy [is] a category of culture rather than behavior, in a class with politics or religion rather than rationality or prudence: not the need-serving activities of individuals, but the material life process of society."[13] However, his argument does not take into account the active production of rationality within a "reflexive modernity," where creating systems based on principles of efficiency and individual competition is an end in itself.[14] Ulrich Beck and Anthony Giddens, who have both considered the importance of modern reflexivity, leave open to investigation the specific processes that pattern reflexive modernization, particularly as it concerns the global circulation of capital. Part of this patterning arises from the design of modern systems that shape behavior and constitute new collectivities and from efforts to correct and improve them. Attention to designers who act as "technicians of general ideas" can help to make the leap between the construction of systems and spaces where, in each, economic ideals of designers work into the material forms they construct.[15] Studying the construction of physical forms and organizations, and the shaping of individuals' conduct can clarify how these cultural processes contribute to market rationality.

Other anthropologists hover at the edges of modern economic practice, seeking sites where "culture" contests "market logic." However, the objects of society and culture, those two spheres that might stand against the economic juggernaut, are now materials for constructing markets. The makers of markets are themselves inspired by social theories. This pattern becomes most clear when new technology inspires managers, designers, and traders to create new ways to realize the ideal of autonomous individuals and a pure economic sphere. The industry's shift from face-to-face interaction to online technologies pushes the existing ethos to the edges of its own practices, creating opportunities for reflection and innovation. In the construction sites of financial markets, social categories are manipulated in the designs of trading rooms and dealing screens. Society and culture do not exist outside the market. Instead, the profit-seeking opportunities they offer are building blocks for new forms of trading, and their challenges to rationalization make techno-social systems seem incomplete even in their moment of implementation. The "edges" these anthropologists search for are already within.

Investigations of the overlapping areas of economics, ethics, and technical specialization fit well with anthropology's cornerstone method, ethnographic fieldwork. Today, anthropology is more associated with fieldwork than ever before.[16] The understanding of what makes up a field, however, has changed. New objects for anthropological study emerge when novel practices and ideas about our ways of life, work, and politics arise.[17] Financial markets are just such objects.

Chicago has always thrived on the tension between the chaos of capitalism and the order it requires. This has never been more apparent than it was during the city's tremendous expansion in the nineteenth century. In *The Jungle*, Upton Sinclair's main characters approach the city by train and experience the sensory and perceptual confusion that commerce creates. "A full hour before the party reached the city they had begun to note the perplexing changes in the atmosphere. It grew darker all the time, and upon the earth the grass seemed to grow less green . . . And along with the thickening smoke they began to notice another circumstance, a strange, pungent odor. . . . It was an elemental odor, raw and crude; it was rich, almost rancid, sensual and strong." Chicago's infamous stockyards belched out an oily smoke, which spread "in vast clouds overhead, writhing, curling; then uniting in one giant river." The sounds from the yards trick the ears of Jurgis, Sinclair's proletarian hero. "You scarcely noticed it at first—it sunk into your consciousness, a vague disturbance, a trouble. It was like the murmuring of bees in the spring, the whisperings of the forest, it suggested endless activity, the rumblings of a world in motion."[1] Sinclair's analogies from Jurgis's rural past jar the reader as he shoots us headlong into the landscape, the necropolis of cows and pigs.

The yards were famous not only for bloody acts but also for the modern techniques developed there. They represented progress and made Chicago the meatpacking capital of the world. Hogs and cattle from all over the western United States converged on Chicago to be killed, dismembered, and efficiently distributed to eastern cities. Chicago turned pigs and cows into money, an alchemy that involved thousands of miles of grazing land, the invention of feedlots, and the all-important technology of the railroad. By the 1880s Chicago was butchering thirteen million animals a year.[2] Efficiency and centralization were vital to the success of the yards.

In the yards, no animals met their end as efficiently as the hogs. Handlers corralled them to the slaughterhouse and arranged them in a neat row on a gangplank. Slaughterhouse workers chained the animals' ankles to an enormous horizontal disc and opened their veins. As the wheel turned, it yanked the pigs into the air, bleeding and squealing, before dropping them into a vat of boiling water that removed the bristles from their skins. Their bodies were then stripped of flesh part by part on the "disassembly line," each section and shred destined to become a commodity. This method was an important inspiration for a later industrialist, Henry Ford, who mimicked this orderly model of death and dismemberment in his automobile plants. His admiration focused particularly on the meatpacking industry's refined division of labor, the intricate order behind the foaming rivers of blood that ran through the slaughterhouses.[3]

The most famous products of this hog's hell were meat, soap, and hair brush bristles for the growing masses of America, and enormous wealth for captains of commerce like Philip Armour and Gustavus Swift. But the by-products of the stockyards overtook the city. In Chicago, capitalism reeked, and the less savory yields of urban growth proved difficult to manage. The odor of rotting animal waste wafted over rich and poor neighborhoods alike. The coal fires that stoked the city's manufacturing painted a "lead-colored sky," as Frank Norris famously described it in his novel *The Pit*. In 1871, city engineers reversed the direction of the river, sending the malodorous waste away from the city and from Lake Michigan, the source of its drinking water. Redirecting nature in the service of the capitalist metropolis saved the noses and health of city dwellers, but the less prosperous towns along the river and downstate paid the price.[4] Nor was engineering able to achieve a perfect fix: during storms, the underside of Chicago's rapid economic expansion surfaced. Sewers overflowed with a noxious effluvium of urine, manure, and blood; despite the best efforts of the city's planners, the by-products of the city's success could not always be eliminated.

Representing Abstraction

The pigs of Chicago's stockyards squealed and kicked on their way to becoming commodities. A physical infrastructure and human hands were required to heave, can, and transport their meat. Across town, a different relationship to the materials of the market also emerged. In 1848, a group of businessmen came together at a flour store on South Water St. Amidst the growing commercial disorder and ever-expanding profit, they founded the Chicago Board of Trade (CBOT), an organization that would help develop both the urban potential of Chicago and the city's distinctive market in futures contracts.

Their "market" was an idea that harnessed time, collapsed space, and ordered prices without spilling a drop of blood. Their challenge was to create the smooth circulation of commodities demanded by their abstract vision. Markets in these "products" had to be imagined and built. First, the members of the CBOT began to construct a site of trade that reconciled an abstract notion of the market with the physical structure of the city and the architecture of the CBOT's marketplace.[5]

Under the direction of the CBOT, the space of the city became the space of their trade.[6] The city the CBOT merchants encountered presented both material opportunities and barriers. The sandy harbor and marshy ground of Chicago clogged trade. An infrastructure that would ease the conditions of trade between Chicago and its hinterland and between Chicago and the powerful cities of the eastern seaboard were primary concerns of the newly formed organization. Beginning in the mid-1800s, influential merchants lobbied for and funded the growth of railways, bridges, harbors, and buildings in the city of Chicago. Under their watch, Chicago grew to support the abstraction of the market, and the market grew to encompass more and more territory. Agricultural markets fused as Chicago's network of railroads, telegraph lines, and trading connections linked the western plains with the East Coast.

Within the city itself, architecture presented another way to shape the space of trade, and merchants created new infrastructures for their markets in the buildings the CBOT erected. They built the tallest and most impressive buildings of their time to give shape to the ideals of centralized, competitive, markets in abstract instruments. The members of the CBOT raised the city of Chicago and their organization together as they created a material form for the market. As the market grew, the CBOT erected new buildings. Each iteration of the market was an opportunity to renegotiate how to make markets in stone, wood, and steel. The story of how the CBOT's members and leaders accomplished their projects demonstrates how politically and economically powerful actors work with the materials of city space and technological infrastructure to create the material form of a market.

Order

Futures made possible the circulation of commodity prices without the physical commodity changing hands. The CBOT built the futures market on the ever-changing value of wheat and corn, and there speculation thrived. But at first, the founders of the CBOT were concerned not with creating a market but with the transportation and banking challenges that faced businessmen in the growing metropolis. Development of the city, particularly its transportation infrastructure, was essential to the circulation of commodities and the commercial interests of themselves and their peers.[7]

These merchants first needed to govern and develop their own organization. The idea of membership was central to the mission of the CBOT. Each member had a single vote. Committees of members investigated the commercial issues of the city and the internal issues of the organization and proposed solutions to the members. At the inaugural meeting, the first committee formed was given authority to draft a series of by-laws. The CBOT also created committees to monitor the activities of the organization's members, guide the development of business in the city, and coordinate efforts with the Boards of Trade in other cities. The members extended the idea of governance by their peers as they drew on mercantile history to argue for self-regulation: rulings on disputes, merchant's law instructs, should be made by other merchants familiar with the customs of business. Separating themselves from the authority of civil law, the merchants and traders of the organization would monitor and adjudicate the actions of the CBOT and its individual members.

The members soon adopted the regulations and elected their first president, Thomas Dyer. Born in the east, Dyer was a manufacturer in Atlanta before settling in Chicago. His pork-packing business put him at the center of the city's traffic in commodities. Other founders had interests in real estate, transportation, and banking. Six of Chicago's first twenty mayors were CBOT members, reinforcing an already tight link between city government and the commercial interests of Chicago's entrepreneurs.[8]

While the members of the CBOT were working to establish the commercial hub of Chicago and develop connections with the cities of the east, they were also beginning to create a new kind of market that would organize the agricultural markets of the nation by establishing a market in the *price* of grain. In 1857, the CBOT began trading in "to-arrive" contracts that established an agreed upon price for grain to be delivered on demand. However, these "warehouse receipts," as they were called at first, never had to be exchanged for grain. Instead, the difference between buyers and sellers could be settled for cash as the price of grain moved. By 1855, the daily sessions of the CBOT were roiling with trade both among merchants and among speculators trading on the changing prices of grain. Just a few years later, government provisioners began trading with CBOT speculators to coordinate the feeding of the Union troops during the Civil War. Their business helped consolidate the already thriving national market in grain prices.

The price of futures set in Chicago unified the nation's commodity markets by creating a single price for wheat for traders and merchants from New York to St. Louis. The grain yields of Kansas and the hogs of Iowa dominated the agricultural trade of the city. But their heft made them difficult to handle. To make a national market in grains and meat, Chicago's merchants forged new tools to trade these physical goods by creating abstractions that transcended geography and time.

A futures contract is a contract between individuals to provide an agreed amount of commodity at the expiration of a "delivery" time set in three-month cycles by the CBOT. These abstract tokens represent wheat and oats from any location—Kansas or Wisconsin, the farms of the Millers or the Taylors, it did not matter. The contracts were a way to trade large amounts of grain even when these grains were still seeds in the ground. Futures contracts enabled traders to set the value of grain months ahead of its reaping with only symbolic reference to the physical commodity. The paper token of the futures contract allowed crops to pass through the hands of speculators without their handling a single sheaf of wheat.

Like money, futures contracts created the ability to buy and sell with ease.[9] As they circulate, they create a new source of value apart from the material goods that lend their value to the contract.[10] As information about the coming harvest changed, so did the price of futures contracts. Each increase or drop created an opportunity for the members of the CBOT to make a small profit on the price change, selling their overpriced contracts or buying into a rising market. The CBOT allowed for trading that had less to do with physical commodities and more to do with the profits to be made from fluctuations in perceived value as the information about future harvests changed.

The merchant members of the CBOT became speculators and disciples of the market both in the movement of physical commodities and in the techniques of speculation that their changing prices allowed. But the speculators of the CBOT did not simply deal for themselves. They had an economic and civic mission. Through the work of the CBOT's members, the organization steered the city's development to facilitate trade and create business opportunities, making strategic connections with other cities that made Chicago the capital of the region and the coordinator of western commerce. The CBOT marshaled economic, political, and technological resources and led the drive to create a capital for American agricultural commerce. They dedicated themselves to the growth of the city's markets and fostered new technologies, primarily the railroad and the telegraph, to secure their city's commerce and their own fortunes.

The Chicago Nexus

That they would succeed in establishing Chicago as a commercial nexus was not certain. As the members of the CBOT well knew, there were other serious contenders to become America's hub. For a while, Cairo, Illinois, seemed poised at the brink of success as rail lines and federal influence converged on the city. According to Charles Taylor, a contemporary historian,

> Great expectations of the future of Cairo were entertained by well-informed people throughout the country. . . . The *American Railway Times*, . . . anticipating that Cairo rather then Chicago would reap the greatest benefit from the construction of the railroad, published an article of which the following is an extract: 'The Illinois Central Railroad will be the largest single railway enterprise in the United States. Cairo, which is situated at the lower terminus of the proposed road at the junction of the Ohio and Mississippi rivers, will in all probability be one of the largest of our western cities.[11]

A federal bill supplied more than two and a half million acres to the State of Illinois to construct a line of the Illinois Central Railroad from Cairo to Galena. Chicago had to fight for a "branch" of the railroad. However, the tributary soon overtook the main trunk line in traffic.[12] With William Ogden, Chicago's first mayor and the nation's first railroad baron, at the helm, the city's combination of water and rail transport cinched the city's success. At the outbreak of the Civil War, Chicago was the world's largest railroad junction, with more lines meeting within its borders than any other city on earth.[13]

Chicago had another, more established, competitor for the position of western gateway city. St. Louis waterways supported its claim to be the great western city and transportation hub. Situated at the junction of the Missouri and Mississippi Rivers, the city's rivers seemed to have natural advantages for transporting grain to market. It had logged seventy-five years as the key western port and principal trading partner for New Orleans. St. Louis merchants cleared furs from the west and trafficked in other commodities on their way to and from the frontier. In addition, a narrow channel north of St. Louis meant that all upstream river traffic had to stop there to transfer to smaller boats. But it was St. Louis's connections that eroded its dominance; Philadelphia was the city's major trading partner, and the eastern metropolis was already losing markets to New York. St. Louis merchants began to switch their alliances to New York, but slowly and too late. New York capital had established ties to Chicago merchants, providing pricing advantages, and railroad money had already helped establish Chicago as the west's rail hub.[14] The great spokes of railroad lines were made far more powerful with the introduction of telegraph lines. The merchants of Chicago could intensify and multiply their relationships with traders in other cities through the wires. The first telegram arrived in Chicago in the same year that leading local merchants founded the CBOT. On January 15th, 1848, at the corner of Lake and Clark Streets, a telegraph in the office of Colonel J. J. Speed tapped out a message from Milwaukee. Soon messages from the east and Chicago's urban kin of the northwest were flowing in. The first greeting sent between Detroit and Chicago read, "To Milwaukee, Racine, Southport, and Chicago.—We hail you by lightning as fair sisters of West. Time has been annihilated. Let no element of discord divide us. May your prosperity as heretofore be onward. What Morse has devised and Speed joined let no man put asunder."[15] The telegraph led to a coordination of commerce, prices, transportation, and politics among these regional centers that had been impossible before.

The members of the CBOT grasped the importance of the city's technological infrastructure. At first a voluntary organization of leading Chicago merchants with no legal status, the board was nevertheless central to promoting the city as a business center. It existed to promote "her commercial interests by more united action then heretofore" and was "the center of deliberation on nearly every question in which Chicago had an interest." Its influence was felt from city hall to the halls of Congress.[16] The board regulated commerce through the region, passed tolls on canal freight to and from the Mississippi, and debated how to manage the ever-increasing flow of information with telegraphic expansions. The men of the board lobbied Washington for land grants to complete the Illinois Railroad. They were so successful that Senators Stephen A. Douglas and General James Shields, both from Illinois, sent special congratulations.[17] In 1850, when sandbars blocked the Illinois River, hampering commerce, the board again sent representatives to Washington to lobby for making the port more navigable.

The CBOT's influence was critical in building and maintaining the city of Chicago and in coordinating northwestern commerce. After a spring flood that destroyed nearly every bridge in the city, the board reestablished communication between the north and west sides of the city to keep the metropolis running. City authorities worked with the board to issue bonds for rebuilding the harbor, and the board shouldered the financial responsibility for negotiating the securities and managing the funds.

By the end of the nineteenth century, Chicago had become the largest grain distributor and the meat-packing capital of the United States. The board's imprint was stamped on its bridges, harbor, and railroads, and local merchants developed new techniques for transporting the weight of grain sacks, beef, and pork through its stockyards. Yet the movement of physical goods was not the greatest achievement of the board. Its greatest innovation was in pricing American provisions—not only for the city and the region but for the entire country and eventually for the world beyond its borders. This project established Chicago as both a regional capital and a site for coordinating the nation's agricultural markets.

The Nation as Market

The CBOT was instrumental in creating a market at the national scale for grains and its other products. Two problems had hampered its visions of connection. First, the distances that separated the prairie from the plains and the seaboard meant that communication was only as fast as the fastest train. The invention of the telegraph addressed this problem by separating travel time from communication time, creating informational bridges between cities and regions that overcame time and distance. It also created a new scale for the politics and market of the nation. More important, the telegraph created a double vision of the market. The first originated in the building of the CBOT with its markets rooted in a particular place and history, and the second seemed to defy location. Suddenly, information emanating from all corners of the United States and all over the world could move grain markets in Chicago. This was a fundamental shift in the concept of commerce. A market was no longer a *place* to buy and sell commodities. The telegraph helped create *the* market, a new entity that existed all the time and everywhere. The free flow of information across space made the market appear as a separate entity simultaneously composed of each its individual participants, and created a single entity that transcended them all.[18] With technology that enables a flow of information disconnected from place, the market appears to be a force outside of and more encompassing than the actions of the individuals that compose it, obscuring the daily acts of coordination, planning, and exchange that shape the market and its circulation. The political and economic work of rationalizing exchange united the commercial space of the nation and cut the market loose from its physical and geographical anchors.

The CBOT did not acquire its singular identity on its own. The country's boards of trade developed standards of reliable commercial news and price quotations that established trusted information sources and consolidated the market's unity. This was done with such effectiveness that in 1884, a prominent historian of Chicago could claim that, "the system of gathering all important commercial statistics has been carried to a point of comprehensiveness and accuracy far beyond that of the Government bureau of statistics." The rhetorical force of the CBOT's efforts in Washington and the Chicago city government belie the discursive opposition between market and government knowledge.[19]

The reliability and accuracy of market information was of keen interest to Chicago traders. At its third annual meeting, in 1851, the CBOT adopted a rule forbidding members to give "untruthful or bogus reports of their transactions, on pain of expulsion."[20] This move toward truthfulness and transparency in commerce was not based simply on moral principles; it was also necessary for making Chicago a center of nationwide commerce. In a national arena, where the reputations of individual traders were not known, commercial agents could only rely on the reputation of the organization. It was imperative for the CBOT to police both the conduct of its members and the information that flowed into and out of its pits, to develop and maintain fair prices and accurate information, and to establish and enforce the regulations that would secure a sound reputation that would allow the extension of commerce beyond the borders of the Chicago business community.

Cities maintained different standards for measuring weight and quality, a technical problem that slowed trade, hampered distribution, and divided commercial regions. Accurate information and interconnection were not enough to extend the boundaries of the market to meet those of the nation. A certain set of standard measures now had to be imposed on provisions in a market where products could move easily across geographical boundaries. The CBOT had created a series of exact standards for the inspection, warehousing, and shipping of grain to make traffic between cities and regions possible, but their adoption in Chicago was not sufficient. They had to be adopted throughout the country to create the fluidity necessary for national agricultural commerce. Chicago worked to standardize measure and coordinate commerce with boards of trade from Milwaukee to Buffalo.

The first innovation was standard grading of quality, a process that made one bushel of wheat classified as "winter wheat" fungible with any other.[21] This allowed for centralization of the grain market in the elevators of Chicago. Farmers and their representatives sold to the elevator owners and released the products of their fields into the vast rivers of "winter wheat" that flowed through Chicago. These standard grades did even more than create new centers for trade. They also helped to make information about oats, corn, and wheat consistent, which allowed for a buyer's easy judgment; winter wheat was winter wheat no matter where it came from or who grew it. The boards of trade scrutinized standards that disconnected commodities from their place of production. With standards in place, information about grain could circulate without reference to individual farmers or particular fields.

The problem of measuring grain matched the more intangible problem of grading its quality. When the CBOT was founded, farmers and buyers measured grain by the bushel, an inconsistent measure of size that maintained the connection between the specific lot of grain and the farmer or owner who produced it. Despite shifting from carriage to boat to train on a trip from Kansas to New York, Jones's bushel remained Jones's bushel until it reached its final buyer. Measuring grain by weight did something miraculous. New standards for measurement allowed shipments of grain to be combined, shifting title from the farmer to the warehouse owner, who could resell a thousand bushels (by weight) of wheat to New York merchants without reference to the farmers who had grown it.[22] This system helped make grain a true commodity, disconnected from the place of its production and its producer. As with grading quality, in order to have this new standard fulfill its potential for easing commerce, other cities had to be convinced to adopt Chicago's standards.

Chicago's prominence in the grain markets lead other inland ports to follow in this reform. The shared standards facilitated transactions and solidified the connections between market centers. New York's merchants, however, who bought much of the West's shipments, remained recalcitrant. Their business remained tied to the Atlantic commerce of the British Empire and the system of standards that bound them to these traders. Forsaking British standards in favor of inland American ones would forcibly redefine their commercial alliances, and American trade had not yet proved more profitable than Atlantic trade. New York was already an end-point for American commerce, and its merchants therefore felt less pressure to adopt measures that would ease trade in vast bulk.[23] They may also have been reluctant to follow the lead of cities they did not feel were New York's commercial equal.

The Chicago Board of Trade and its allied associations in Milwaukee, Toledo, and Buffalo bristled against this impediment to commerce. The grain merchants of the west chose Buffalo to lead the charge on New York. Trapped between buying in the west by weight and selling in New York by bushel, these merchants fought to impose their standard. In June 1854, the Buffalo BOT adopted a resolution that put pressure on New York to capitulate:

> Resolved, That this Board of Trade strongly disapprove[s] of the practice of measuring grain as now existing in the city of New York, and view it as detrimental to the interest of produce dealers generally, and particularly to those making shipments direct to that market, occasioning thereby unnecessary delays in unloading boats, and vexatious disputes and losses to shippers and owners of grain.
>
> Resolved, That this Board view the antiquated custom of measuring grain as practiced in the city of New York, as an incorrect and illegal method of ascertaining the number of bushels and the practice ought to be abolished and an uniform system of selling and delivering by weight, adopted.[24]

But pressure from inland cities could not sway New York. When it did break down in 1870, it was a crucial step in integrating the geography of the grain market, but by then, the capital of the grain market was not in dispute. It was Chicago.

The Architecture of Finance

As the CBOT and its markets grew in size and significance, the members committed themselves to carving out a place in the city that would match their growing stature. The directors built a succession of three buildings in the heart of Chicago. These buildings were not simple containers for the labor of traders; the buildings themselves shaped the market within their walls. Just as the bridges and railroad tracks created a material infrastructure for Chicago's commodity markets, the CBOT building's dealing floor, trading pits, and corridors established a material form for the market. The flow of information, the shape of competition, and alliances between firms were all shaped by the interior geography of the CBOT buildings. The executives of the CBOT and their architects were conscious that each building was an experiment in the social shape of the market, its symbolism, and its civic significance. The struggle over the shape and meaning of the market created the CBOT's most poignant symbol—the 1930 building that stands at the intersection of LaSalle and Jackson in the heart of Chicago's Loop (see fig. 1.2).

Buildings are unusual technological artifacts because they require enormous sums of capital investment and can last for hundreds of years.[25] The CBOT buildings provided an unusual opportunity for experimenting with the physical form of a market. Because its business expanded so rapidly and continuously over the course of a century, the organization built structures to keep up with the pace of growth. Each structure bears the imprint of its many constituencies and their ideas about the proper arrangement of their marketplace. The building constructed by the CBOT in 1930 and its additions bring these stories together.

LaSalle Street is one of Chicago's most important avenues. It cuts through the heart of the Loop, in the center of Chicago's business district. Like Wall Street, its New York counterpart, Chicago's financial world takes its name from this thoroughfare. LaSalle Street may define Chicago's financial heart, but derivatives, like the CBOT's futures contracts, define LaSalle Street. The Chicago Board of Trade, the Chicago Board Options Exchange, a spin-off of the CBOT that has grown to rival its progenitor, and the Chicago Mercantile Exchange, now the largest futures exchange in the world, are LaSalle Street's global players and some of the world's busiest derivatives exchanges. Financial tales are etched on its architecture.

Although Chicago's working shoulders are most often connected to hog butchery, the derivatives story is just as defining for the city. None of these stories is more important than that of a building that does not carry a LaSalle Street address: the 1930 building at 141 W. Jackson Boulevard. From the layout of their trading floors to the decorative details of the elevators and the façades, the designs of the Chicago Board of Trade buildings reveal a fundamental transition from a market based in the abstractions of the midwestern grain trade to the markets for financial instruments based on abstractions of government debt.

But the importance of architecture goes beyond this modern story. The buildings, trading pits, and technologies of the CBOT shape the ways that dealers conduct their business within the confines of the Board.[26] The CBOT buildings create markets by arranging bodies and communications in space and guide their movements through channels of concrete, metal and stone. They assemble the information technologies, the speculators, and the organization in one space, define the actions that *can* happen there and the actions that *must* happen there to produce successful deals in futures contracts.[27]

: : :

The 1930 Board of Trade Building shows how new configurations of place, space, and time organize the mechanics and symbolism of trade. The buildings, trading floors, and dealing pits themselves were the outcome of a complicated process of growth, quarreling, and the exercise of power. The finished building renders the designers' vision of the market durable, fixed in stone and cable; it cements the role of the CBOT in Chicago; and it imposes routines on the conduct of traders as they make the trading pits churn, linking the physical form of the building to the proper operation of the market. The 1930 building held two significant promises: it would make the market more efficient by allowing more business into its halls, arranging the trading floor according to market principles, and channeling the arrival and dissemination of information. It would also anchor the board's place in the city of Chicago as a key financial institution inseparable from its host. There were conflicting ideas about how to move forward with the ten-million-dollar project. The stakes were high.

The building completed in 1930 was the third building dedicated to the exchange. The first space specifically designed for the CBOT was the Chamber of Commerce, which was destroyed in the Great Chicago Fire of 1871. The exchange rebuilt the structure, but it soon outgrew the space, and in 1885 the CBOT built its first structure at Jackson and LaSalle.

Height was a key design element for each of the buildings that have stood

1.1 Completed in 1885, this CBOT building was the first to stand at the corner of Jackson and LaSalle. Courtesy of Special Collections Department, University Library, University of Illinois at Chicago.

on this site. At ten stories, the 1885 building cut an impressive figure on the Chicago landscape. It was the tallest building in the city and the first commercial structure to have electric lighting. A tower jutted from the building, an image of Chicago's financial power that linked the national and international aspirations of the city with the commercial prowess of the CBOT. As the designers must have intended, the structure's luminous bulk was a defining feature of Chicago. It awed Frank Norris, whose prose practically trembles as he describes the structure in *The Pit*, "The lighted office buildings, the murk of rain, the haze of light in the heavens, and raised against it the pile of The Board of Trade Building, black, grave, monolithic, crouching on its foundations, like a monstrous sphinx with blind eyes, silent, grave — crouching there without a sound, without sign of life under the night and drifting veil of rain."[28] Norris notices the Board of Trade Building not simply for its financial power (he describes the building after hours) but for its monumental physical presence in the "great gray city" of Chicago.[29] The building embodied Chicago's project of urban greatness through private commercial strength.[30]

Its great mass was divided into three elaborately adorned parts, each crowned with a pyramidal tower. An enormous clock hung under the eaves of the most prominent gable, lending a modern touch, and reminding Chicagoans of the connection between time and money. Seventeen elegant stained-glass windows offset its unwieldy design. The most significant of these connected the business of the board with forces beyond the control of even the most masterful traders: the morning sun shining into the trading room illuminated the allegorical figures of Agriculture, Commerce, Fortune, and Order. The windows were designed by John La Farge, a nineteenth-century artist, critic, and designer, and fabricated by Tiffany in New York. La Farge's works in glass and paint still hang in Harvard Memorial Hall, Trinity Church in Boston, and the Metropolitan Museum of Art in New York. Such art aimed to express the CBOT's cultural prominence through commerce. The Sunday *Chicago Tribune* (February 4, 1929) reported that the mayor and a committee of federal, state, and city officials who presided at the opening of the building in 1885 were suitably captivated.

Several objects and documents were deposited in the polished cornerstone as the foundation was laid in 1882. The tokens fixed the time and place of the building's creation and memorialized the citizen merchants of the city who built it. They included a list of members of the CBOT, a city directory for 1882, a copy of the *Chicago Inter Ocean* for December 31, 1881, containing a statement of the trade and commerce of Chicago, and a set of United States postage stamps. The building, however, ultimately fell victim to expanding business. In the early 1920s the CBOT's leaders began making plans to erect a skyscraper on the site.

The Art Deco tower that replaced the initial building rises forty-four stories above the street. The lines of the building draw the eye straight up. Several stories up, a stylized stone eagle guards an enormous clock that is buttressed by two figures. On the left, a stone image of a hooded ancient clutching a sheaf of wheat. Three stories tall, the icon represents the farmers of the Fertile Crescent, who first cultivated grain. On the right, a figure

1.2 The CBOT's Art Deco tower, completed in 1930 and crowned with a statue of Ceres, the Roman goddess of grain, remains the exchange's signature building and a Chicago landmark. Courtesy of the Board of Trade of the City of Chicago.

of a Native American, adorned with stylized feathers, grips stalks of corn. A pyramid crowns the top of the building, supporting a thirty-one-foot cast aluminum statue of Ceres, the Roman goddess of grain and the harvest, who guards the business interests of the men below. Every morning, traders and the clerks, office staff, and managers who support them file through heavy brass doors adorned with images of agriculture. This skyscraper, designed by Holabird and Root, the first of two buildings that now house the Chicago Board of Trade, was finished in 1930 and dominates LaSalle Street with an imposing grace. Its vertical limestone ribs and its stylized, machine-worked details, evoke an era of commercial brilliance and individual flash.

But the finished building hides as much as it reveals. The New Building

Committee had considered and rejected several other designs for the building that also satisfied city setback regulations and provided ample office space
for the CBOT to rent.[31] The competition was fierce. Architects from Chicago and New York lobbied for the contract. One eager architect wrote to the
New Building Committee to support his plan with flattering arguments for
its symbolism and future profitability:

> I believe this proposition merits serious consideration because, first—a build-
> ing of this type will be a monument to the City of Chicago as well as the home
> of one of the basic industries of the country; second—the project can be eas-
> ily financed because of the substantial value of your . . . holdings; third—
> because if properly handled the project will show a substantial return on the
> money invested.[32]

Of course, every competing architect might have made the same claims.
The differences were in the drawings.

The offices of famed Chicago architect Daniel Burnham submitted drawings of a building adorned with neoclassical ornaments. Their design frames
the building's main entrance with an arcade of Corinthian columns, each
topped with a classical figure in full round and elaborated with Latin commentary. Enormous windows garlanded in stone swags face LaSalle Street,
overwhelming the doorways, which appear miniscule in comparison. In the
drawings, the street bustles with sketchy figures of pedestrians, but the imposing neoclassical details seem to shut them out of the edifice. It is a clumsy design that confounds the civic meaning that Burnham had achieved in designs
for the Chicago World's Fair. The cornices and pediments on the CBOT
building strike the wrong balance between civic purpose and finance.

Alfred Alschuler, on the other hand, favored a neo-Gothic design complete with ornamental buttresses, reminiscent of the recently constructed
Tribune Tower just a few blocks away. In his drawings, a flag tops the skyscraper's central spire. In a medieval city, the flag would be a signpost; it
would make urban space legible by marking a palace or center of commerce.
The giant flag, however, is superfluous. By its sheer size, the forty-story building, which would have been easily visible for miles, would need no other
adornment to signal its place in Chicago's landscape.

More Modern

Holabird and Root's modern skyscraper won out.[33] Their design brought together the high style of capitalism with the board's modern project—profit
through distilling and abstracting nature into circulating commodities. Rather

1.3 The Burnham firm's submission for the architectural competition buries the modern mission of the CBOT behind enormous neoclassical columns and statuary. Courtesy of Special Collections Department, University Library, University of Illinois at Chicago.

1.4 Alfred Alschuler's skyscraper design appealed to the CBOT's taste for history, adding medieval details to this cathedral of capitalism. Courtesy of Special Collections Department, University Library, University of Illinois at Chicago.

than harking back to the Middle Ages or classical times in its symbolism, the building's direct and forceful lines swept into the future. Like the financial work of the CBOT, the building was dressed in the symbols of an ongoing project—making trade faster, more efficient, and more far-reaching, ultimately supplanting nature with a man-made system of trade.[34]

The story is in the details. As the 1885 building came down, the icons of Agriculture, Commerce, Fortune, and Order gave way to machine-tooled nickel decorations that acknowledged the centrality of technology in the contemporary practice of agriculture. The Goddess of Grain and the ancestors of cultivation may seem pure emblems of an agrarian past and present, but the new building's adornments suggested the relationship between the CBOT, modern technologies, and the future.

Art Deco made its official debut at the 1925 Paris exhibition. In 1930, such architecture was cutting-edge design for the "cathedrals of capitalism" like the CBOT building and the Chrysler Building in New York. Unlike the avant-garde architects of the time, who bared the structure of their buildings in the spare aesthetic of the International Style, Art Deco designers flaunted the power of money with the glamour of variegated marble and extravagant lighting systems that made the interior glow. The sumptuous materials and copious, lively decorations of Art Deco invoke a modernism that explicitly links design to the worship of capital. More is more modern at the CBOT.

The details of the building highlight the board's particular technique of capital accumulation. Abstract images of plants and flowers swirl with a machine-precision finish. These decorations are geometric and angular, accentuating their stylized, man-made quality. The images express a distance from the organic world even as nature is exploited, much as do futures contracts themselves. The details bring this denaturalization to life, showing off the transportation technologies that brought grain to market and people across oceans to engage in commerce. The building's lower floors are adorned with granite inlays of stylized zeppelins and ocean liners. The paneled gates that guard the entrance to the 1930s trading floor show intricate scenes of the planting, harvesting, threshing, and milling of grain, and at the end of the cycle are depictions of the transportation technologies that bring the wheat, corn, and other grains to market. These images reveal the importance of machines to agriculture. In the planting panel, two men and a woman sow a field while smoke curls out of two tall smoke stacks behind them. In the second panel, a threshing machine spews out wheat as the two human harvesters seem to be retreating from its presence. The ship's panel contains no representations of either grain or human presence; rather, a silo's contents are unloaded into the cargo hold of a ship via a chute without the intervention of human hands.

The design of the Board of Trade Building tells us that human abstractions, like futures contracts, and technology now dominate nature. No longer is the trade in grains symbolically linked to the gods of Agriculture, Commerce, Fortune, and Order. Expertise and technological equipment are the essential conduits of commerce.

Gathering Constituencies

Even though the New Building Committee thought that the Holabird and Root design clearly drew together the board's missions of modern commerce and urban grandeur most effectively, they had to gain the CBOT membership's approval before they could hire the architects. Henry A. Rumsey, chair of the committee, set about assembling a constituency to support their decision. As with every major plan at the CBOT, the members had the opportunity to vote. Whether or not each member preferred the Art Deco splendor of Holabird and Root's building was less important than the way the vote brought together the collective opinion of the members. After the vote took place, the varied opinions of the membership were solidified into a single choice that sealed the shape of the building and reinforced the network of traders. The vote gave the members a collective investment in the design.

In addition to representing the consolidated and ordered opinions of traders, the building was also a site for bringing together and arranging alliances between organizations, and individuals, and for making concrete their commitments to futures markets. The destruction of the 1885 building eradicated an older set of alliances and opened an opportunity to reconfigure the network of actors that made up the CBOT and reconstruct markets. It was an opportunity to reinforce some connections and sever others.[35] Henry Rumsey selected the associations and interpretations to be established and strengthened.[36]

Rumsey began a chain of communications with members in Chicago and in other key cities. His far-flung supporters whipped up the vote, persuading other off-site members to send in ballots. Rumsey, looking to enlist the influential Dennis & Co. of Baltimore, wrote to emphasize the symbolic role that the building could play in the Maryland company's business. "If we have the wonderful building which is projected you will certainly be proud to visit us some day and take your friends into the new building or put its picture on your letter-head."[37] Others didn't need convincing. E. P. Peck of the Omaha Grain Exchange simply sent congratulations, as did H. F. Shepherdson of the Minneapolis Grain Exchange. Rumsey replied to Peck with gratitude: "Handsome is as handsome does. May I say once more that we have had a worthy representative, mentally, physically, financially and spiritually in your good self in recommending the erection of the finest structure grain business knows or Chicago has ever had. You know the Committee thanks you for this splendid work and personally I am more appreciative that [*sic*] I can tell you."[38]

Grain traders and bankers outside Chicago used their votes to link themselves and their businesses to the future of the CBOT and its building. Rumsey and the board's leadership clearly wanted to make the building the symbol of the organization's national commercial strength, worthy of support and investment.

What Is in an Address?

Planning the new building had helped Rumsey draw together the board's constituencies of traders outside Chicago, as would at least two other moments in the building's early life. The opening of the new building provided an opportunity to establish and sustain ties with other businessmen and their organizations. The CBOT was clever about buttressing its trade and influence through alliances. To announce its opening, the CBOT sent clay models of the new building to officers at financial, transportation, and technology corporations, including the president of the Chase National Bank in New York, the president of American Steel Foundries in Chicago, the superintendent of the Little Rock Cotton Exchange, the president of the Omaha Grain Exchange, and the President of the Erie Railroad in New York.

The board also used the majesty of the new building to claim its place among the nation's most important institutions. Laying the cornerstone provided an opportunity to bring together representatives of organizations that worked with the board and institutions whose financial stature the board matched or to which it aspired. The ceremony included the president of the New York Stock Exchange, the president of the Chicago Stock Exchange, the governor of Illinois, the mayor of Chicago, the secretary of the Department of Agriculture, and the governor of the Federal Reserve Bank. The ceremony allowed each of these institutions to show its support.

Some connections were made more material by sharing space with the CBOT. From the beginning, the Chicago Stock Exchange was housed within the CBOT's walls. In addition to creating a place for its own financial operations, the board's new building provided vast rentable space. The CBOT did its best to fill the offices with desirable tenants, emphasizing in its advertisements its physical and symbolic location in the heart of Chicago and the part it played in America's growing financial prowess. The promotional booklet that the CBOT distributed to potential tenants juxtaposed a photograph of LaSalle Street ending in the imposing, modern CBOT tower with a drawing of Wall Street, obliquely presented and ending in Trinity Church. The images are accompanied by the caption, "At the head of LaSalle Street. The Board of Trade Building dominates the financial center of the middle west." The juxtaposition makes clear its claim for inclusion in the company of the great financial institutions of America, if not the world.

The CBOT building committee banked on such a reputation to draw tenants, confident in the claim of their architects that, "In spite of the rather large amount of office space on the market at this time, we consider that the enormous prestige of the Board of Trade coupled with its unique advantages of location in the heart of the financial district justify the erection of a building of maximum capacity."[39] Renting space in the CBOT building, they thought, would create opportunities for companies to maintain close ties, both symbolic and real, with the eminent institution.

Apparently, many organizations agreed and set up offices in the building. Listed on the 1931 roster of tenants are newspaper companies such as *Barron's Financial Weekly* and the *Wall Street Journal*; transportation companies, including the Canadian Pacific railway and the Duluth South Shore and Atlantic Railway; and telecommunications companies, including Western Union and R.C.A. Communications Radiograms; and industrial and agricultural powerhouses like Armour and Company, and Cargill Grain Company. Offices in the Board of Trade Building not only provided ready access to the CBOT markets, but also allowed tenants to be part of the expanding influence of Chicago's financial world.

The city itself had an interest in connecting to its workings. The Chicago Transit Department sought office space in the new building, and the Chairman of the CBOT Transportation Committee worked to secure it. Going over the head of the New Building Committee, he wrote directly to the board of directors to ensure that Rumsey would provide substantial space for the Chicago Transit Department. The chairman argued that it had always had headquarters in CBOT and that the Transit Department represented "all of the Chicago railroads in transit shipment matters. It maintains the records pertaining to the in- and outbound shipments of grain, seeds and the products of our mills and factories and certifies the freight rates. Our shippers are necessarily in constant contact with the Transit Department and having it located in our building is a great convenience to them." He reiterated the connection between the CBOT and the city's services and infrastructure, which the organization had worked so hard to build in the nineteenth century.

The CBOT also emphasized the advanced technologies incorporated in its new building in order to attract tenants. Elevators and telephones connected the trading floor with office workers both inside and outside the building, short-circuiting the distances between them. As the CBOT advertised, their Otis elevators were "[t]he finest vertical transportation in the world." In addition to speeding workers to their desks at the literal heights of commerce, the elevators accelerated communications, helping clerks to whisk messages between the board room and the offices of trading companies. Elevators had an even more powerful counterpart in the telephone. Skyscrapers are only possible because elevators allow rapid and effortless movement between the upper floors and the street and to the upper floors of other buildings.[40] But with the telephone, distance and height were no impediment to communication.

In addition to forging business connections, establishing communication with the market, and distributing market information, the CBOT building was a place for traders to congregate as men. In between rounds of dealing, they could visit the tailor to keep up with the latest fashions or stop in at the barber shop to get a haircut. A cigar stand and a soda fountain area were also included in the original building plans. Such amenities offered additional opportunities for the board to exercise its connections with city government. In typical Chicago fashion, Christopher Paschen, Chicago Commissioner of Buildings, wrote to Rumsey asking for assistance in securing the cigar stand and fountain space for a friend.[41]

The connections and services available to the new tenants were crucial. But symbols of the building's prominence were not yet set in stone. Even though the CBOT building was located in the heart of the financial district, its mailing address was not yet firm. Such a common detail as a street address was a subject of keen discussion between representatives of the board and the tenants, all of whom sought to stabilize the building's symbolic potential. Writing to another official at the CBOT in 1930, H. Rumsey recounted a conversation with a representative of Quaker Oats over the proper address of the building.

> Dear Mr. Clutton:
>
> In talking with Mr. Murray of Quaker Oats after I had suggested to him that they use as their address Board of Trade Building, LaSalle at Jackson, he intimated that he thought it would be a splendid feature on the letterhead of everyone connected with the Board of Trade or in the Board of Trade Building.
>
> This would tie the Board of Trade Building up with LaSalle Street, the world's greatest financial highway west of Wall and a street having something that Wall Street has not namely: The Board of Trade Building.[42]

All official CBOT communications were headed with a graphic of the building. Eventually, a phrase was added to the logo—"Serving the Nation since 1848." Rumsey and his counterpart at Quaker Oats were both conscious of the commercial and urban connections that an address crystal-lized and used that to draw a specific connection between the organization of the CBOT, its city, street, and building. The CBOT tenants piggybacked on this connection and used the board building to claim a place of com-mercial and cultural significance that could rival New York's.

The Trading Floor: Element of Design

However lucrative rental income was, the board's main mission was the pro-duction of markets. The skyscraper was constructed around the hangarlike trading room that defined the building. But the design of the trading floor was a source of conflict.

From the design of the trading pits to the placement of the telephones and the material of floorboards, the architects, board officials, and members debated the proper arrangements with intensity. The construction and lay-out of the trading floor guide the daily paths of the traders and configure whom they can see and hear, their access to information, and what com-munications technologies they can use instantly and which they must stretch to procure. These spatial arrangements mean money, and the CBOT's mem-bers had fiery opinions about how it should work. The trading floor that was finally built was the product of competing interests and the powerful figures that mediated them. Rumsey, the board's negotiator and decision maker, swapped letters and conducted innumerable conversations with the archi-tects, builders, and members of the board over the years during which the building was conceived, planned, and constructed.[43] His correspondence shows how he mediated between traders, customers, architects, and con-cerned members of the city bureaucracy, who all had an interest in the shape of the building. The CBOT that now stands is an artifact of Rumsey's skill-ful handling of these exchanges. Once it was erected, it consolidated a net-work of individuals, commercial interests, and urban planning concerns in its stone form.

Rumsey's committee recommended plans to the chair of the board of di-rectors, who had the final say. But there was little disagreement between the board of directors and its committee. Rumsey was the guiding hand behind the building, synthesizing interests and making the final decisions about what would be built and how. He made sure not only that the design al-lowed for compromise between interests, but that assembling physical plans was an opportunity for experiment. During the design process, he could bring the marketplace more closely in line with the ideals of commerce, shaping the pits to reflect market principles of individual competition and smooth circulation, and making them literally durable.

For Rumsey and the building's designers, the trading floor, or the board room, as it was called, was the central concern. In the board room, traders produced futures markets, but producing the board room took some feats of engineering. First, it required a vast open space at the building's core. Six huge trusses, each weighing 227 tons, held up the skyscraper over the enormous hall, eliminating the need for support columns that would block the movement and view of the traders. The wide-open arena allowed traders to circulate easily between pits, the telegraph and telephone operators, their offices, and the smoking room where traders met clients. This space, at 165 feet long by 130 feet wide, with a 60-foot ceiling, gave each trader equal access to the markets and to the information he needed to trade. The design applied the market principles of order and equal access to information.

The board room of the older building had strayed from the ideal and had become chaotic as the CBOT grew. In Holabird and Root's 1927 memorandum on the older board room, the architects observe that "[i]t may be of some interest to note the changes that have come about in the board room in the last eight or ten years. First, the board room looks more dingy, more cluttered up and less orderly than it did some time ago. This is due to the demand for increased facilities." A cotton pit, a trading post for oats, several telephone stations, and a coat room for telegraph operators crowded the floor. More and more Western Union operators packed the desk surrounding their office. Companies overcrowded their telegraph stations with illicit operators. Swarms of clerks also congregated by the telephones, creating "a very unsightly condition" as the messengers elbowed their way to the phone lines.[44] Quotation boards, where the changing prices of commodities were recorded, were raised off the ground to make more room and operated from a balcony. The News Bureau was shunted into the smoking room as the markets they reported on ballooned.

The architects, builders, and New Building Committee debated how to turn this haphazard arrangement into an ordered whole. Creating a rationalized board room meant both providing good arrangements for the traders, giving each equal access to the market and its sources of information, as well as providing efficient conduits for prices between the board room's markets and the outside world. Each demanded close attention to the construction of physical space. Letters to and from Rumsey detailed disagreements over the kinds of communications technologies to include, where to place them, and how to set up the pits to optimize their operation. Luckily for the New Building Committee, an experiment in marketplace design was already under way. Before the builders began to wreck the 1885 building, the board reestablished itself in a temporary trading space not far from the new construction site. New arrangements and materials could be tested there. The experiment showed that traders' concerns focused on their access to other traders' eyes and voices.

In the board room, hand signals and shouts conveyed prices and dealing offers, placing the body at the center of traders' dealing strategies. Floor trading was taxing physical labor. To take full advantage of the markets, a trader stood for hours a day among throngs of competitors jostling each other for advantage. For the interim trading floor to work, it had to provide a certain level of physical comfort for the traders and allow them to hear and see the sounds and gestures of their trading partners and the market as a whole. The acoustics of the hall were crucial to the operation of the market and to profits. Rumsey conveyed this to Holabird and Root in a request to use a flooring material for the permanent trading room that would absorb excess sound and be "easy on the feet." The architects dismissed wood, rubber tile, cork, and linoleum as options. The softer materials would quickly give way under the floor traffic and would, "in a short time present a dilapidated appearance."[45]

Unhappy with the architects' aesthetic intransigence, the board turned to a scientist for help. Rumsey hired Professor F. R. Watson, a physicist at University of Illinois, to analyze the acoustics on the temporary trading floor. There was apparently much room for improvement. A letter to John Hola-

1.5 Before the day's activity began, the trading floor of the 1885 building appears calm and orderly. Telephone stations and proliferating trading pits do not clutter the space yet. Courtesy of the Board of Trade of the City of Chicago.

1.6 Traders at the CBOT pose for a group portrait on the crowded trading floor. Courtesy of the Board of Trade of the City of Chicago.

bird from the New Building Committee conveyed the sentiments of the traders and communications workers from the experimental trading floor. Traders in the corn pit were especially piqued:

> Conditions are terrible, far worse than it was at the old Board; can't make yourself heard across the pit; in the old Board could stand on edge of pit with back turned and pick out and distinguish voices, impossible now; majority of traders are experiencing throat trouble since they began trading here; go home at night actually tired from the exhaustion of shouting in order to be heard and from the continual uproar and noise in the trading hall; in the old building were able to distinguish outstanding voices of men in the wheat pit or whever [sic] they might be, can't seem to now; . . . one could pick pit voices readily and locate their origin, but that is difficult now.[46]

Clearly the experimental space had failed to improve the market. The cacophony even threatened the accuracy of the price information coming out of the pits. A Mr. Chronister, who managed the CBOT's Quotations Department, reported that the new space was "500% worse than the old building. The reporters have difficulty in getting quotations correctly and the traders themselves are unable to hear properly across the pit."[47]

If the quotations were incorrect, false price information would flow from the trading floor by way of the telephones, telegraphs, and pneumatic tubes that connected locations as near as offices in the building and as far away as England and Argentina. Demand for information from the CBOT was growing rapidly. For the new building, the architects expanded the electric wiring capacity of the floor and opened larger channels for telegraph cables to run from the board room to the offices of the Cleveland Telegraph Company, the Western Union office, and the postal telegraph stations. Although these companies provided the major public access to CBOT quotations, many firms maintained their own dedicated lines to the trading floor.

How to arrange the informational conduits of the trading floor was a hot button issue. Rumsey and the New Building Committee had to mediate arguments between traders, telegraph companies, and the architects over where the telegraph and telephone stations were to be located on the floor, and how to allot them to Western Union and other telegraph companies. Noting that "[a]t present there is more demand for telegraph facilities than ever before," the Holabird and Root plan provided for sixteen telephone booths in sight of the quotation board. Traders suggested configurations for the telegraphs and telephones. Arthur Lindley of Clement, Curtis & Co. suggested that the CBOT imitate the New York Curb Market and install stadium-style telephone banks to ensure that "every telephone man has a very clear view of the whole floor." Rumsey filed his letter and photos with "all the others of like nature."[48]

Holabird and Root were also concerned to make market information available to all participants. They noted that the haphazard arrangements that had grown up on the older trading floor had obscured the quotation boards. A fair market where skill and speed would determine profit required equal access to information. The firm set out to construct a board room that would give no inherent advantage to place. However, not all participants were willing to give up their privileges. Some member firms tried to manipulate access to telephones, aiming to gain advantage in the market by influencing the arrangement of space and technology on the trading floor. They pressured the board of directors to secure extra telephone lines that would support their own business. The president pressured Rumsey to accommodate their requests.

Rumsey objected to this departure from the ideals of an apolitical market developed under the direction of experts. He replied to the president's attempt to influence his plans with ire:

> Your Committee on New Building has been advised of the wishes of your
> Honorable Board . . . relative to . . . the installation of equipment for fourteen
> private telephones adjacent to the Wheat pit to the South.
>
> We must respectfully, but nevertheless earnestly, protest against such a
> plan. Two years of study and thought were dedicated to the main floor arrange-
> ment, for handling the business of the entire active membership rather than
> the few. The best architectural and engineering talent have counseled us in
> determining the best possible arrangement for our floor facilities, including
> private telephones. Two Boards of Directors have reviewed and approved of
> the lay-out, sponsored by your Building Committee.[49]

Some raised aesthetic objections to the new telephones. "It is the unan-
imous opinion that it would be a serious mistake to mark the superb Exchange Hall floor with this limited number of telephones," the building
committee wrote. But mainly the committee objected on the grounds of
equal access to information. Some firms had begun "flashing" their orders
to the pit from the telephone lines, relying on the rapid hand signals that
would become an integral and identifying part of financial pits. The New
Building Committee saw this as introducing informational disorder. Flashing blurred the boundary between the pit and the outside market. The hand
signals made customers' orders visible to attentive traders who could see
them before they reached the open market. Rather than acting only with information available within the market borders of the pit, these traders could
act with information from outside the boundaries of the physical market.
Adding new telephones would therefore not only favor a select group of
trading houses but also allow the market to spill over out of the trading pit.
Rumsey's letter continued:

> It appears that the preference for these telephones is confined entirely to cer-
> tain houses flashing their orders to the pit, and . . . this practice has been
> frowned upon in construction plans due to its possibility for special prefer-
> ence. Customer orders should have privacy, and it is a notorious fact that alert
> pit traders soon become aware of the signals of different houses and can thus
> define the character of orders before they actually reach the pit.
>
> Therefore, . . . there is no justification for making any variation in the
> plans for confining the private telephone privileges to the East and West wall
> of the building, as this plan avoids highly discriminatory positions, while ben-
> efits, if any from change, accrue to comparatively few firms.[50]

The New Building Committee stood by its responsibility to define the
kind of information available. They had assembled the expert opinions that

showed them how to engineer information and shape the space of the trading floor. The design process they favored reflected the process of the market itself. They worked with the idea that conflict produced the truest and best design, just as it allowed the market to "discover" a price.

The 1930 building was the symbol of the board's place in the city and nation. The monumental design of the board room and the care that went into its construction asserted its central importance to the organization and the city. Rumsey and his committee had worked to create a board room that would draw traders, firms, and information into the pit. The design of the floor anchored the market inside the pit and created lines of communication that stretched away from it.

When the new building opened, the connection between Chicago and futures markets was undeniable. The Chicago newspapers crowed, declaring its central place in the city. The *Chicago Daily News* ran a photograph with the caption, "Impressive when viewed from any angle, the Board of Trade Building stands like a tall sentinel among the older structures that flank it on the east and west. On clear days it is visible to motorists starting northward from Hyde Park on the outer drive." The *Chicago Daily Times* for November 13, 1931, devoted a spread to the building with the following headline: "NEW BOARD OF TRADE BUILDING IN FRONT RANK OF CHICAGO'S POINTS OF INTEREST."

Smaller headlines defined other sections.

> THE SENTRY—LaSalle St., financial center of the west, stretches before this handsome temple of trade. The architectural marvel rises 44 stories into the sky; it value—land and building—is $22,000,000. Limestone is the predominant material used in its construction.
>
> BEAUTY GALORE—Inside and out, the Board of Trade Building challenges its fellows the world over.[51]

The Board of Trade Chapter of the American Legion offered yet another suggestion for making the building a spatial signpost for Chicago. John Fisher, the post's commander, wrote to recommend a beacon light for the top of the building, which would serve as a guide-light for the U.S. Air Mail pilots and would, "help to bring the name of the Chicago Board of Trade into greater prominence, not only among the people of Chicago, but of the United States as well." Finally, it would be the only beacon light west of New York atop a major building.[52] Although it is unclear whether a light was ever installed, it is certain that the American Legion officers had the right idea. The CBOT building was a beacon for the City of Chicago and its financial nexus for years to come.

Architecture of Circulation

The story of the CBOT and architecture does not end in its Art Deco halls. The differences between the 1885 and 1930 buildings arose from a renegotiation of the material form of the market; the expansion of the 1980s provided another opportunity for the CBOT to reconsider the form and symbolism of its marketplace. Some fifty years after the construction of the Art Deco tower, the CBOT raised more questions about how best to express its markets and mission through its architecture, making plans to redesign its market space.

The room for expansion allowed for in the 1930 design could not contain the explosion of trade that followed the invention and development of Treasury futures markets in the 1970s and 1980s. By the late 1970s the expanding Board of Trade was stretching its machine-polished seams and began planning an addition and an improved trading floor that would be constructed behind the 1930s building. They commissioned Helmut Jahn, of the Chicago firm Murphy/Jahn, to design it. The differences between the Art Deco building and the new glass and steel addition reflected the evolution of the CBOT from its origin in industrial technologies and agricultural trade to an exchange built on the profitability of financial futures contracts — abstractions upon the abstraction of the U.S. economy.

The CBOT's place in the post-1970s global financial markets is represented by its material presence on the streets of Chicago. The new architecture embodied the emerging identity of the board, crystallized its alliances, and created a futures market outfitted with the latest technologies and guided by new principles of market action. These had changed radically since the wheat market dominated the trading floor. The gleaming new building, with its airy offices and sunlit interior, was appropriate for an organization centrally engaged in global financial networks. Illuminated from the inside, the building seems to float. Even though trading takes place in the hangarlike dealing room, the building's transparency expresses its connections to the markets beyond its halls.[53] No longer is the Board of Trade a financial space contained within Indiana stone, declaring its connections to agriculture and proclaiming its seemingly immovable place in Chicago. The new building's open environment replaces limestone solidity with an aesthetic appropriate to global network connections; its spaces bear little trace of Chicago's specificity.[54]

Instead, the 1980s building establishes a space of circulation that creates an image of swift, unobstructed flows, the market ideal for digital dealing, the newest market technology. The neon lighting and the boxy spaces of the 1980s addition retain little of the careful craft and local detail that established

1.7 The modern glass extension and airy atrium mix inside and outside, symbolizing the unobstructed flow of abstract financial futures contracts. The Art Deco portrait of Ceres that once graced the 1930 trading floor and reminded traders that their commerce was based in grain is now framed for nostalgic effect. Photo by Bob Davis.

a sense of urban solidity and regional significance in the 1930 building. Attachment to place can tie down the economic organization and individual; in financial dealing this threatens to draw attention from the space of trade and into the realm of civic obligations such as family attachments and city life, all of which threaten to impinge on financial judgments. Instead of dedication to place, the architecture of the Jahn building exudes abstraction and distilled commitment only to the circulation of colorless capital. The Board of Trade once reorganized the space of the city in order to build a market. Jahn's abstract structure reveals how organizations like the CBOT now understand the market as detached from place, a "disembedding" aligned with market ideals of unobstructed flow.[55]

Yet at the core of the building is a contradiction to the architecture of circulation. After fifteen years, the CBOT added still another trading floor, an amalgam of digital information technologies and trading pits at the center of the exchange. A heavily guarded turnstile gives access to the fourth floor—a space with two separate sections: the agricultural room, where traders still deal in contracts for wheat, corn, and soybeans, and the now more powerful financial dealing room. From the grain room, a narrow passage opens into the enormous new space where financial contracts are traded. Pat Arbor, chairman of the Board of Trade in 1997, when he built this state of the art, $182-million trading facility, made it clear that the board's commitment to pit trading was unshakable. But the new trading floor already seemed trapped between its commitment to place and its mission of creating endless circulation.

Blair Kamin, the architecture critic for the *Chicago Tribune*, emphasized the connection between the city's master modernist architect and the new trading space designed by his successors, Fujikawa, Johnson, and Associates. "Anyone who ventures up to the trading arena itself cannot help but feel Mies's influence. The master almost surely would have been pleased by the straightforward power of the room's big, column-free space, by its flexibility to accommodate both expansion and future technologies, and by its lack of visual clutter—no small achievement for a building with about 27,000 miles of low voltage cable."[56] Yet elements of the new trading floor were more akin to the fortress architecture of contemporary Los Angeles.[57] It is an aggressively private space, a huge stone block just to the side of the main building. There are no windows. The walls of the new trading floor create a boundary for the market, severing it from the city streets beyond and ensuring that no information can be exchanged between inside and outside. There is no public entry to the building. The revolving doors are tucked under the overpass between the old and new buildings. The doorway opens onto an atrium where members exchange their street jackets for trading coats. There are no chairs or places to linger. It is a clearly defined passage pointing to the trading floor. Traders pass through the guarded turnstile and ride up the escalator to enter the network of hallways surrounding the trading floor. The walls are unadorned granite, shiny, cold, and imposing. Short and shallow passageways cut through banks of phone desks to open onto a trading room the size of Grand Central Station. Diffuse, bright, fluorescent light comes from the fixtures four stories above. The walls of the financial room are covered in tall, gray panels covered with metallic-looking material. There are no internal walls to break up the space.

Circular structures raised above the floor level have steps inside and are ringed with padded railings for the clerks and brokers to lean against. Within the pits there are no places to sit. Long phone desks abut the pits, where clearing-firm clerks take orders and relay them to traders. When there is no one in the room, the sense of vacancy is absolute. There are no photos of family or friends such as might be found on cubicle walls in offices anywhere in the country. Nothing suggests what kind of commerce occurs at the exchange. The only signs of life outside this enclosed space are three flags on the east wall—the American flag, the Illinois flag, the City of Chicago flag, and a banner that says, "Welcome to the CBOT" on the north wall.

Despite its fluid, abstract architecture, the trading floor reveals a com-

1.8 The flags of the United States, Illinois, and the City of Chicago hang in the financial futures trading hall, marking the exchange's commitment to local and national identity, despite its global orientation. Photo by Bob Davis.

mitment to a particular market form: the trading pit as the nexus where commodities and information converge. With this new and costly structure, the CBOT leadership invested the organization in a particular vision of the Chicago market nexus. Arbor and his supporters argued that the millions of dollars spent on space and technologies to support the floor traders was nothing compared to the advantages their unique skills brought to the work of pricing and creating liquid markets. Digital technologies were excellent conduits of information to and from the trading floor, Arbor argued, but the essential technology of the CBOT was still the trading pits. All trading in American Treasury futures was channeled through these market arenas. Even when the board implemented an electronic trading system in the mid-1990s, it functioned as a supplement to the pits, operating when they were closed for business. This commitment to the pit, a specific place, and the local population of traders contradicted the logic of ubiquitous circulation.

The trading pit remains the CBOT's emblem and key tool for making markets. An image of a trading pit is emblazoned on the stone façade of the new trading floor, declaring the board's dedication to its method of trade. The same symbol is imprinted on CBOT business cards and on every publication that leaves the CBOT's central offices. The trading pit as a place and a technology at the heart of the exchange remains a defining feature of Chicago's distinctive commercial life. In the late 1990s, as the global futures industry was implementing digital dealing, the CBOT had to defend its commitment to the trading pit. The trading floor hidden within the architecture of circulation exposes the challenge that the CBOT faced. The meaning and function of the 1930 building had gradually given way as developments in technology and changes in financial markets allowed the board to reshape the material form of its marketplace. By the late 1990s the board was no longer able to sustain the contradiction at its core. Electronic technologies were replacing trading pits around the world. The price of a membership plummeted, and the board began to plan how to integrate electronic trading technologies, but the CBOT's historical attachment to open-outcry trading was not easily broken. The members' collective commitment to the cultural life and form of labor based in the trading pits was as fierce as the spirit of Chicago commerce. Although many of the arguments in the 1990s placed the computer at the heart of the problems of technology, we have seen how technological innovations, from bridges to telephones and architecture, have reshaped markets and raised challenges to older forms of exchange. Creating a material form for abstract exchange has always been a fundamental problem of the CBOT, and the shift from pit trading to electronic trading at the end of the twentieth century was only the latest phase in the modern project of creating the abstract space of mar-

kets. From standardizing contracts and commercial measures to establishing the city as a commercial space, creating circulation is a project based in
the manipulation of the physical world through technology and architecture. Revising the material form of the market to conform to the shifting
ideals of abstraction can never be complete.

In July 1998, Pat Arbor, the chairman of the CBOT, called a members' meeting to discuss rumors circulating in the pits, lunchrooms, and bars in and around the CBOT. Every day new tales surfaced about Arbor and his supporters pursuing electronic trading and creating a global trading network with other exchanges. The CBOT had already instituted its own electronic trading system, Project A, which operated after the trading floor closed, and word was that the managers were considering leaving it on all the time. More worrisome were Arbor's reputed intentions to bring European-style electronic trading to Chicago. He was pursuing an alliance with the all-electronic German-Swiss Exchange, which had recently wiped out the pits in London. The Chicago traders knew their chairman was making plans, and the traders speculated constantly on exactly what they were and what kind of changes they would bring. Each bit of gossip stirred up their anxieties. What costs would this transition involve? How would they train themselves to work on screens when their work had been rooted in the human action of the pits? Was Arbor going to give their German rival power over the course of the CBOT? Was their way of life and labor at risk? The outcome of arguments over the implementation of electronic technologies and cross-Atlantic alliances would shape the exchange's trading networks. The history of Chicago, allegiances to the trading pit, and the close ties of CBOT members came together to direct the actions of the largest futures market in the world.

The thirty-year Treasury Bond futures pit was the stage for the meeting. That July day, scraps of paper from the last hours of trading littered the floor as the clerks and other employees filed out, leaving only members in the quiet pits. Traders from the grain room across the hall joined the financial dealers. Arbor was already waiting to preside over the meeting, literally, from his perch atop the market reporters' stand, which hung over the pit. From the outset, the members were tense and their chairman was defensive. Arbor opened the meeting saying that he wanted to dispel the "rumors du jour" and allow the members to ask questions in the open, bringing what was already being talked about into the official discourse of the exchange.

First, he said, the CBOT would use its reserves to update its technology. Members would not be required to pay out of pocket for the electronic technologies they feared would relieve them of their livelihoods. The next rumor was wishful thinking. "Hasn't the Eurex agreement fallen apart," someone asked. No, it had not foundered, Arbor told them. The members noted that the wider public lacked confidence in the CBOT's future course. Over the last year, the value of CBOT "seats" had fallen almost half a million dollars off their peak. This loss in value symbolized the declining significance of the exchange, but it also meant that each full member of the CBOT had lost $500,000 (in paper value, at least) in this collapse. Arbor had to dispel the hope of the next questioner, explaining that the CBOT was not buying up seats to boost prices.

Other questions danced around the central issue, and then someone raised it directly: "What good is a seat without open outcry?" Another asked rhetorically, "What is the appeal of computer trading, besides some cost savings? Traders can get into the pit and *see* a true bid/ask. They can *see* exact size. Bigger, deeper, better markets is what open outcry can give." But Arbor refused to acknowledge what the speaker meant to pass off as a self-evident truth. He replied curtly that computers could provide deep and liquid markets and then pushed ahead. The members were committed to open outcry, but they had never before had to justify or defend their trading system. Traders' allegiances and profits were tied intractably to the trading pit, but, until recently in the history of the CBOT, these attachments had remained in the background, part of the invisible structure of assumptions. The threat of electronic trading, even in its vaguest forms, forced them to consider where open outcry fit in the nascent technological future. The members fought over the implementation of electronic technologies and cross-Atlantic alliances to preserve the place of the pits, the future of their craft, and, they hoped, the role of Chicago as a center of global trading. The stakes could not have been higher.

When they spoke among themselves, traders defended open outcry by saying it created efficiencies in the market that no electronic technology could ever replicate. They believed that the "liquidity" of the pits was deep: any bank or strategist could do business at any time, no matter how large the order, ensuring the circulation of capital through its markets. The pits provided speculators, and speculators would always trade. Chicago traders also believed that the open-outcry system of the pits protected markets from catastrophe, since people working face-to-face could maintain stability in turbulent times.

In its advertisements, the CBOT reminded the world's financial managers that these markets were the only ones to stay open during the 1987 crash. Their strength, they argued, came from a potent source—the dedication of the Chicago floor trader. Their perseverance in making markets, even in the face of their personal financial peril, kept the exchange sailing through the storm. The relationship between Chicago's traders and their distinctive technology is reciprocal—just as the men make the pits work, work in the pits shapes these men, creating a process that solders self, technology, and organization together to forge a market.[1]

They asserted that it was the relationships among the traders and the roots of the market in open outcry technology and in the city of Chicago that created the deep, liquid markets that had always drawn business to the CBOT. In other words, they believed that the premodern elements of the CBOT were still at the heart of this modern financial exchange.[2] The impersonal nature of electronic trading posed the greatest danger to the market, they argued. New technologies that linked actors who were decentralized and dispersed would remove the energy and excitement that could only come from face-to-face competition. Traders worried that with rivalries and friendships far removed, computer trading would not give the rush or provide the intensity of competition they experienced in the crowded pit. They insisted that the more abstract and analytic approach to the market would cause screen-based markets to be illiquid; that is, the online exchange would be unable to provide continuous circulation.

Defenders of the CBOT pit technology also argued that the open-outcry tradition was better suited to handle the human irrationalities that cause panics in the market. Even the forward-thinking Arbor declared, "Nobody does it better in times of market stress." Traders inhabit, identify with, and develop responsibilities to the market. The conservative traders argued that this unique combination of attachments kept the CBOT markets liquid. Sean Curley Jr. told a story from the bond pit that illustrated the responsibilities of the trader and his professional identification with the market. It was March 1995 and the government was about to release employment statistics for February. Even though traders were expecting a stronger job market by about a hundred thousand jobs, the number that appeared on the electronic ticker tape showed an additional five hundred thousand jobs. Conventionally, bond prices drop a when economic signs, such as unemployment data, indicate a healthy economy. When job growth is strong, investors see more profit opportunities in the stock market. They sell treasury bonds, driving down the price, and reinvest the money in the equity markets, a logic that can be dangerous for bond-futures traders.

Sean remembered the day vividly: "And the bonds traded down, down, all the way to limit down. . . . The big bond locals didn't leave the bond pit. They *couldn't*. You can't. That's what you're there for. Certain bond guys won't leave, even when they're losing a lot of money, until their friends pull them out of the pit. But, you know, they just were there to make markets, that's what their job is."

Advocates of open outcry even contested claims that electronic markets provide greater transparency. They argued that the social environment of the pit, where traders know and watch each other, is a more effective forum for identifying illicit market activity. The responsibility shared by competitors and friends alike creates a social transparency that no accounting procedure can match. "With the eyes of competitors on you, you are unlikely to do something dishonest. . . . On the screen, how do you know who the criminals are?"[3]

The traders argued that the technological tools of market abstraction, the direct connections between electronic trading screens, would hinder the market's operation. This discussion positions technology as a force of efficiency that dampens emotion and facilitates calculation based solely on prices and other financial abstractions. The argument belies how social ties and emotions are always part of the market. The market ideal of technological abstraction sets the terms of the debate—one that the floor traders were sure to lose as the market made the transition from an earlier modern form to a contemporary one.

On regular work days, though, the scene on the financial trading floor gave no hint of the threat the traders were facing. The Chicago Board of Trade markets had a banner year in 1998. The pits were packed. The thirty-year U.S. Treasury Bond futures pit, the largest in the industry, hit its daily record on August 27—1,121,634 contracts. The hall vibrated with the shouts of active business. The traders did not fear that the CBOT would fail but that the pits and their jobs would be swallowed up by the new logic of world markets they had helped to create. The members and the exchange leadership faced a vexing problem. How could the CBOT update its technologies and remain a global player while maintaining its commitments to Chicago and its traders?

Traders and managers had a set of fierce and contradictory commitments, first to the market and then to their way of making the market—the trading pit. In their vision of the trading nexus, the pit was the physical location for the market, putting flesh and bones on the abstract market, peopling it with bodies, voices, personalities, and colors. Digital technologies upset the delicate balance between the abstraction of markets and the materiality of the pit. Yet proponents of the new information technologies asked what seemed to be a straightforward question about efficiency. Why should big banks pay fees to Chicago's brokers for carrying out their orders when electronic networks could connect traders directly? Electronic networks could obviate trading pits entirely and provide direct access to the market. The possibility of electronic trading undermined the traders' working assumptions about the production of markets by challenging their efficiency—the fundamental reason given in favor of the CBOT pits. In response to this threat, the members and managers of the CBOT defended their form of exchange.

The technologies of digital trading "problematized" the reigning market form and forced market planners and managers to reimagine and reconstruct what markets should be in light of the new possibilities of technology and geography. The mere *idea* of electronic trading made the constitution of the market—the trading pits and the personal interaction that brought them to life—"into an object of reflection" and made it "available for analysis of its meanings, its conditions and its goals" when it had not been before.[4]

The screen would replace personal relations with abstract associations. Men laboring to create liquidity with their voices and bodies in the pit would be replaced by numbers. The logic of this process of "disintermediation" redefined the landscape of the futures markets. Everyone knew, and many feared, that digital technologies could circumvent the trading floor entirely, setting the market loose from the pits. Traders' on-screen interactions would be recorded on servers they never saw or felt, allowing the market to float freely among the electronic nodes of a global network. Screen-based trading not only threatened the traders' links with the market but also put the identity, economy, and business culture of Chicago at risk.[5] Electronic technologies could remove the market from the marketplace and relocate it outside the Chicago nexus. According to estimates at the time, Chicago's exchanges provided, either directly or indirectly, more than a hundred thousand local jobs—many of them high-end service functions such as banking, law, and insurance.

The traders themselves were wedded not only to open outcry but also to the cultural practices and forms of social organization associated with it, from the skills honed over generations to the institutions that brought it to life. Traders growing up in Chicago and its suburbs learned specific ways of engaging the market through networks of friends, family, and neighborhood ties. Members of Chicago's "trading families" learned about open-outcry methods of competition and strategies in their youth. Thousands of others are connected to the market through looser ties with friends, colleagues, or clients who work at the exchange. People who work downtown saw the garish, colorful coats that traders wore to make themselves visible in the crowded pits. The CBOT building was just one of the ways that the marketplace made a visible contribution to the city's atmosphere.

During its hundred-and-fifty-year history, the pit had garnered a singular place among trading technologies, too. The CBOT defined the market in futures every day. Chicago traders were proud of their part in modern market history. Losing open outcry threatened their role in global finance. The Chicago Board of Trade resisted digital technology when other central financial institutions in global cities were willing to submit themselves to rapid change.[6] The CBOT's fight for the distinctive technology at the center of its exchanges was a struggle to define the singularity of Chicago and establish its special importance in the systems of global finance and among global cities, as well as to establish its own terms for how the markets in financial futures would be spun into a web of global markets.[7]

How did the CBOT become so entangled with open-outcry technology? To understand this, we must first understand how traders' techniques are wedded to a single technology of exchange. But this is not a simple question of skill. The affective ties of the members to family and to Chicago extended to their method of trading. When new technologies and exchange techniques presented a global challenge to open outcry trading, traders struggled to find a viable way to navigate the terrain of electronic efficiency that digital technologies carved out. The combination of technological conflict and local history played out in the 1998 contest for chairman of the CBOT, the man who would plot the organization's course in the new technological landscape.[8] To understand this decisive moment in CBOT history, it is helpful to examine the layers of technology, social institutions, and cultural practices that formed the market's foundations.

Technology and Performance

Open outcry trading brings the market to life.[9] The pit's steps arrange the market as it organizes traders' shouts and hand signals. Each trader brings his bids to buy and offers to sell to the open pit. The auction that follows does not have a central coordinator. Each deal is a communication between the individual trader and the market as a whole. Brokers and local traders, or "market makers," form agreements that move contracts. If the trade is not accomplished inside the pit according to the specific set of performances that qualify as a trade, the exchange does not legally occur. This specific performance unites the physical location of the CBOT and the particular skill of the traders and brokers who work in the pits. The physical and social organization of the pits supports the technology of open outcry trading.

For the CBOT's believers in open outcry trading, the market begins and ends on the trading floor. The space of the pit defines the market, and its octagonal steps organize the arena of exchange. Temporally, the market is what is happening that moment in the pit, and is apparent in whatever deals are being made. Once trades have been written and verified and their prices inscribed on the quotations board and sent out on the electronic ticker tape—all of which takes only seconds—the market has moved on. The traders' work is to locate the market, a process that discovers the price of a commodity, and it can be found only within the boundaries of the pit. But the work of the pit does not end here. As an economic device it is a site for identifying the contours of the market, but that process is entwined with trading hierarchies, and the pit operates as symbol for the CBOT, not just as a mark of the organization. It is a defining object that must be defended.

The abstracted image of three concentric octagonal rings is the official symbol of the CBOT. The pit wrapped the commercial glory of Chicago within its concentric steps; it tamed the swirl of commerce and sucked it in to return market information as concrete prices. It is the commercial nexus of Chicago's financial world. The pit is more than a place where prices were set; it is a symbol of a city and its global connections.

Since 1870, the stepped, ringed structures have been the distinctive feature of the Board Room. Just as redesigning the trading floor of the 1930 building offered an opportunity to rationalize the marketplace, the pit itself was originally an effort to rationalize the space of the market. Its design worked to solve a problem of the fragmentation of the marketplace. Within twenty years of its founding, trading at the CBOT became so popular that crowds inundated the CBOT space. Unable to see potential deals across the room, traders scaled heights to improve their sight lines. Market reporters began to complain in the pages of their daily papers that traders were climbing onto their desks and obstructing the reporters' vision.[10] As auctions, futures markets are effective for manufacturing prices and producing profits when all the participants can see and hear all bids on offer. The crowded trading room hindered speculators from getting to all the available trades. Since traders could do business only with partners in their immediate reach, the market broke up into cliques, each producing its own price based on whatever information was available from its vantage point. This was a weakness both for individual traders and for the CBOT, whose mission was to create a central marketplace that set a single price for a commodity.

The pit offered a solution to the problem by rearranging the space of the market. Rather than distributing participants over the flat surface of the floor, the pit raised them up in tiers, as in a stadium, an arrangement that produced considerably better views. After trying out several shapes for the raised structure, the CBOT introduced the octagonal pits in 1870, and these tiered steps have organized the open outcry market ever since.

Within this trading arena, the choreography of a trade links the pit technology to traders' techniques. The fixed steps of open outcry trading shape shouted numbers into a legally enforceable contract between traders. Material devices structure trading, but just as important are the systems of conventions regarding their use. Formal regulations require certain movements to offer and close a trade. Within the physical confines of the pit, these movements seal a legal reality, a binding, enforceable contract. The action of the pit rests on them as much as on the rubber-clad steps. But the requirements are flexible, and traders use these limitations creatively. Practitioners manipulate the conventions and their bodies in ways that sometimes support and sometimes subvert the choreography of a trade. Norms of use among traders grew up around the pit and became fused with it and the Chicago trading floor. These norms of use can change over time, but while they last, they seem necessary and intractable, the only methods that work.

The norms and legal regulations came together at the CBOT and fused into the open-outcry system, a complicated mix of material objects—the trading pit, paper records—and the specific physical motions that create futures prices. The choreography of a trade is a technology because this set of movements is a device for producing a binding trade. This procedure, embedded in particular motions (discussed in the following section) that accomplish a task, is a legally defined technique.

Choreography brings legal and material technologies together with individual and collective techniques: the dance of dealing uses not only the prescribed movements but also the artistry necessary to bring that performance to life. There is room for creative play within the binding rules in the tone of the voice, the flair of the hands, and the timing of shouts. In the pit, the legal rules that define the movements of a trade both circumscribe technique, by constraining traders' bodies to certain moves, and establish the boundaries for inventive work. Not any movement can create a trade; only a limited set of actions can do this. Yet, there is still room for trading norms and individual manipulations to develop.

This interpenetration of technology and members' performances ties the fate of the CBOT to the vitality of open outcry. Tom Donovan, the president and CEO of the CBOT in 1998, expressed this intertwining in a powerful statement marking the exchange's one hundred and fiftieth anniversary: "To be number one, number one for the past 150 years. Not a day, not a week, not a year. Every year. Number one—this says something. This says that the world, and this is a global market, comes to the Board of Trade daily because they believe in us. They believe in the members and they believe in the Chicago Board of Trade."

He directs the listener to recognize that the success of the organization and its markets is directly tied to the skills of the membership. In order to understand how the success of these markets became coupled with the specific, fixed skills of the locals, we must first understand the structure of trading and the rich social life of the pits.

How Trading Works

The succession of stages that make up a trade rely upon the tight orchestration of individuals. Each person controls diverse types of information and operates with a different communications system. The ordered interaction among the players is built on and generates relations of dependence, familiarity, and apprenticeship that shape traders' networks and create channels for career advancement. Learning to master the intricate interplay between traders, clerks, phone-bank managers, and outside clients is the secret of pit traders' success and a key to profit. The interactional order of the pit is as important to the economic reasoning of floor traders as the price information they acquire. To understand how traders became so tightly entwined with the pit, we must examine the performance of trading.

Into the Pit

A trade originates outside the pits with managers and traders from banks and hedge funds. From their bases in major financial institutions, strategists monitor financial markets in search of profit opportunities, either within a single market or between financial markets. One common tactic used by strategists is to exploit differences in the pricing of bonds for sale in the present against the price of bonds offered in months ahead in the futures markets. For example, the strategist might consult a mathematically complex bond-pricing model and see a discrepancy between past and future price. The price of a futures contract for thirty-year treasury bonds might be high in comparison to the price for the same bonds in the present. Perhaps the futures contract is trading at nine when it should be trading at three, according to the model. Deciding quickly that the price of the futures contract is about to fall, this heavily funded player presses the speed dial buttons on his telephone to call the desk managers or clerks who manage business for his firm on the floor of the CBOT.

The clerks are usually high-school educated workers who act as channels to the brokers in the pits. Desk managers are traders themselves who may trade company accounts in addition to serving clients. Whoever answers the strategist's phone call will "flash" the order to a broker's clerk in the pit. A series of hand gestures at the level of chin, brow, or crown of the head indicates the exact price and numbers of contracts to be bought or sold. If the trade is above or below the current price, the clerk writes the order on a slip of paper, stamps it with a "time in" mark, and hands it to a runner. Runners, the lowest paid of the floor staff, weave their way through the maze of phone banks to bring the order to a broker's clerks. They may be traders in training, learning the inner workings of the markets by moving through the apprenticeship system. In contrast to these usually white, male runners who have connections in the pits, there is also a few "career" runners, whose minimum wage and outsider status leave them navigating the packed pathways between the pits without the possibility of becoming traders.

After receiving the order, the clerk taps his broker, or shouts in his ear, communicating the new order. The broker either executes the transaction immediately at the current market price, or slips the order form into his deck, a fat pile of paper slips indicating at what price customers have commissioned him to buy or sell contracts. He holds the deck, folded in half like a hot dog bun, close to his body. The flow of orders in the deck contains valuable information. A large order could push the price of a bond down. A trader who knows such an order exists before it is brought to the market could sell ahead of the lowered price and profit from his insider access.[11]

Inside the pit, there are two levels of trading choreography—the legal requirements for a trade to occur and another level of verbal communication and physical action that sets agreements into motion. The legal template for the actions of a trade is brief: one trader signals an offer or a bid with his voice. The responding trader vocally agrees to fill the opposite side of the trade. After one check for price and quantity ("I sold you 5 contracts at a half") the trade is legally completed and enforceable.

In practice, however, this short sequence is elaborated by the local methods of communicating and occurs in the context of a pit packed with six hundred men. The initiating trader yells his bid or offer into the pit, using the leverage of the stiff soles of his steel-reinforced shoes to push past any obstacles on the step that would block him from the view of other traders. Thrusting his arms forward over the shoulders of traders on the steps below, the trader curls his hands into position, indicating the number of contracts he would like to bid or offer. In a "fast," or busy, market, where prices are rapidly rising or falling, the trader may be joined in his bid by hundreds of other bodies and voices. A trader who wants to "hit the bid" or "take the offer," strains his neck toward the initiating trader. He tries to make eye contact while yelling a terse agreement: "Sold." According to the CBOT's rule 335.00, known as the "first" rule, the initiating trader is legally bound to give the desired number of contracts to the trader whom he perceives as having responded first, distributing the remaining contracts among the other bidders. Because the trader can exercise discretion in his perception, personal relationships between traders are significant in gaining (or losing) access to crucial trades.

The successful respondent verifies the trade with a flick of the wrist, check mark in the air. The initiating trader responds with a nod. Each trader marks down the three-letter identifying code imprinted in bold letters on the other trader's membership badge. Because this system relies on verbal agreements between members to cement each trade, it also requires trust and honor between members. The worst offense against both the formal and informal honor codes of the pit is for a trader to deny a trade on which both parties have agreed. As Sean, a broker for twelve years, told me, "I trust that you are going to card it up that I sold you ten. I have faith in you that you are going to make that trade good." Pat Arbor described it in another way: "Honor is the lifeblood of the system." Trust and technology are tied together in the face-to-face exchange.

This choreography is not simply a *pas de deux*. As the trade makes its way back out of the pit, another set of players launches into action. If he employs a clerk to check his trades, the trader hands his trading cards, marked with his three-letter code and the name of the clearing firm responsible for his accounts, to his trade checker, who circles the pit to find the initiating trader's clerk. Leaning over an empty trading desk or supporting the cards on an available knee, the two confirm the trade. The trade checker then deposits the cards in a basket for desk clerks to bring upstairs to the company's office. There the flying fingers of back office staff will enter the trades into the clearing apparatus of the CBOT, where the deals will be matched and accounts settled. These skills do not come automatically. Learning to use these sets of signals is a challenge everyone working in Chicago's futures pits must meet.

Locals and Brokers

From the perspective of the outside observer, the trading floor seems chaotic, but in fact the frenetic activity of the pits masks a finely tuned organization. Open outcry trading is based on the relationships between locals and brokers in the pits, the most important connection in the arena of trade. Brokers are traders who accept orders from outside the market and complete these transactions in the pits in exchange for a commission on each trade.

They execute buy and sell orders for brokerage houses or corporations for whom they generally work on informal, fee-based contracts. Desk managers are free to direct their business to any broker working in the pit. Brokers are the link between outside market participants and the trade in the pits, the conduits for orders from traders outside the pit to the speculators inside.

The locals, also known as "market makers," are concerned with risking money for profit. They are traders who deal for their own accounts, speculating on price changes in the market. The presence of locals allows outside market participants to trade at any time because they are always there to buy and sell. In the market's own terms, the locals provide liquidity. They are entrusted with responding to any bid or offer that money managers bring to the marketplace. Locals are "market makers" because they support the central assumption of the marketplace—for every buyer there is a seller, and for every seller there is a buyer. In exchange for this service, they gain a time and place advantage by inhabiting the heart of the market.[12]

Local traders hope to profit from correctly predicting the movement of the market up or down and risk losing their own money in the process. They are speculators in the most pure sense—individuals making money purely on the changing prices of financial commodities. Although locals have a variety of trading strategies, most of them are known as "scalpers." Scalpers trade in and out of the market within seconds or minutes, profiting from small price fluctuations. Making hundreds of trades during the course of the day, the scalper never goes home owning contracts.

The word *local* makes this type of trader sound small and provincial, but this is often not the case in the CBOT pits. The skills and wealth of the major traders at the CBOT are especially important when markets are plunging. If there are no buyers in the outside market, the locals can take command and support the market. As the market weakens, the professional ethic of the trader fills the breach. One bond trader described the job and attitude of the market maker:

> When you're a local, your job is to make a market. So make the damn market. What is [the bid/ask]? Give me a number. [Using the voice of a broker] "I got a customer here who needs to be filled." When you get a cascading market or a rallying market, [the challenge is] who's going to be the first one to step in and say "no more"? Who's going to be the first one to say when the market is breaking? . . . OK, that's . . . where the market is. Here is where it is going to stop. In the pit, you look to the guys that you know are going to be the ones to do it. You know when you are in the bond pit that everyone looks to Tom Baldwin. . . . There wouldn't have been a trade there without a local there to "step up," that's what they call it on the floor. Who's going to step up and be the market?

Locals and brokers cultivate relationships with each other and generate a flow of trades from friends and colleagues that is strong enough to support traders in tough times. Trading regulations allow for gray areas, where traders can use their networks and their judgment to assist friends and cultivate bonds. At times brokers rely on locals to take on trades even when the local will lose money, cultivating a relationship with an implied, if nonspecific, reciprocity.

The interpersonal organization of the pits is tied to the social universe of Chicago. Membership at the CBOT is mediated through the networks of traders. Buying a seat in the CBOT that allows access to the trading floor is a large investment. For example, a full membership traded for $350,000 in October 2001. In addition to finding the capital to purchase a seat and set up a trading account, aspiring members must get sponsorship from an existing member.

Within the hierarchy of runners, clerks, traders, and brokers on the floor, a system of apprenticeship creates a channel for vertical mobility. Traders often train their clerks in trading techniques. Clerks watch the traders, learn the signals, and plug into their networks. Under the supervision of the broker, a broker's clerk can take his first steps into the pit by executing a few trades during slower periods in the market. Traders can "back" younger, promising traders by lending them capital for their accounts and "guaranteeing" their trades. The backers agree to cover their losses in return for a (usually very high) percentage of the profits they make. These arrangements are often quite informal, arrived at through mentoring relationships or by ties of family and friendship.

Given the informality of these ties, it is not surprising that the CBOT is an insular environment. Knowing a family member or someone from the neighborhood who can give you a job as a runner or a clerk (a low-paying, entry-level job) can put a hopeful trader's foot on the first rung of the ladder.[13] Ethnic loyalties and family ties run strong. The CBOT has spawned many trading families, and Irish surnames like Brennan, Hennessey, McBride, Cox, O'Daugherty, and O'Brian head the list.

For example, Sean Curley and his father Sean Curley Sr. share an office in the older portion of the CBOT building. A laminated feature article about the older Curley published in *Futures* magazine decorates the walls. On his desk are two gifts recognizing his contributions to the CBOT—one is a miniature version of the statue of the Roman goddess of grain that tops the CBOT building, the other a Mont Blanc pen in an inscribed marble stand. Both Curleys are dedicated to the institutional life of the CBOT and have served on the organization's board of directors. The clothes of the majority of traders in the pit reflect their maverick attitudes, but the Curleys wear neatly pressed shirts and ties under their oversized trading jackets.

The Curleys trade soybeans. Sean Sr. has been a member at the CBOT since 1962 and Sean Jr. since 1996, when he left an unsatisfying career in law. The father described his family's involvement with the CBOT.

> My Uncle Matthew and Geoff Curley were the first two who came down here. My Uncle Geoff came down in the early 1950s. And a third uncle, John. Several nieces and nephews have followed. So we have probably fifteen family members down here—if I were going to enumerate—most of them in different parts of the business. Sean and I work in the bean pit. We have two girl cousins who work in the [soybean] oil pit. We have two other cousins in the bean pit. We have three cousins in the meal pit. So just on the grain floor in oil, meal, and beans, we have nine . . . and a couple in the financials.

The Curley family has branched out, helping each other to secure the necessary capital and learn the business.

Traders' ties can keep them in the business when losses and frustration take over. Henry Mueller runs his own small brokerage business in the Dow Jones pit and has sustained his trading through the connections and dependencies that support open-outcry technology. The Mueller family's roots in the trading business and agriculture brought him to the CBOT. Through years of successes and failures, his connections within the exchange have supported him and allowed him to survive his mistakes in the business. Henry's father was a wheat broker for thirty-five years at the CBOT, so Henry got to know the markets over conversation at the dinner table. He knew he wanted to make a career in the pits, and when, after his third year of college, a family member fell ill, Henry left school and never returned. For a while he worked on the family farm in western Illinois, where his father was trying to perfect a breed of cattle. But he quickly migrated back to the city to become a trader.

Henry held a series of jobs and traded in many different products and across exchanges before landing in the pit, where he now makes his living. When he first arrived at the CBOT, he leased a membership and tried his skill in the index, debt, gold, and energy markets. Trading did not come easily to him, and he lost steadily. A job in the back office offered an opportunity to learn the business from the accounting perspective and to make some risk-free money. He checked "out trades," beginning at 5 a.m., before the day's trading bell sounded, untangling problems in matching buyer and seller to specific quantities and prices. He traded in the afternoon and checked more out trades in the evening. After another series of losses, he abandoned trading completely and took a 5 p.m. to 5 a.m. job in the back office of a brokerage firm. He saved his money until he had enough to begin trading wheat options in the slower-moving grain room. He lost everything and then some; it took him about seven years to pay off his debt from those trades. After managing to gather another trading stake, he went to work as a clerk in the Eurodollars pit at the Chicago Mercantile Exchange.

When the CBOT announced that it would open a pit to trade in futures on the Dow Jones Industrial Average, where trades would come in smaller denominations than the established (and more lucrative) bond futures complex, Henry saw his opportunity to reenter the pit without the risks of trading outright for his own accounts. Like his father, he would become a broker, gathering commissions on trades executed for the brokerage firms whose trading desks surrounded the pit. Many people with whom he had traded were now moving to the Dow Jones. He felt he could rely on them for business.

To generate a coterie of brokers who would "fill paper" for the surrounding desks, the CBOT required each broker to show that he had enough clients to command a top step position. Henry approached Iowa grain and negotiated with them to fill their orders. The owners knew his father. As a kid, Henry was a fixture in their offices. They were happy to give him their business. Henry used their business to argue that he needed a good spot in the pit. His location in the pit gives his clerks sightlines to the desks of two other firms. They have directed their business to him and he has finally assembled a stable place in the trading business.

Such ties develop over the course of a trader's career both in and out of the pit as well as between pits and exchanges, and tie the technology to the individuals who make that pit work. The interpenetration of organization, family, friends, and neighborhoods links the CBOT to open-outcry trading as a way of life.

On the August 13 edition of *Chicago Tonight*, a local PBS television show, Pat Arbor put this point bluntly. "Chicago breeds futures traders," he said. Citing the family connections that support the market and create allegiance to open outcry, he stated, "There is a great deal of tradition attached to open outcry trading in Chicago, and that will help sustain this form of trade. . . . Chicago is truly the open-outcry exchange capital."

Leo, a veteran of the Bond pit, agrees: "We all started here. It's really become an industry in Chicago. There's like nine thousand traders who are part of the industry, and it's gone from generation to generation. . . . So it's become part of Chicago. I mean you could go to a city like Atlanta, Georgia, wonderful city. You can't open an exchange there—or you could, but where are you going to get the traders from?" Sean Curley points out that the fine-tuned operation of the pits leans on a group of men he calls "pit rats," with a mix of admiration and revulsion. To Sean, it is as if these men,

Chicago locals, "can smell where the next trade is coming from. [These are] the kind of guys who you wonder if [the pits] weren't here what these guys would be doing."

Chicago's traders have much in common — particularly their choreography and a technology of trading — but there are also deep rifts that divide the membership of the CBOT. The corridor that divides the financial room from the grain room defines a split along lines of age, voting rights, and trading etiquette. Most important for the fate of the CBOT are the splits in membership categories that define each room. Traders at the CBOT can invest in different types of memberships that give them access to markets in specific products and exclude them from trading others. Political rights are also tied to each type of membership. Full members, who can trade in any pit at the CBOT, dominate in the grain room, their yellow badges showing their investment in full voting rights. The Associate members, who can trade any of the financial products, but whose votes are worth only one-sixth of a full share, show little deference to the grain room traders despite their power within the organization. Whereas a gentlemanly trade rules in the grains, an aggressive style and hyper-masculine ideals mark the ethos of the financial room. The macho bond traders refer to the floor that lies on the other side of the corridor as the "old man's room." Yet the weighting of votes engineered by the grain room traders allows them to control the politics as the exchange.

Because the membership ultimately ratifies major decisions of the CBOT board of directors, threats to the value of full members' seats generally have a short life at the Board of Trade. The members value their investments in the price of the seats and in their relationships in the pits. Any decision that would change the fundamental structure of the CBOT or weaken open-outcry trading opens the door to conflict. So when the abstract and anonymous forces of electronic technologies threatened their technologically and socially bounded world, Chicago's open-outcry traders were apprehensive.

Politics

With trading setting a record pace, the CBOT seemed very much in a position to control its fate. Open outcry was strong, but developments in the European exchanges were sending undeniable signals that the supremacy of pit trading was in jeopardy. Earlier that year the French futures exchange, MATIF, had closed its open-outcry floor. The introduction of electronic trading had drained the flow of orders from the pits. Soon thereafter the London exchange, LIFFE, had lost its most-traded contract, the ten-year German bond future, to an all-electronic German exchange. The Deutsche Terminborse (DTB) then merged with its Swiss counterpart to form Eurex, the CBOT's most threatening competitor. The growing volumes at CBOT affirmed the vigor of its markets, but faster growth in Europe raised questions about how long its dominance would last. By the end of 1998, the CBOT had traded 281 million contracts, an increase of 16 percent over the year before. Despite the impressive growth of trading volumes, seat values were plummeting. Falling from their 1997 high of $857,500 for a full membership, values stabilized around $490,000 in 1998. The even more astonishing growth at the all-electronic Eurex was partially to blame. Although the German-Swiss exchange still lagged behind the CBOT at 248 million contracts in 1998, the German-Swiss exchange's 63 percent growth over the prior year swamped the board's expansion. At the same time, a company that kept an office on the twelfth floor of the CBOT addition initiated a challenge to its host's monopoly in the U.S. Treasury bond futures market. At the end of September, Cantor Fitzgerald, one of the world's largest dealers in the primary bond market, launched its online T-bond futures market. At home and abroad, the CBOT's hegemony was under assault.

Floor traders and financial experts alike began to question the traditional methods of exchange. The speed and efficiency of electronic trading set the standard against which even the traders now measured their own work. The CBOT traders could no longer absorb the technological challenge of electronic systems into preestablished ideas about the consummate effectiveness of their local open outcry system and the self-evident superiority of the CBOT as a trading institution. The force of the technological disruption required the CBOT to take a new stance toward its most fundamental trading operations. However, it was slow in responding to external pressures and inconsistent in its actions. As the members tried to protect their place in the industry, divisions reflecting seat values and voting rights emerged within the Board of Trade.

Since 1998, the CBOT has struggled to remain in control of its own entry into the electronic marketplace and at the same time define the shape of electronic markets for the global futures industry. The CBOT's functional monopoly on trading T-bond futures, a key tool for financial managers, along with the sheer size and prominence of the organization, positioned it to be a key player. However, the membership of the CBOT had yet to decide on a way to balance their interests and the market values of technological efficiency. The future of futures trading was in the balance.

Given the deep ties between the Chicago traders and their technology of exchange, it is not surprising that the challenge of electronic systems spilled over into institutional politics during the 1998 election for the chairmanship of the CBOT. Advocates of electronic trading were set against the defenders of the open outcry pits, and the conflict peaked in the weeks leading up to the December 9 election. Both contenders were soybean traders. Patrick Arbor, the chairman of the Chicago Board of Trade for three consecutive two-year terms, was running on petition after the board of directors denied him their nomination because of his pro-electronic trading stance. Instead, they endorsed David Brennan, a third-generation member of a prominent CBOT trading family and a staunch defender of the open outcry system.

The contest for chairman was played out in halls, offices, trading floors, and wherever traders met to debate the fate of the CBOT. But discussions of the issues were not limited to the organization's boundaries. The Board of Trade's business came from around the world and was affected by market events in Frankfurt and Sydney, and the political contestants also used a global stage. The financial media provided a forum where CBOT leaders and members could voice their ideas about their piece of the global marketplace. Coverage in the financial media is important for the CBOT, especially for the chairman, who is an envoy to the financial world.

Pat Arbor, whom CBOT traders alternately lauded and derided for his media savvy, made ample use of this forum. He had already taken a stance on the role of the CBOT in the emerging shape of the futures industry. This included championing the introduction of more digital technologies into the CBOT marketplace and pursing alliances that would enhance the exchange's ability to compete in electronic markets. However, exchange politics demanded that he hedge his strong support for electronic technologies by reaffirming his commitment to open outcry. In the June 20 edition of the London-based *Financial Times*, he played to these politics while sending a message to Board of Trade clients that their demands for efficiency would not be subjugated to the will of the local traders: "The Chicago Board of Trade, the world's largest futures exchange, is positioning itself for a move to full electronic futures dealing if its customers demand a switch from traditional open-outcry trading. 'We see no reason to change from open-outcry trading. But we will make certain we are ready so that if we have to move to electronic dealing, we can,' Pat Arbor, CBOT chairman, said."[14]

As both the CBOT and Eurex were registering record trading volumes, Arbor began to roll out details for a proposed alliance with Eurex. Arbor's goals for an alliance between the world's two largest exchanges were to expand the reach of the CBOT across the globe by increasing traders' access to its products, to improve technology, and to prevent Eurex from competing in the U.S. debt futures market. The CBOT and Eurex would collaborate to develop a platform that would carry both exchanges' products and share the cost of improving and expanding their electronic networks. Arbor was poised to bring institutional life to the idea that markets should connect participants around the globe into a single, real-time market.

In contrast to Arbor, many members, especially in the grain room, began voicing fears that an alliance would compromise their autonomy and leave the Chicago exchange beholden to the Germans' superior electronic technology. The floor traders' desire to protect their open-outcry markets opened an opportunity for a candidate who would champion the direct interests of the membership. David Brennan, already experienced in exchange politics, filled the available slot.

During the melee that led up to the vote, Pat Arbor called David Brennan "President of the Flat Earth Society." The slur referred to a disagreement between the two over the pitch of the trading desks on the new floor, but the comment was equally useful in characterizing Brennan as turning a blind eye to the pressures of electronic markets. Arbor remained concerned with how the exchange would maintain its competitiveness in the global environment. He believed the CBOT would benefit by treating the markets as an expanding global network. Arbor took a long-term view that could, in the short term, imperil the interests of some of the CBOT members who were committed to their daily work in the pits. Arbor advocated embracing the new technologies and moving toward alliances that would extend the organization's reach while creating markets that would link traders together through CBOT terminals across the globe. However, the structure of the membership organization and the distribution of voting rights made this a difficult position for an elected leader to sustain. Arbor's main constituents, the Financial Commission Merchants (FCM), large firms that hold memberships in the CBOT, and the associate members who dominated the financial room, were at a political disadvantage.

Brennan committed himself to protecting the value of the full members' yellow badge, which meant defending open outcry. The more conservative members agreed. These traders were also concerned that the proposed alliance with Eurex would give away the CBOT's control over its own destiny. Brennan told the *Chicago Tribune* that "[n]ow it looks like we are following the Germans around. We look like we're struggling. . . . The Board of Trade is in a position to set the agenda. We should pounce on it." This nativism opened an opportunity for Arbor. He spun Brennan's die-hard allegiance to open outcry as evidence of his Luddite nature. The press exploited the clear division that Arbor had drawn. Yet this depiction did not fairly represent Brennan's policy positions or experience. Brennan had served on committees for implementing Project A, the exchange's electronic system for after-hours trading, and on the designing committee for the new $182-million trading facility.

His position did not waver from assignment to assignment. Brennan always fought to secure members' advantages by strengthening the open-outcry

Special Issue

Chicago Board of Trade

the trader™

Annual Election 1998

November 1998   Volume 22, Number 9

Arbor, Brennan Vie for Chairman Post in CBOT Annual Election

Balloting Set for December 9, 1998, Candidates Elected To Take Office January 4, 1999

Patrick H. Arbor

Patrick H. Arbor is a candidate to serve a two-year term as Chairman of the Board of Directors of the Chicago Board of Trade.

Arbor currently is serving his third consecutive two-year term as Chairman of the CBOT, a position to which he first was elected in December 1992, again in December 1994, and most recently in December 1996. Concurrently, he also is serving his third term as Chairman of the MidAmerica Commodity Exchange. An independent futures trader, he is a principal in the trading firm of Shatkin, Arbor, Karlov & Co.

Arbor has been a member of the CBOT since 1965, serving three years as Vice Chairman and another 10 years as director. In addition to having had more than 100 exchange committee appointments, he also sat for three years on the Board of Governors of the Board of Trade Clearing Corporation, two of those years

continued on page 2

The Chicago Board of Trade Annual Election will take place Wednesday, December 9, 1998. Polls at the fourth floor entrance to the exchange trading floors will be open from 8:00 a.m. to 3:00 p.m., Chicago time.

To be elected are the Chairman, a full member, to a two-year term, and a Second Vice Chairman, a full member, also to a two-year term. The nominating and election procedure for the First Vice Chairman and Second Vice Chairman was established under a member-approved proposition for staggered two-year terms of office for these two positions. After the 1995 Annual Election the First and Second Vice Chairmen are to be elected to two-year terms in

continued on page 4

Please turn to the inside pages for biographies of nominees and candidates for Second Vice Chairman, Director, and members of the Nominating Committee.

David P. Brennan

David P. Brennan has been nominated to serve a two-year term as Chairman of the Board of Directors of the Chicago Board of Trade.

Brennan, an independent member of the exchange since 1980, was elected to serve two three-year terms on the CBOT Board of Directors, from 1988 to 1990 and from 1992 to 1994. He also served as a member of the CBOT Executive Committee in 1990. As a CBOT Director he also served on the Board of the MidAmerica Commodity Exchange, a CBOT affiliate.

Brennan most recently served as the Chairman of the New Trading Facility Task Force and Design Subcommittee. Currently, he is on the Ceres Advisory Committee.

He also has served on or chaired numerous committees since he joined the exchange, including Technology, Finance, Membership, Business Conduct, Floor and Floor Traders, Common Goals, and

continued on page 2

⬤ **Chicago Board of Trade**

2.1 Biographies of Patrick Arbor and David Brennan, final candidates for the position of chairman, are presented to the CBOT board members in the exchange's internal publication. Courtesy of the Board of Trade of the City of Chicago.

2.2 Completed in 1997, the new, technologically enhanced trading floor was known as "the Arboretum," after chairman Pat Arbor. Courtesy of the Board of Trade of the City of Chicago.

system. In his bid for the chairman's seat, Brennan campaigned for electronic technologies to enhance the main open-outcry business of the exchange. He believed that the CBOT had to continue to draw business to the pits of Chicago by creating a more efficient version of open outcry. In contrast to Arbor's vision of an expansive network, Brennan's perspective was that the global market for U.S. futures should resemble a whirlpool with Chicago at its center. He made his position against the Eurex alliance clear and criticized Arbor for expenditures relating to it.

In the press and among the membership, the "flat earth" attack created a clear division between Brennan and Arbor. However, this neat categorization obscured the fundamental agreements that bound their positions together. Both candidates saw that the CBOT had to respond to electronic trading. Both men advocated using digital technologies to make open outcry more efficient and expanding some electronic capabilities of the exchange to achieve global distribution of products. But while Arbor advocated pursuing the Eurex deal to expand the reach of the exchange, Brennan supported increasing the number of terminals on the CBOT's own Project A network. According to Brennan's plan, Project A would remain entirely under CBOT control and would always be subservient to the open outcry pits.

Each backed an approach that mixed technological regimes. In "electronic open outcry," digital "clerks" would route orders from the outside market directly into the pits, bypassing the army of clerks and runners. Electronic technologies would provide greater speed in filling orders and greater accuracy in accounting procedures. The possibilities of these new efficiencies were central to arguments both for maintaining and for abandoning the open outcry system. Brennan and Arbor's essential agreement that some degree of digitalization was necessary exposes their assumptions about technology. Each justified strategies that would eliminate human mediators from the market. Adding digital technologies to bring orders to and from the trading pits would decrease the cost of human labor for clients while allowing the traders to remain in the heart of the market. Arbor and Brennan's disagreements, and those among the members, focused on how well suited each technology was for achieving those ideals.

Election day arrived, and the traders brought these arguments to the ballot box. Their ties to the pits proved unbreakable. When the debates ended and the votes were tabulated, David Brennan won by only the narrowest of margins—608 votes to Pat Arbor's 598. David Roeder of the *Chicago Sun-Times* reflected on the significance of the election, "He won because the trading floor struck back, but his victory raises questions about whether the CBOT is stepping dangerously away from the global stage" (December 7, 1998). Within a month, the membership had reaffirmed the vote by scrapping the alliance with Eurex. Brennan moved quickly to dismantle the deal in favor of expanding Project A and to focus his attention on increasing electronic order flow to the pits.[15] Pat Arbor left to found an electronic trading firm of his own. He eulogized his last term in office in the *New York Times* business section on December 11: "The push for technology, I think, was maybe too much for the membership to digest right now. . . . This means that the old guard is back; they thought we were going too far" (December 10, 1998).

The election proved that pit traders were still in control in 1998. The exchange had created a method for hedging farmers' risks and perfected the related trading technique. One hundred and fifty years later, the pits had become much more than a rationalized and elaborated form for handling risk. Open-outcry technology and the daily performance of the market had linked Chicago's traders to its method of exchange.

While the CBOT debated whether to go digital or retain the open-outcry trading system, Perkins Silver, a firm founded by Chicago locals, was maneuvering to take advantage of the electronic upheaval. The two directors, Eric Perkins and Philip Silver, founded the company in 1985 as a clearing firm managing the accounts of Chicago locals. Both men were closely involved in CBOT politics and management, and both watched with frustration as the CBOT swerved to avoid the coming of electronic trading. At the same time, they recognized how their company could take advantage of the opportunities in the emerging overseas electronic markets.

Eric Perkins saw a shift occurring in the global futures industry. The Chicago exchanges no longer dominated the futures industry in trading skill and knowledge. Perkins noted that both São Paolo and London had successfully adopted "the Chicago trading culture" during the past ten years. In London, moreover, the financial futures exchange had been built on the Chicago model, and the market was already populated with scores of Chicago traders. Although this may have posed a threat to organizations like the CBOT, Perkins knew that local trading populations in financial centers outside Chicago could provide human materials for Perkins Silver and other entrepreneurial Chicago firms. Silver and Perkins positioned themselves to take advantage of this experienced work force. They intended to hone the skills of the British futures and foreign exchange dealers along the Chicago model and train new ones who would ultimately supplant them according to their plan for diversity. They planned to set up an electronic dealing room in London that would bring Chicago techniques of trading to the electronic financial frontier.

Europe, in particular, presented a clear opportunity. Without the constraining attachments to pit trading that held back the CBOT, in London Perkins Silver would be able to bring Chicago-style speculation to the new world of online markets in European futures. Perkins and Silver planned to provide market makers to these electronic exchanges, but with a crucial difference. The CBOT markets remained largely based in tight networks reinforced by friendship and family rather than the values of education and diversity. The pits did not necessarily reward formalized knowledge or professional commitment, and this financial shop floor was dominated by white men. Perkins and Silver decided that their company would improve on the CBOT markets by welcoming groups that had previously been excluded and set out to create a dealing room that was more efficient and open than the pits they were leaving behind. They brought in educated professionals, including women and minorities, to replace the working-class traders who had manned the London pits. They assumed that traders with these backgrounds and experiences—often the ones that prevented entry into the CBOT pits—could provide profitable readings of the market. According to the Perkins Silver philosophy, the academic approach of the new traders would help them to see new ways to interpret market activity. Their multicultural vision and neoliberal logic trusted that sound market behavior would have beneficial results. These criteria guided the Perkins and Silver's hiring practices as they began organizing their European expansion.

Perkins Silver opened an office in London to train traders to deal in European futures products and provide market makers to Eurex, LIFFE, and MATIF, the European exchanges. London's time zone is only one hour earlier than that of Germany and France, and it is populated with native English speakers. London already had traders who were well seasoned in the foreign exchange (also known as FX) and futures markets of the City of London, the financial district of England's capital city. Perkins Silver planned to use established London traders to seed their new operation, while training new ones who would change the social composition of the dealing room and thus generate diverse points of view on the market.[1] This plan was itself part of a broader pattern, and the Perkins Silver executives were not the first to bring Chicago-style speculation to London. Throughout their twenty-year history, financial futures exchanges in England had been planned and populated by Chicago traders and administrators. By the 1990s, the London futures market was an assemblage of economic forms from both sides of the Atlantic.

This chapter provides an account of Perkins Silver's entry into London and an introduction to London markets. It describes how the City's financial futures markets began with working-class actors and then began to replace them with university graduates. Next, it examines what happened when the Perkins Silver executives implemented their strategy to profit from new market actors, particularly by developing a professional cohort of traders that included minorities and women. The managers adjusted their goals to the London context and implemented them in their hiring practices. But their ideas did not play out neatly. The traders who already worked in the London financial markets had their own ideas of economic action, and they, too, would have their say on the trading floor.

New LIFFE in the City

Although London had its own homegrown commodities exchanges for tangible goods such as metals, coffee, cotton, and sugar, the Chicago exchanges—the Chicago Board of Trade and the Chicago Mercantile Exchange (the Merc)—had been the powerhouses in commodity futures trading since the nineteenth century. The Chicago and London exchanges differed in the way they had established financial futures markets. The London futures markets had drawn their clients from firms, which discouraged the retail business of smaller players.[2] In contrast, the Chicago markets were heavily populated by local speculators trading mostly for themselves. The designers of the London market identified these locals as the source of the Chicago markets' famed liquidity, and they explicitly set out to develop such local talent to staff the pits of the new London exchange.

The development of the London International Financial Futures Exchange (LIFFE) and the cultivation of new London locals were part of a financial revolution that was taking place in England in the 1970s and 1980s. A move from "gentlemanly capitalism" to the new order of the "Big Bang" was in progress and supported by Margaret Thatcher's policies.[3] The Big Bang was technically a series of regulatory changes outlined in the Financial Services Bill that were put into practice October 27, 1986, and opened the City to new kinds of firms and traders. This transformation aroused conflicts that focused on the entry of new players and new organizational forms—particularly on the foreign ownership of formerly British banks such as Warburg and eventually Schroeder's and Barings—and on new financial products and the companies and individuals that traded them.

The death of an older style of British capitalism was marked by the demise of a figure that represented the values of the old city—that of the gentleman capitalist who, as political commentator Will Hutton describes,

> does not try too hard; is understated in his approach to life; celebrates sport, games and pleasure; he is fair-minded; he has good manners; is in relaxed control of his time; has independent means; is steady under fire. A gentleman's word is his bond; he does not lie, takes pride in being practical; distrusts foreigners; is public spirited; and above all keeps his distance from those below him.[4]

These characteristics may have fit well with finance before the Big Bang era, as Hutton asserts, but they did not describe many of the new actors who entered the City, least of all the new traders brought in to staff the foreign exchange rooms of merchant banks. The market in currencies led the way, welcoming working-class men with relatively little education. Soon financial traders were considering developing a financial futures exchange staffed by Chicago-style speculators to complement the currency markets thriving in London's banks. In 1977, John Edwards wrote a piece in the London-based *Financial Times* entitled "Speculators Are Made Welcome," lauding Chicago traders and considering the potential of such risk-takers for London markets, "It is the 'locals' operating exclusively for themselves, who make the U.S. markets so different from London, where all the business is channeled through member companies of the exchange," he wrote.[5] The article was a challenge to London to build an army of such traders. Leaving behind its own models of financial activity and organization, London focused its sights on the American Midwest to find the kind of trader who would populate the open outcry pits of the newly envisioned London International Financial Futures Exchange (LIFFE).

On July 27, 1981, an article appeared in the *Financial Times* entitled, "Can Financial Futures Traders Out Shout the Old-Timers in Chicago?" The reporter felt that "British bankers and other supporters of the London International Financial Futures Market are confident they can create a respectable complement for the more difficult financial futures markets in the USA." But these new British traders would be operating on Chicago turf. Traders who ended up on the LIFFE floor had "to adjust to an environment firmly based on the Chicago model," especially the pits, which were the key technology for the liquid market in American financial futures. The LIFFE managers, with consultants from the CBOT and the Merc, seeded the floor with a dozen "natives of Chicago" and implemented an educational program in speculation.[6] When the trading floor opened in 1982, a new kind of London trader had been ushered into existence.

The *Mail on Sunday* described this social shift: "The City has produced a new breed of broker. He swaps millions at the flick of an eye in the rainbow-hued Financial Futures Exchange. He's young and brash and sometimes without an O-level to his name."[7] The wild behavior and spending practices of the mostly working-class traders became legendary. In his autobiography, *Rogue Trader*, Nick Leeson, the most infamous of these traders, chronicled his exploits in the futures markets and bars of Singapore, which ended in the collapse of the venerable Barings Bank.[8] From the mid-1980s, London was no longer driven by English commerce and class ideals. The models for proper financial conduct derived from relations and tensions between City norms and the new organizational forms like the LIFFE and the American- and European-owned banks. With the Big Bang, the City officially deregulated not only its securities markets but also it social space.[9]

Barrow Boys and Essex Men

As London opened up to new ownership of its merchant banks and became a more cosmopolitan hub, the City's futures and foreign exchange dealers were a strangely parochial group. These newcomers to the life of the City were known as "barrow boys," streetwise dealers from East and South London without the education and class of the "white shoe" financial firms and the Bank of England. The newspaper-reading public could also identify the barrow boys as representatives of the species "Essex Man." Simon Heffer, writing in the conservative *Sunday Telegraph*, coined this phrase to describe those who had delivered Margaret Thatcher to power and kept her in power. Essex Man signified the heightened entrepreneurialism and conspicuous consumption associated with the economic styles of the 1980s among a rising stratum of the English middle and working class. Essex Man was a key figure in the London of the 1980s and 1990s — so much so that the *Guardian* could admit, in an article entitled "Barings Blood Spreads Wider," (March 4, 1995), that in the initial analysis, "it seemed simple enough to blame the downfall of Barings on Essex Man."

The County of Essex, just to the east of the East End, became the migration site for working-class families whose crowded London neighborhoods were razed during urban renewal. Essex Man was a type related to images of an uprooted working class committed to bettering its economic prospects and showing off its success in its clothing, houses, cars, and women. Simon Heffer was quoted in an article by Nicholas Farrell in the *Sunday Telegraph* for November 10, 1991, saying that his interest in Essex Man had been piqued by a minister of Parliament who "had long been fascinated by the grim landscape of South Essex and its atavistically Cockney people. . . . It was his view that the affluent, industrious, ruthless and caustic typical inhabitants of South Essex were the shock troops of the Thatcherite revolution, the incarnation of the new economic freedoms she had bestowed upon a broadly ungrateful nation. I was inclined to agree."

Essex Man represented an intertwining of politics, class, and styles of consumption that confounded the appreciation for restrained behavior of England's tastemakers and social commentators. It seemed that deploring Essex Man on the LIFFE floor and in his home county united the commentators of the Tory *Daily Telegraph* and the liberal *Guardian*, who normally sniped at each other in their columns. The commentary concerning

Essex Man and his air-headed, Gucci-clad counterpart, Essex Woman, coded differences around consumption styles, language, and self-presentation as biological, implying that social conduct had a racial component.[10] The caustic terms imagined a new species that had resuscitated an earlier and more primitive form of humanity, presumably one better left to die. Heffer's "atavistically Cockney people" invoked a life form revived by a combination of free-market policies and City innovation.

Stories from the floor of the LIFFE made this discomfort understandable. In fact, the barrow boy traders seemed to pitch their raucous spending and new wealth directly against the dictates of upper-class taste. While British cultural commentators railed against him, Essex Man played against upper-class conventions.

The LIFFE floor traders spent lavishly what they earned—and, from their stories, some of what they may not have earned. Tony Healy, an ex-LIFFE trader working at Perkins Silver, told me that many floor traders treated "their trading accounts like bank accounts." Expensive lunches were the order of the day. The Mercedes showroom around the corner from the exchange thrived. Essex men famously donned designer clothes, particularly from Gucci (and now, with a swing in fashion, from Prada). Essex Man turned the virtue of thrift on its head. Barrow-boy traders spread the wealth they acquired, tilting the balance between saving and spending that creates a productive tension in a working capitalist economy.[11] Tony neatly summarized this ethic: "The more money you spent, the bigger a man you were."

The Perkins Silver traders who had worked on the floor of the LIFFE told tales of their erstwhile colleagues. There was Dickey, a South Londoner who ran his pit with an iron rod, and was reputed to have made 18 million pounds in one year. There was Frankie the Frenchman, a wealthy man who would repeatedly lose all his money and then return to France to plead with his father to refill his accounts. Other traders were given nicknames reflecting their personalities or appearances, such as Knobby and Freddy (like Freddy Krueger of *Nightmare on Elm Street*). In these tales, the British floor traders outstripped their Chicago counterparts in raucous revelry and under-the-table dealing. As one veteran told me, it was "a playground for grown-ups," and a paradise for "opportunists for wheeling and dealing."

The Perkins Silver traders who came to the City in this first wave of financial innovation mostly lived in Essex and claimed the working-class heritage Essex Man was reputed to have. They exaggerated the styles of working-class London. Having family that worked the docks on the Isle of Dogs (now covered in towering office buildings and called Docklands) lent legitimacy to their brash style and halting speech with its Cockney accents. Even those whose background was far removed from manual labor appropriated the style. Billy, whose father is the manager of a soccer team, worked hard to prove his allegiance to these rude manners.

Others, like Trevor and John, came by their working-class style by being born into it. John, originally a South Londoner and an ex-FX dealer, had crooked and yellowed teeth, was skinny, and dressed with little care. His accent was so riddled with glottal stops that there seemed to be no meaningful utterances. Martin, on the other hand, embodied the successful Essex Man. He was in his early thirties and Perkins Silver's most prosperous trader. His elegant sweaters and expensive haircut trumpeted his success. He wore his success in his clothes, arrogance, and aggressive style and in the way he used humor to dominate his fellow traders with metaphors of homosexual penetration.

Knowing that the association of their occupation with such characters would tar them, other traders positioned themselves in explicit opposition to Essex Man. Darren, a currency trader at a large multinational bank around the corner from Perkins Silver, actively resisted the Essex moniker by explicitly defining his relationship to money, family, and style. Darren told me that he loves having the money that his success as an FX dealer brings, but he was quick to emphasize that he does not spend lavishly. He appreciates the potential of money without having to be a conspicuous consumer. He was disdainful of what he considered to be the obscene spending practices of many of the other foreign exchange and futures traders he knew. One had filled his garage with three Ferraris. Now he has nothing.

When and where the purchasing potential is or is not realized is critical to the aesthetics of capitalism, class, and masculinity.[12] The spendthrift ways of the City's newly wealthy traders were a positional claim about the value of money in relation to their upper-class neighbors who, as Hutton suggests, were no longer able to assert social distance from those below them. The claims to East and South London heritage and styles oppose yet are intimately connected to the members of the city's social clubs, just as the servant classes were (and are) connected to their employers. They redefined this relationship by embracing a working-class affect, accent and the linguistic turns of phrase of a market version of Cockney rhyming slang.

Representatives of the well-meaning middle and upper classes once ventured with reformist fervor into East London neighborhoods like West Ham and Bethnal Green to civilize the inhabitants, but in the trading rooms of the City, the reformers' vision of crude, base, unrefined humanity had already triumphed—and the Perkins Silver crew wore this badge of affiliation with pride.[13] The barrow boy traders of Perkins Silver purposely cultivated a crude aesthetic and made gritty, foul-mouthed masculinity a central part of their trading selves. In the dealing rooms of London, Essex Man reigned, skimming undisguised filthy lucre from the global market.

Yet their opportunities did not last long. In 2000, LIFFE evacuated their trading floors under the competitive pressures of the German-Swiss exchange and online technologies.[14] The locals dispersed to the trading rooms and unemployment offices of London. All that is left of the LIFFE floor traders is the bronze cast of a man on the corner of Walbrook and Cannon Streets. The figure poses, legs widely planted, one arm flung out and head angled toward an outsized cell phone. His loose trading jacket is permanently spread in the wind that streams through the glass and stone funnel of the City's streets. The statue was erected in 1997 to mark the fifteenth anniversary of the London financial futures markets. Just three years later the pits were gone. The metal statue gives material form to the transition from open outcry to electronic trading in the City of London. By the millennium, the LIFFE floor trader had become the most recent casualty of the ascendance of electronic markets in financial futures.

At the same time that the LIFFE trading pits were closing, dealing rooms at large banks were replacing the barrow boys with more educated employees. The original barrow boys were associated with currency and futures dealing, markets that used fairly simple trading techniques. As financial instruments got increasingly more complicated, with swaps and options becoming more widespread, banks recruited university graduates to deal in these complex markets.[15] The ascendance of the educated group reasserted the class character of the City that the barrow boys had challenged. Many of these original currency dealers and futures traders found themselves without jobs as the LIFFE floor closed and dealing rooms in the City were reconfigured. These cast-off traders were very pleased to find work at Perkins Silver as their opportunities at other City venues closed.

A Perkins Silver trader who had been a LIFFE fixture explained to me that many of his buddies from the trading floor had tried and failed to make the transition to online trading. Freddy recounted the career trajectories of his friends who had left the LIFFE. Some had gone belly up and some were driving minicabs. "It is very hard to go from making ten thousand pounds a month to that," he lamented. He assigned dire percentages to the possibilities of success—40 percent of them had tried to move to screen trading, and about 85 percent of those had now quit. Freddy himself was struggling with the transition. I later learned from him that he had had recently had his best month yet on the screen. He had made a scant eight hundred pounds in profits. Joshua Geller, whose experience as a trader, trainer, and manager lent more credibility to his estimates, painted a similarly bleak picture of the transition from pit to screen; 5 to 10 percent would succeed, he offered. Yet

3.1 The LIFFE floor traders are memorialized by this bronze statue that stands on a corner near the defunct trading floor. Photo by author.

at the same time that Perkins Silver was hiring the barrow boys to try their luck in online futures, the managers were also participating in the professionalization of the City that was displacing these same actors.

American Trading in European Markets

As LIFFE went digital and the old markets closed, Perkins Silver sought to step into the void and supply some of the liquidity that the London locals had supported in the rough and tumble pits. Not only the LIFFE but also Eurex and MATIF needed online market makers to ensure that customers would find consistent markets on their exchange. Focusing on Eurex, the largest and potentially most lucrative of the three markets, Perkins Silver planned to capture 5 to 10 percent of the business on that exchange. More than that and "we would be trading with ourselves," Adam Berger, the lead Perkins Silver manager and strategist, told me. With the expertise of Chicago locals, Perkins Silver was positioned to skim profits from the transactions that flowed through these exchanges.

As Perkins Silver was opening its office next door to the LIFFE, the pits that writhed below its windows were slowly dying, and the Chicago model of speculation was disappearing from the trading floor. But it was reappearing online as the Perkins Silver dealing room adapted to the new context of electronic markets for European financial futures. Yet the pit-trading techniques by which Chicago traders and Perkins Silver founders flourished were not easily transposed to the London marketplace or to the new regime of online trading. The face-to-face auctions, where the Perkins Silver founders had developed their talents, thrived on the controlled chaos in the pits. In contrast, electronic futures markets link traders in a neatly networked web of dealing rooms, in which market transactions are played out not in shouts and frenetic hand gestures but through the boldface type of constantly changing numbers on a graphic user interface. Yet neither the Perkins Silver executives nor the futures and foreign exchange traders who staffed their dealing room had much experience with online trading. At the same time, this radical break from open outcry trading technology provided an opportunity for Perkins Silver's managers to advance their ideas for improving the composition of the dealing room by recruiting new kinds of traders. In this new technological and social environment, what resources could Perkins Silver draw on to pursue its ambitions in the new markets?

The challenge facing the managers and trainers of Perkins Silver was to translate Chicago-style speculation not only for the London lads who would staff their dealing room, but also for the emerging technologies of online trading. The Perkins Silver executives were not content simply to reproduce the population of the Chicago pit, which they perceived as composed of destructive cliques. In their view, the insular networks corrupted the purity of the market and excluded potentially profitable traders who lacked the personal contacts or did not fit the ethnic or gender profile that allowed access to trading jobs. Perkins Silver wanted to build a trading team that would be most effective in the market and that would correct imperfections in the Chicago markets. They would substitute abstract principals for personal recruiting networks. Their recruitment and training strategies were based on professionalization, American-style multiculturalism, and meritocracy. The Perkins Silver managers planned to engineer the social content and context of their dealing room to create an efficient trading machine.

Recruiting Futures Traders

The new traders were the raw materials from which the managers constructed a Chicago-style trading room in London, planning the social content of the trading room to draw profits to the firm. Particularly, the Perkins Silver managers sought to take advantage of the underutilized trading talent of new university graduates, minorities, and women. They believed that individuals from these groups would bring new perspectives to reading the market, allowing Perkins Silver to profit from their elimination of barriers to participation based on race and gender. The Perkins Silver strategy was based on the idea that education, experience, and membership in different racial, ethnic, and gender categories and levels of education shaped each individual's vision.

The Perkins Silver trainers set out to recruit traders. Adam Berger and Joshua Geller, the two leading Perkins Silver managers, had clear ideas about who would make a good futures trader. The most obvious were those who already had some proven record in the industry. In London, these were mostly currency traders recruited from investment banks and futures traders from the floor of the LIFFE. With their dealing skills in place, these traders would have to reorient themselves from the telephones of foreign exchange dealing and the face-to-face world of the pits to a new focus on the screen. Perkins Silver recruited many barrow-boy traders who had been laid off as the City labor market sought university graduates.

Adam and Joshua interviewed some who applied in response to newspaper ads or word of mouth. The managers sought people with certain "personality characteristics" that they used as proxies for undeveloped trading skill, even while acknowledging that, as one of the codirectors of the firm told me, "no profile assures that someone will be a good trader." Joshua had a list of traits they required, drawn from the executives' collective experience and knowledge of traders on the CBOT trading floor. They looked for recruits who worked with aplomb under pressure, were "dogged," ambitious, and had decent math skills. The managers preferred their recruits to be single. They observed that trading was a more difficult and stressful task when a family's budget was on the line. A speculator should not be worried about such "extraneous" matters as whether he will be able to pay for his wife's car or the family vacation.

The Perkins Silver managers were also looking for risk-takers. Joshua told me, "Give me a room full of outsiders. Immigrants. People who came to the city with no friends. People who are hungry." Some of the traders he had recruited for the Chicago dealing room served as models for his London endeavors. Two prime examples were a woman who had worked on attack helicopters in the Persian Gulf and a young man who had grown up in one of Chicago's most notorious housing projects and was determined to escape his poor neighborhood. Joshua saw material desires as evidence of ambition and drive. One of the directors of the firm was impressed with a woman who told him she wanted to be a trader because she had expensive taste. For their newest cohort of traders—the one that I was to join as an anthropologist and neophyte futures dealer—they were bringing in "graduate trainees," a group of young men and women between the ages of twenty-one and twenty-five with university degrees. The Perkins Silver innovation was to build a group of traders that would have diverse ways of reading the market.

In mid-September of 2000, the new group that Joshua and Adam had assembled was gathered in the conference room in the Perkins Silver office. From appearances, it was a truly motley crew. Sitting next to me at the back of the table was Paul. He slouched in his chair with his knees wide apart and arms crossed, showing off his thick rings, one with a polished black stone set against his pale skin. His cagey style masked his rigorous training in math and science at Imperial College. Next to us, two neatly dressed white women were flanked by a thirty-something man with an early Beatles-era haircut and a tall, round-faced black man with short dreadlocks and a Midlands accent. Two small Asian (Indian) men, a sleepy, male Orthodox Jew, and I, "the American girl," completed this group. The thirty-something man was our group's sole representative of the barrow-boy traders who dominated the trading room we were all about to enter. Trevor had worked for eleven years as a foreign exchange trader, been laid off, and spent a year traveling in Asia to tourist spots already filled with British vacationers. He broke the silence in the room by spitting out a question in a thick Cockney accent: "OK, so who are the drinkers here?" He assumed he would get a ready, affirmative response. But instead of pointing to themselves and making a date to go to the pub after work, many of the new traders looked furtively around the room. "Drinker" was apparently not the image they wanted to declare to their new employers and colleagues in their first day on the job. Matt broke the uncomfortable silence with a soft chuckle and a light statement of self-incrimination. Sarah chimed in, "I've been known to have a few." The rest of us fidgeted while we waited for the managers to appear and take control.

After about twenty minutes of early morning quiet, Joshua Geller and Andrew Blair, the London risk manager and trainer, entered the room. They complemented each other. Joshua's energy spilled out of his wide smile. His fringe of hair circled his head electrically. Andrew, himself a currency trader in London markets for sixteen years, meandered through his introductory speech, finishing his statement by articulating, with a schoolmistress's stridency, a zero-tolerance policy for drinking during work hours. Alcohol, the managers believed, gave traders a sense of false confidence, and the traders' weakened judgment could cost them profits.

After the initial introductions, the training started. Many of the recruits had never been in a dealing room before and had little experience with finance. But the Perkins Silver trainers understood that deep knowledge of the financial products was not necessary to trade successfully. According to the Perkins Silver executives, and many other traders I interviewed, a good trader could deal in any product. The particulars of the contract itself were not important; a good trader has mastery over the techniques of speculation. So the Perkins Silver trainers focused on producing speculators, not experts in government debt products. Their techniques emphasized creating new relationships to the self and instructed the new group in the particular skills that futures dealers use. They did not insist on technical mastery of the internal workings of financial instruments or their theoretical bases.

The lessons started out simply, with questions like: What is a bond? What is a futures contract? But the curriculum quickly moved beyond that to explain the two techniques that most of us would use to trade in our own accounts: "scalping" and "spreading." Both techniques focus on the profits to be made in the daily fluctuation of futures markets. Scalping focuses on the price movements in a single contract. The scalper buys contracts that he expects to rise in price, or at least that he anticipates being able to make money by buying at the bid and selling at the asking price. Spreading, in the form we were to practice it, takes advantage of the difference in volatility between bonds of different durations. The Perkins Silver managers directed most of their traders work with spreads in ten-, five- and two-year German Treasury bond futures nicknamed the Bund, Bobl, and Schatz. The price of a ten-year bond is more volatile than that of a two-year bond because the longer time frame presents more opportunities for changing economic conditions and involves greater uncertainties. A spreader takes opposite positions in each of two instruments, using the more stable contract to limit the loss potential of a position in the more volatile product. These techniques take no more than a day or two to master conceptually. For traders whose computation skills were slow, "cheat sheets" were available that did the work of calculating the initial position of the spread.

Joshua advised that we pursue other training techniques on our own time. Particularly, he suggested playing video games. Minefield was a favorite of Joshua's. We spent the mornings in class and the afternoons in developing our skills on a program that simulated an arbitrage market. Glued to our screens, we simulated buying and selling cotton futures in New York and London. Later we graduated to trading with real data from past LIFFE markets. Each program tallied up our wins and losses in discreet rounds, as in a video game. These mock markets allowed us to develop online trading skills before "going live," armed with Perkins Silver cash. These programs taught the group some fundamental lessons about the gamelike character of trading and the intense focus necessary, as well as sharpening our hand-eye coordination.

The physical demands of online trading centered on the ability to recognize visually a profit opportunity and implement a decision to buy or sell by clicking a mouse. One crucial problem we had to surmount during this period was known as "fat fingering"—clicking the right button on the mouse rather than the left. Although this has little consequence in a word processing or spreadsheet program, in a live market it is critical. The left button allows the trader to join the bid or offer. The right button, the danger button, sells directly into the bid or buys the offer, establishing a position opposite to the one the trader intended. Establishing control over these opposite intentions embodied in a quick, sharp twitch of barely separated fingers at first took much concentration. Even the more experienced traders sometimes suffered from lapses in manual control. "Ahh, I've fat-fingered it," an unlucky trader would cry with disgust, desperately trying to get out of his position before the losses mounted.[16]

After these basic physical skills were established, trainers provided techniques to help the new recruits evolve from malleable university graduates into seasoned, Chicago-style speculators. The managers recognized that this required creating a bridge between the Chicago and London offices to bring the techniques of the Chicago managers into the London trading room and make their British recruits subject to inspection and evaluation by Chicago management.

Andrew was in charge of managing the London traders. Philip, the cofounder, had recently moved his permanent residence to London and spent his days in an entirely glass-enclosed office. Rumors about him circulated more quickly than futures contracts. He had a mansion in Belgravia, an extensive art collection, and more women than he could fight off. Philip would occasionally venture into the dealing room and trade on a terminal at the edge of the room rather than the one in his office, to get a sense of what the "room was doing." He was also available for advice and discipline. Even with Philip present, the traders had contact mostly with Andrew, Joshua, and Adam. Joshua and Adam were based in Chicago but spent one week of each month in London. Their visits maintained a connection between the London and Chicago offices and established a virtual presence in London. The Chicago managers had constant live access to the trading accounts of all their traders in both Chicago and London. Adam dropped in daily on tape to give lessons on the techniques of speculation. On the television screen, he paced back and forth in front of a group of fledgling traders in Chicago, pausing to write statements of trading philosophy in capital letters on the board behind him.

But neither these techniques nor the Perkins Silver vision of a professional, egalitarian market were easily implemented and absorbed. When the graduate trainees entered the trading room, they encountered the sixty traders already stationed at their trading terminals. The tensions between the Essex Men, the graduate trainees, and their overseers were high. The graduate trainees represented the educated classes that were replacing the barrowboy traders throughout the City and were part of an American, multiculturalist program that the barrow boys rejected. Perkins Silver compounded these distinctions by creating special arrangements for the new group. The managers dedicated two rows of trading desks to the graduate trainees, separating them from more experienced traders. This separation helped the new traders cohere as a group and it also worked to preserve their unique work habits. The managers wanted the graduate trainees to adopt some of the existing dealing techniques and attitudes, such as adopting aggressive postures in relation to the market, while avoiding others.

The Perkins Silver managers changed the pay structure for the graduate trainees to avoid some other problems of managing an independent workforce. The barrow boys' pay was based on the model of the local trader; as independent contractors, most of the traders in the room traded the firm's money for a percentage of their profits. This percentage was individually negotiated between the trader and the management on the basis of the trader's success. This structure gave the barrow boys a lot of control over their work hours. They could come in when they wanted, leave when they wanted, and vacation when they wanted. They were subject to reprimand if they were chronically absent, if their profits fell off, or if they were not practicing the firm's techniques of speculation, but many maintained loose schedules. I would arrive at the trading room at 6:45 in the morning, but the room was

sparsely populated until 10:00 a.m. The glow of computer screens that normally illuminated the room came only from the full row of graduate trainees
at that early hour.

This flexibility was frustrating to the Perkins Silver managers, who wanted
to develop a workforce committed to practicing speculation as a profession.
Some of the best traders did not come in until close to 1:00, when the Chicago markets would "wake up," or come online at 7:00 a.m. Chicago time.
Among them was Pat, one of Perkins Silver's best earners. She had been the
only woman on the trading floor before the managers brought in our group.
She'd stride in after noon on painfully high heels and plunk herself in the
chair at her workstation, which was adorned with fuzzy pink beasts. She was
always gone by 3:00 when the market began to slow. After she left her desk,
her screen saver reminded the room in three-dimensional swerving letters,
"I've cleaned up."

The arrangement for the new recruits was meant to remedy what the
managers believed was a lax attitude toward producing profits for Perkins
Silver. The graduate trainees were required to be at their desks before the
market opened at 7:00 and remain there until 4:00. They received a set
number of vacation weeks and a bonus determined by performance. While
the graduates accepted this arrangement, it enraged Trevor. With his eleven
years as an FX dealer, he believed that he deserved the straight percentage
deal on which his buddies in the room operated.

The tensions between Essex Men and the new forms of Chicago-style interaction played out in their relationships with the graduate trainees. The
older traders assigned nicknames to the new traders. Two in particular stood
out. The first was "The Fetus," their name for Paul, the young, arrogant, and
seemingly natural trader. The barrow boys saw themselves in his swagger.
The other was for Jason, the Orthodox Jew who would leave around 2:00
p.m. on Fridays to make it home before sundown. Jason got the nickname
"son of Adam," supposedly because he bore some physical resemblance to
the disliked top manager, though I could discern none. The barrow boys'
discomfort with the characteristics of the new cohort were played out in the
marking of Jason and Adam as Jews — different from the barrow boys and
beyond the boundary of the acceptable types of traders, according to their
own definitions.

Women in the dealing room also challenged this boundary. One of the
issues that dominated the management of the trading floor in the fall of 2000
was the use of the word "cunt." Although it is used more blithely in Britain
than in the United States, it was particularly obnoxious to Perkins Silver managers. They insisted on excluding the word from the trading room to make
the atmosphere more comfortable for the newly minted female traders. In

the service of profits, the managers believed that the women should have a space where they felt comfortable in expressing their views.

The barrow boys, however, tried to keep the women feeling "out of place" in the dealing room. The saturation of sexual language of male domination demands of women "a physically impossible performance."[17] In an all-male trading room, "cunt" could be construed as a metaphor for the market or for a particular competitor, usually a man. However, in the presence of women, the insult slips uncomfortably, but perhaps intentionally, toward its referent.

This slippage did not seem to bother Pat, the original female trader at Perkins Silver. She took up the cause of the word with fervor. She rejected the management's idea that the term might disturb her. She did not want to be singled out as a woman, but kept her identification with the barrow boys with whom she shared history, class, and, of course, Essex. In the conflict, the word became a protest against the feminization of the dealing room and, therefore, the social experiment of the Perkins Silver managers. The managers' challenge to their swearing was a signal of the barrow boys' dislocation. Women in the dealing room were an assault on their already tenuous position in the City. The barrow boys and Pat protested by defending their market lingo.

Essex Boys, Germans, and Chicago

While these conflicts exposed divisions in City trading rooms, another set of competitors was emerging online. The Perkins Silver traders were not trading exclusively with people whose habits and fears they knew, as they had on the LIFFE floor or over the telephone networks of foreign exchange dealing. Online trading networks stretch over the globe. Traders rely on knowledge of their competitors to orient their own trading strategies; in the rhythms of the changing numbers on their screens, the Perkins Silver traders constructed virtual competitors. They identified the competition by drawing conclusions about their trading styles from national and regional characteristics that they observed.

In the market for German bond futures, the groups that the Essex traders competed with were "the Germans" and "Chicago." They had daily nationalist battles with their German and Chicago counterparts. Essex was a locus of identity for Perkins Silver traders who felt their trading prowess was related to their social origins. They drew on their own national and urban identities as streetwise English lads to do combat with their Chicago and Frankfurt counterparts in a market that operates on foreign territory—the German Treasury bond futures market.

The language the traders used to identify these groups linked local identities with trading styles. The Germans were closely associated with an imagined set of national qualities such as dishonesty and inflexibility. The Essex traders suspected them of collaborating with their government to gain market advantages, especially in what they saw as the absence of street-smart trading skills.

The market is ruled by the logic of time zones that are coded by national and regional participation in the German bond futures market. The Perkins Silver traders often griped that the timing of market movements conveyed that the Germans had inside information from the Bundesbank or the group of banks that sets rates for German bonds. The Germans were the subjects of the Perkins Silver traders' narratives in the hours between 7:00 a.m. and 1:00 p.m. London time, when the Essex Men and the Germans were seen to be the majority of players in the market.

This changed daily at 1:00 p.m. Unlike the Germans, "Chicago" was not identified with its national government. Instead, Chicago traders were identified as a collective always referred to by the name of the city where financial futures trading originated. Perkins Silver traders admired members of the Chicago group for their aggressive style of speculation. The markets were often said to be "more interesting" after 1:00 p.m. Along with Pat, several of the most successful traders chose to arrive shortly before then. These traders claimed that the afternoon hours gave the best opportunities for competition because Chicago brought larger volumes and more skillful trading to the market.

Chicago's involvement also gave clues to the identities and strategies of yet another set of market actors. In the Perkins Silver dealing room, a cable line connected Perkins Silver to the pits in Chicago. When the bond futures pits were open for business, a speaker on the Perkins Silver floor funneled the bids, offers, and final prices into the dealing room. A man with a flat-voweled Midwestern accent called out the bids and offers and occasionally the identity of a bank. The Perkins Silver traders derided the predictability of the big financial houses' strategies. When the nasal voice called out, "Merrill's a seller," a jaded reaction followed. "Did you hear that, Billy, Merrill's selling?" Billy responded in mock surprise, "Yeah, fancy that." In fact, Merrill Lynch's selling became an ongoing joke. This information oriented the Perkins Silver traders to the players in the market and added to the notion that these actors were consistent. These clues helped traders imagine and identify patterns of action in the market.

Displacements

Tensions between a particular kind of localism and the effects of the globalization of populations and markets were felt simultaneously within the

Perkins Silver dealing room and in Britain more generally. While the Perkins Silver traders were negotiating the tensions between barrow boys and the new recruits, the shape of British multiculturalism was being debated in the government and in the newspapers. An independent think-tank called the Runnymede Trust delivered a report developed by the Commission on the Future of Multi-Ethnic Britain to Home Secretary Jack Straw. The two-year study called on Britain to reconsider the concept of "Britishness." Objecting to the racial coding of the nationalist term, it stated that the idea of Britishness was "southern England-centered" and that it potentially excluded millions from the "national story and national identity." The race-based language and concerns of the report elide the British concern with class. The usurpation of the privileged category of underprivilege was echoed in the tension between the Perkins Silver barrow boys and the new, multi-ethnic graduate trainees. While this report framed the tension between inclusion and exclusion in terms of the political identity of the nation, the Perkins Silver managers were importing the same logic of race and difference under the mantle of the market.

The Market and Multiculturalism

The Perkins Silver managers constructed their dealing room to create a cohort of professionalized traders within an American-style, multiculturalist paradigm that resonated with the Runnymede Trust report. Perkins Silver hired Asians, blacks, and women, all of them educated, to bring in different views of the market. According to this logic, the categorical differences of each trader would lead him or her to interpret the market differently, providing a range of insights into the market's actions. This committed and diverse professional staff (certainly different from the population of the Chicago pits from which the Perkins Silver managers came), coupled with Chicago trading techniques, would, they hoped, help their fledgling operations prosper.

The Essex traders, their new colleagues, and their bosses clashed over defining the appropriate economic subjects for a global market. What characterizes the kind of person who operates responsibly and effectively in electronic financial futures markets? This was not an obvious question for Perkins Silver, the CBOT, or the London financial world. Early in the process of building the financial futures market, Chicago had a dominant role. In the first wave of innovation, the LIFFE set out to copy the Chicago model. But the electronic environment demanded further adjustments. Rather than reproducing the Chicago model, Perkins Silver set out to correct for the market imperfections of the pits by creating a dealing room more closely in line with market ideals. The Perkins Silver founders and managers worked to make their trading room conform to the image defined by their market ethic, using ideas at the intersection of American multiculturalism and capitalism.[18]

Just as electronic trading forced the CBOT to reconsider its commitment to open-outcry technology, the ascendance of futures trading outside of the Windy City forced a new perspective on Chicago's cultural resources. To create their own trading room based on electronic technology and physically distant from their home institutions, Perkins Silver managers had to isolate the key characteristics of Chicago-style speculation that they would bring to London markets.

These displacements gave the Perkins Silver managers a new perspective on the norms and practices of the CBOT. The London traders and electronic markets were simultaneously familiar enough and different enough to show Chicago traders what was unique about their own methods, techniques, and the mushy but significant area that Eric Perkins identified as "Chicago culture"—the set of relationships to the self and to competitors interwoven with the trading techniques and the orientation to risk that were rooted in pit trading. The synthesis of nearness and remoteness enabled the Perkins Silver executives to develop their own trading techniques, modifying them for new technologies and geographies while identifying and retaining what they viewed as the key elements of Chicago-style speculation.[19] Their approach blended Chicago techniques with new techniques and practices rather than simply transferring them to a new location.[20]

Perkins Silver tried to perfect its approach to trading by professionalizing speculators while establishing a cohort of mixed ethnicity, race, and gender. According to crude anthropological notion that the Perkins Silver managers implemented, these differences would generate novel perspective and interpretation, a process that they believed would lead to more profits. The Perkins Silver managers were linking a basic market notion—that opposing views build a liquid market—with the values of professionalism and diversity.

Risk is the business of the futures industry. From the trading floors of Chicago to the corporate Eurex offices in Frankfurt, futures markets manage risk.[1] The temporal nature of risk, particularly the way disjunctions between the present and the future create situations of fundamental uncertainty, is a central problem for planning and control.[2] As hedging tools, futures contracts work to "colonize the future," limiting dangerous exposure by bringing the problem of future prices under the influence of the present.[3] Futures exchanges are quintessential modernist institutions: the contracts traded there bring the contingencies of passing time under human management.[4]

Yet there is another side to risk. Risk reaps reward—in money, status, the elaboration of the social space of markets, and the construction of a masculine self. A close examination of the uses of risk on the dealing room floor at the Chicago Board of Trade shows the productivity of risk in the construction of financial space and in the elaboration of economic selves. Financial speculation is an active, voluntary engagement with risk. Risk-taking and thrill-seeking behavior can be seen as challenges to the constraints of bureaucratically organized social routines.[5] In this light, it is a dissident practice, a critical contestation with the regimentation of modern life. To work with risk is to engage fate and to play with the uncertainties of the future. Engagements with risk are more powerful than an interpretation that emphasizes spontaneous actions in the context of bureaucratic control would imply. Risk is a constitutive element of contemporary power and economic practice. The work of speculation shows that the complex practices of economic risk-taking are exemplary acts of contemporary capitalism that configure markets and shape speculators.

The productivity of risk takes several forms in the organization and practices of financial futures markets. The first aspect of productivity is located in the infrastructure and organization of futures markets. Following actuarial logic, financial risks require management, a service that the CBOT provides. The CBOT creates the contracts and establishes a market in financial risk that allows bankers, agribusiness, and others to protect themselves against changes in interest rates, exchange rates, and the weather. Economic organizations like the CBOT define, support, and routinize risks as they bring financial markets to life. They create contracts, match orders to buy and sell, perform accounting functions, and operate worldwide markets. The CBOT packages and channels financial hazards, providing risk management to shift the danger and the potential of the market from its clients to individuals or groups that specialize in profiting from risk. The organization creates both markets in futures contracts and a population of speculators who trade in risk products.

Rationalized risk-management markets establish the conditions for speculation in financial contracts. But risk-taking does not become routine for speculators. It retains the thrill of gain and loss. Traders must learn to manage their own engagements with risk and the physical sensations and social stakes that accompany the highs and lows of winning and losing. Traders come to these markets, hotbeds of profit and loss, to try their skill on the financial high wire. In the pit, they work to perform a kind of alchemy—turning risk into profit. The tightly regulated markets of the CBOT create the conditions that make speculation possible. Aggressive risk-taking is, therefore, established and sustained by routinization and bureaucracy; it is not an escape from it.

In the trading pit, risk-taking helps to generate two levels of action. First, aggressive economic risk-taking is crucial to the social and spatial constitution of the marketplace. The conflicts and contests among traders constitute the competitiveness of the marketplace. The traders sustain the market and, at the same time, the market produces risk-takers. In the pit, a particular kind of self is manufactured in relation to financial action. Risk is the object that traders use in their individual projects of self-creation and re-creation. Traders manipulate risk to manage their identities and establish status in the eyes of their competitors. These practices produce subjects who can sustain themselves under high-stakes conditions to draw profit from economic risk. The ascetic practices and social displays of virtue enacted in the pit describe a capitalist ethic that centers on the mastery of the self under conditions of hazard and possibility.[6]

The perspective on risk generated in the trading pit diverts attention from the negative consequences of uncertainty and refocuses it on what is to be gained by taking risks.[7] In futures markets, the obvious reward is money. Risk-taking includes the potential of creating wealth. But even in financial institutions, it does not end there.[8]

Financial futures traders work within a carefully defined market sphere and within radically short time frames, often moving in and out of a single trade in a matter of seconds. The self-fashioning of these risk-seeking actors is not an ongoing process of reorienting calculations to a market logic; financial calculations are always present. However, with each trade, dealers wager much more than money. Their market engagements are significant social games, a form of "deep play" in the heart of capitalism.[9] Each trader displays a risk-taking self that his competitors, the market, and he himself will judge. The pit is an exemplary situation where character is gambled along with money.[10] In that space, traders subject themselves to the judgment of their peers, who will see them as successful risk-takers or as ineffectual losers unable to engage the market productively.[11] These games of risk gain their significance from the fact that a trader voluntarily places himself under threat of annihilation. The potential reward of success is the creation of a newly defined person in the eyes of the pit.[12]

On the trading floor, Foucault's "limit experiences" meet daily market reality; traders meet a situation of "maximum intensity" in face-to-face competition, and confront the "maximum impossibility" of seeing into the future. Futures markets as risk-management organizations identify the limit of economic reason—the impossibility of calculating future events—and provide methods to contain, objectify, and understand that uncertainty. Yet there is an ecstasy in expressing and engaging these limits.[13] The passionate play with the boundaries of the self and reason—on the edge of financial possibility—is the social stake of the trading pit. Traders who operate at the heart of modern capitalist economies take risks with money and self everyday. For speculators, retaining their integrity and identity is often a mark of successful work at the limit. At the edge of annihilation, surviving financial peril is enough. Situations that package and circulate well-defined risks, like the CBOT markets, are stages where modern actors play out these critical games of self-definition.

A futures contract is a binding agreement to buy or sell a commodity at an agreed-upon price several months in the future:[14] a farmer can lock in the price to be paid for his crop, or a mortgage broker can know what price he will have to pay for bonds at year's end. Futures contracts can be used to neutralize the possibility of loss from unpredictable events. Hurricanes, floods, interest-rate hikes, a falling Euro, or a presidential embarrassment can all affect prices in agricultural and financial commodities. Futures exchanges around the world provide products that harness the risk of these potential events. Futures contracts render the future subject to planning.[15]

As hedging tools, futures contracts protect against the negative effects of risk by formulating specific price risks and constituting rationalized techniques for their avoidance. From this perspective, we can view futures contracts as insurance, or as technologies of risk management, and this depic-

4.1 A grain trader quotes a price to the pit. Prices for the CBOT's agricultural contracts fluctuate on the electronic boards in the background. Photo by Bob Davis.

tion of risk management is how futures exchanges justify their markets.[16] The video that the CBOT shows in its visitors gallery begins with an interview with a farmer, followed by shots of his corn field, before it finally cuts to images of a mortgage broker at work in his office helping his customers purchase their homes at low interest rates.

The use of futures contracts to alleviate risk for farmers and users of grains soon spawned a secondary speculative market in contracts. The original members of the Chicago Board of Trade made and lost fortunes on the variations in Midwest commodity prices without having a stake in the contents of a grain elevator. The CBOT became a place where professional risk-takers gathered to buy and sell contracts, not grain. As the Chicago futures markets consolidated and grew to encompass contracts based on U.S. Treasury debt, these speculators created a continuous, or liquid, market where anyone who wanted to trade could buy and sell futures contracts.[17]

Economics tells us that liquid financial markets, like those in Chicago, London, and Frankfurt, transfer economic uncertainties to speculators, the market's risk specialists. In the language of futures markets, these speculators perform a critical function: they "absorb" the risk that hedgers want to "lay off." The organizations that provide the opportunity to avoid the effects of risk also generate the ability to make a living by taking risks.

In the past, speculators had often been in the business of producing the commodities before they entered the speculative melee.[18] But, this connection between commodity production and futures trading has become more and more abstract. Traders joke about the attenuated connection between speculators and the underlying commodities they trade. Grain traders kid each other about forgetting to sell all the contracts they own. A truck, they declare, will show up at the trader's home and dump a container-load of corn on his front step. This image is funny to traders because the trader's relationship to the physical commodity is so distant. Contracts based on the Dow Jones Industrial Average Index and the debt of the United States government (now the most widely traded markets at the CBOT), rely on an abstraction similar to that of contracts based on future yields of Kansas wheat, a distance from production that points to the central place of exchange in speculation. On the grain floor or in the financial trading room, knowledge of oat markets or macroeconomics is of limited use.

Speculation is a skill of its own that comes from the ability to negotiate the social layering of the pit and create a self that can read and react to rapidly changing market information. These are the keys to mastering risk and taking profit. Each pit and product has its own distinct characters, power dynamics, and rhythms. However, traders claim that a good speculator can trade in any market.

Speculators use futures contracts to exploit rather than to allay risk.[19] Speculators do not fully own the contracts they buy and sell. Instead, they buy and sell contracts "on margin." The CBOT requires each trader to keep a bank account with a balance correlated to the value of contracts they trade. This balance, or margin, assures the trader's ability to pay for losses he may incur during the trading day. Margins are adjusted every night. A trader who has sustained major losses may get a margin call requiring him to deposit funds into his account if he wishes to continue trading. With margin, traders do not have to commit to buying the product and do not need to have the cash necessary for the complete purchase of the contracts. They look for the short-term gain in price fluctuations apart from any ownership of a financial or agricultural commodity. They reap the rewards (or sustain the losses) from the price changes as the contracts pass through their accounts.

In March of 2004, more than 51 million contracts changed hands in CBOT markets. The CBOT estimates that only 3 percent of the trades made on its exchange end in "delivery," when the manager, farmer, or corporation actually takes possession of the bonds or grain shipments that lend their value to the futures contracts. Thus, almost all of CBOT trading business can be considered speculative.

Watching and Being Watched

The strategies traders use to make a profit develop in the specific social and informational contexts of CBOT markets. In the pits, traders watch each others' moves and create a public definition of themselves as risk-takers by performing for the watching eyes of the other traders in the pits.[20] Traders constitute their marketplace by examining each other's risk-taking and acting on their assessments.

Under such watchful eyes, risk reaches beyond the calculation of the possible financial loss and gain. What is at stake besides the cash that a trader places in a market position? A trader submits himself to the vigilant attention of the hundreds of others who will witness his successes and defeats in the pits—what he risks and what he reaps. With money, he wagers his reputation and his self-definition in the eyes of others. His status is always on the line.

Traders scrutinize each other, but not all traders are considered worth watching. Pit traders watch the movements of successful traders closely: whether in order to emulate them or to evaluate them as competitors or potential allies. These kinds of watching are tied to evaluating the risks a trader is willing to take and are a direct indication of the trader's "size."

Technology defines the potential audience for risk-taking performances. The pit is an exchange technology intentionally designed as an arena where a trader can see and be seen by every other trader. Online markets reconfigure the audience for traders' performances because they transform the ability to watch. Online markets enable risk managers and company executives to watch any trader's transactions from the screens at their own desks. Only the managers have access to the full picture of risk-taking; they can see each trader's size and control it. In the trading room, managers walk the floor looking over the shoulders of the traders. But they do not always seek to limit a trader's risk-taking. They are monitoring the company's exposure to loss, but they must also balance potential losses with risk-taking strategies that make profits possible: they may witness a trader's hesitancy in a market—a sign of a failure of nerve. Under the eye of the risk manager, the trader tries to ride the line between taking on too much risk and not taking on enough.

In the pit, risk surveillance operates much more in the open, and it interacts with the ambitions of the traders and the social topology of the space. There are two major divisions within the pit. The first is between brokers who execute orders from outside the CBOT and locals, who buy and sell contracts for their own accounts. Brokers make transactions for financial houses or corporations in exchange for a commission on each trade, linking the outside market to the internal world of the pits. In contrast, locals focus their energies on the pit itself. They speculate with their own money.

The second major division is between "big" and "small" traders. This is referred to as "size," a measure of how much risk a trader is willing to take on in any given moment. A "small trader" may trade from two to five contracts at a time. A big trader may trade in lots of five hundred. Traders identify themselves and each other by their trading size — "I'm a two-lot trader," "He's a fifty-lot trader." "He does size" is a description laced with respect and a degree of awe. The ability to take on greater and greater risks by increasing size defines success among traders. As the mark of risk-taking skill, size is the most important factor in organizing the social and physical space of the pit. The locker room overtones of the language of size are unavoidable.

The hierarchy of size translates itself to the ascending steps of the pit's octagonal structure. The social divisions within the pits define the pecking order and the structure of opportunity for profit. The newest traders stand at the center of the pit, the area that is least desirable and most obscured. They are literally and figuratively beneath the vision of the bigger traders and brokers, who control the largest flow of contracts. The bigger traders stand on the step above the newest and "smallest" traders. The truly "size" traders stand closest to the big brokers on the top step of the pit. The biggest traders are legendary figures who serve as models for all of those who stand beneath them. As a trader named Victor explained:

> Big traders are guys who are actively in there at all moments, and these people are *watched*. . . . You know, Tom Baldwin, Joe Niciforo, and all those guys. They know that they have developed their authoritative presence in the pit, and they know that when they just stick their hands in the air, everybody sees them. You watch them. We watch the players. We watch the risk-takers; we watch the big guys. We watch the shooters, as we call them. We don't sit there and watch the little Mark guy who stands next to me who's never really good or offered a market at any given time. . . . These developed risk-takers, the big guys, have the presence.

The little guys, the Marks of the pit, revere these captains of risk. They aspire to the top step. But the move from the center to the top step is not easy or obvious. In order to become "bigger" and move out of the center, a local must increase his size by trading more contracts and assuming greater and greater risk. This is not just a matter of deciding to trade more. A small trader must navigate the divisions that separate him from the financial action. Moving toward the top step where the biggest opportunities lie requires a strategy.

Traders use risk-taking as a strategy for gaining status and securing access to the physical positions and social standing that are crucial trading resources. They use the flexibility of the trading processes to their advantage. The rules of the pit dictate that the first trader who responds to a call has a right to the order, but brokers and traders exercise discretion over whom they see or hear "first." Such regulatory gray areas provide opportunities for traders to use their networks and judgment to assist friends and cultivate bonds with other traders.

Within the flexible procedures of the pit, locals and brokers cultivate relationships with each other. At times brokers rely on locals to take on trades, even when the local will *lose* money. This establishes a relationship of reciprocity with the implication that the broker will use his discretion to benefit the local in the future. Sean Curley Jr., a broker, describes how the ties between brokers and locals operate:

> There isn't any quid pro quo. But of course a local will be more willing to do things that would seem on the surface to be irrational [because they cost that local money] on the understanding or on the belief that later this human being he's trading with will remember. This happened to me the other day. I got an order to sell from a big local trader in the pit who I have a great relationship with. He [the local] bought it from me at the high[est price] of the day. I know that he didn't make any money on that trade. The next time I get an order to sell and there are a bunch of people who are bidding together, well, I'm going to remember that he bought it from me up there. So if I have to pick someone out of the litter, maybe I'll pick him. . . . There is a lot of discretion.

The local took a loss to the benefit of the broker and his client, and by doing so, he strengthened his relationship of reciprocity with the broker. By making it possible for the client to complete a trade, the local has added to the liquidity of the market, and the broker will reward him at some future time.

Brokers are able to execute trades for their clients with better results when locals are willing to take on financial risks. Ambitious locals wish to make a public demonstration of their risk-taking skill and actively seek out trades to integrate themselves into the society of risk-takers. Brokers reward those traders seen as risk-takers with increased business. The challenge for small locals is gaining the attention of the big traders.

To do so, small traders must convince the bigger traders that they deserve a place among them. Because status in the pits is directly linked to their position as risk-takers, traders who are not content with a small stature must take on greater size. Bigger risks might be out of proportion to the money that they keep as margin, but this is invisible to the traders who watch him. What they see is his size in relation to what he normally trades and to the size of the traders around him. What is seen is more important than what is hidden from the eyes of the pit.

So traders manipulate their risk-taking to curry favor with the traders above them. Because of the spatial constraints of the pit, moving up onto the steps means displacing a trader who is already there. Each trader stands in his own spot, and the social order of the pit strictly enforces the owner-ship of spaces. If a trader stands in another trader's spot, he will likely be hu-miliated, spit on, or literally shoved off the step. Yet despite the vehement defense of space, younger traders do manage to ascend in the hierarchy.

Small traders know that brokers reward ambition with business. As one broker told me, "There's Joe Schmoe, he trades five contracts at a time, but I know he's got that ego where he wants to trade fifty. And knowing he pos-sesses that, I'm going to use him." When a younger trader is ready to ascend in the ranks, he begins to try to gain a spot on the next step up. Paul, a top-step trader, told me how he made his first move. Every day, he would step up to the next level, and the traders there would shove him off. But Paul, from the lowest level, used an informal alliance with a top-step broker to be-gin increasing his size. The traders above Paul became embarrassed when he literally began going over their heads to complete his big trades. Even-tually he stepped up, and they let him stay. He increased his "size" by mak-ing successful trades with the help of the broker. In the eyes of the pit, he gained the respect necessary to move up to the next step.

Even when a trader gains a better spot, holding on to it requires main-taining the recognition of the other traders. The experience of one of the few women who have worked in the thirty-year bond pit illustrates how this works. Although she is now a highly esteemed trader, for her first two years in the bond pit Theresa had to fight to hold her position. She would come in every morning at 6:30, nearly a full hour before the pits opened for busi-ness, to sit in her spot. If she did not make an early appearance, another younger trader would displace her because she was perceived as a weak link, and her spot was a place where newer traders could establish their positions.

As a woman, Theresa's vulnerability was extreme. The mutual scrutiny of the pit is between men. Women are not worth watching, and there are few to lay eyes on. In 1998, when business was vibrant in the financial pits, there were only two women among the six hundred regulars who took to the steps of the thirty-year pit most mornings. The women who survived in the pit, like Theresa, could consider themselves as successful, respected traders. But there was not a single woman among the "top dogs" of the financial pits. At the time, more women traded on the agricultural floor. There, family connections and the clubby networks of established CBOT traders allowed a number of women to operate. But the high-risk games associated with the financial trading floor were decisively masculine. Successful women traders spoke of themselves as being outside the risk-based status competition that raged around them, even when upstart male traders made incursions into their spots. One woman who worked in the agricultural markets described herself as living off the "scraps" of the trading pit. But these financial remains were good enough to support her and her two children and get her home in time for their return from school. As a woman, Theresa was simply outside the pit's rules of challenge and riposte. As a subordinate in the world of risk, she was simply invisible in the pit.[21]

Competitions over space are critical in the pit. Traders will defend their spaces against any new bodies, whether they are unknown neophytes or well-seasoned traders who migrate between pits to try the market in a new product. Financial traders pride themselves on cutthroat competition and deride grain traders for using connections. Even in the bond pit, however, the connections of friendship and family can be especially helpful when trying to gain access to a good place to stand. Dennis, a seasoned trader who usually deals in corn futures, told me about the day he decided to try his hand in the thirty-year bond pit, where contract size and volume offered great opportunities. He entered the pit and took a spot on the third step, the same place he stands in the corn pit. He didn't go unnoticed. The trader to his right got angry that Dennis was forcing him to turn his body sideways to stand on the step. A shoving match started. But during the exchange, Dennis realized that the man battling him for space was the son of an old friend from the North Side neighborhood where he grew up. The younger bond trader stopped fighting and made room for his father's friend.

While smaller traders fight to ascend in the ranks, bigger traders cultivate their own strategies to create and maintain their "neighborhood" of risk-takers.[22] One broker described how he gets rid of encroaching traders whom he doesn't think will help absorb the risk his clients bring to the pit: "I've had guys stand next to me and I've bumped them literally two or three hundred times a day with my elbow. . . . I can do it and not even blink an eyelash, like I'm not even doing it. And they just don't like that. They're gone. They're standing somewhere else."

Brokers promote risk-taking locals as active partners. Smaller traders try to attract the attention of brokers by displaying a desire to "make the market," which means being available to trade with the broker's clients. This creates the conditions for what one broker called "ego liquidity," trading made possible by the desire of a trader to show off his risk-taking prowess. Craig, a broker, acts out an engagement with an aggressive local: "[Speaking as the local] "I'm the market. You are not going through me." [Speaking as the broker] "I'll sell you a hundred at six." [Imitating the aggressiveness of a local]. "OK. I'm the man." [Commenting in his own voice] That guy was the man at six. And everyone in the pit saw him."

The local acted out his desire to make the market and to gain position in the pit by taking on risk. And even as the market went against him, he gained recognition by taking on the risk of the broker's clients. The aggressive local shows that he is "the man" by his willingness to engage with market forces when others are unwilling to do so. And even more critically, he puts it on display for all the other traders in the pit to see, establishing his risk-taking in the public arena. In stepping up to make the market, he shows his willingness to assume risk. His ability to gain the trades he needs will be supported by the broker, who now identifies him with the sort of "ego liquidity" that sustains his business.

New locals try to create opportunities to impress the brokers. They stay in the pit when others leave for lunch or golf, taking advantage of opportunities to be seen. "When everyone leaves, you're in there, and you step up, and the guys see you, and they know you are in there every day. 'He's been in here every day for years. Maybe we should throw him a trade.'"

Brokers challenge the locals to prove themselves. Victor, a young and ambitious broker in the financial room, describes a technique called "jamming" that brokers use to test the risk-taking fortitude of locals.

> I've got an order to sell 20 and I call out "20 at 6" and somebody will say "sold," and I sell that guy 20. Then this little five-lot trader starts yelling like, "Sold, sold, sold. I want that trade. That's mine." And then my clerk says, "Hey, sell 50," and I know this guy doesn't trade 50 contracts at a time, and he's aggressively bid 6 to me and I know he's a [small] trader. I say, "I'll sell you 50. Just stuff 50 contracts down on you guy." And the guy's usually sitting there and panting, staring into a couple of bright headlights, freaking out. . . . So a lot of times we just stick guys with quantities that they don't want, and you make them take it.

Victor wields his discretion as a broker to test the local, who collapses under the pressure of the risk. He cannot rise to the challenge of increasing his size. Instead of mastering the potential gain that fifty contracts carry, the fear of the potential loss incapacitates him. Victor depicts the trader's collapse as a bodily breakdown exposing his inability to handle the risk. He is unable to move and hot with anxiety. He has proven himself useless to the broker and an embarrassment to himself.

A trader's movement through the ranks of the pit allows us to see the interplay between risk-taking and its social returns. The possibilities and perils of every trade link financial and social rewards. Traders play at the boundary between decisions and consequences that lies at the heart of the futures markets and determines the difference between social success and failure, wealth and bankruptcy. Risk-taking orders the social space of the pit. Traders use engagements with risk to maneuver for social and physical position on the steps of the trading arena. However, taking risks is not only a problem of social strategy and display. Learning to successfully handle financial risk requires managing the self under the conditions of imminent gain and loss.

Managing the Risk-Taking Self

Traders proudly identify with their role as risk-takers. They describe "absorbing risk" as their job, their place in the division of financial labor, a job description that indicates how locals see themselves as taking risk into their selves and bodies. This intimacy with risk links risk-taking and self-determination.[23]

Direct engagements with risk are at the center of traders' understandings of their own labor. During my first days at the CBOT, the locals in the pit where I worked insisted that I would never be able to understand trading without putting money on the line. The experience of placing a stake on the line was critical to their self-perceptions, and they did not believe I could understand it by just talking about it with them. They asserted that risk-taking was intensely personal, something that can be felt only in the immediacy of the moment and could not be properly translated.[24]

Since I lacked the $10,000 minimum stake I needed to enter the pit, Henry, a broker, offered to help me learn about working with risk. He suggested that we "paper trade." I would "buy and sell" contracts by marking each decision on a trading card. If I made a successful trade, Henry would give me a penny for every change in the price. If the market turned against my trade, I had to pay Henry in pennies.

Henry taught me that risk-taking requires total focus.[25] There is no room for distraction. I spent hours with my neck craned toward the price screen with a pen in one hand and a trading card in another. Quickly, other traders too—both those I knew personally and those I had only known by sight—began to train me. Mark tutored me in his system of limiting losses by placing orders about fifteen ticks below the market. Ethan told me about trade trends. Traders passing me on their way in and out of the pit took the opportunity to school me in the adages of trading, "Ride your gains and cut your losses." "The trend is your friend."

By insisting that my knowledge of their task would be inaccurate without a personal experience of risk, the traders taught the anthropologist an important fieldwork lesson: abstracting the task can limit the analysis. A trader pulled a book of sociological essays about financial markets out of my pocket and told me that I might as well throw it away. The book was not going to help my trading. Observing from a reflective distance is antithetical to traders' norms of practice. As Henry directed my attention, my direct engagement, even at low stakes, helped me notice specifics about the market. Paper trading showed me the connection between risk-taking and the techniques of discipline that traders described to me.

Trading is a profession that thrives on action undertaken for what is felt to be its own sake.[26] The intensity of focus, the thrill of testing my wits against the market, the utter absorption in the moment-by-moment action, the absolute nature of being right or wrong, of making or losing money on every trade helped me to understand the importance that traders place on engagement with risk for its own sake, not just for profit and loss. One trader told me that with discipline, "you can experience the market and become a part of this living thing, intimately connected to it." The economic incentive is not enough to explain the attractions of trading. The significance that traders draw from their risky work involves financial pleasure.[27]

For speculators, fate lies in the time gap between the present and the future. The risk-taking trader assesses the market, places a stake, and faces the time that must elapse between each decision and its consequence. The market moves and determines his gain or loss, and the result is disclosed. In Erving Goffman's description of the moments between placing the stake and reaping the consequences, the trader "releases himself to the passing moment, wagering his future estate on what transpires precariously in the seconds to come."[28] His skill lies in determining when to place his stake and how large it should be, and then in facing the consequences of his action undaunted.

The consequences of taking risks evoke excitement and complete absorption into the action. This state of being in the present is similar to the experience of mob violence and shares the condition of immediate consequences. Bill Buford describes the pleasure of participating in a riot with British soccer hooligans. "I am attracted to the moment when consciousness ceases: the moments of survival, of animal intensity, of violence, when there is no multiplicity, no potential for different levels of thought: there is only one—the present in the absolute."[29]

The volatile atmosphere of the trading floor also links risk-taking with fighting. Trading often erupts into contests of shoving and swearing, joining together literal and symbolic violence. The CBOT hired two paramedics to staff the trading floor against the possibility of everyday violence erupting into something fiercer. During my time on the trading floor, shouting matches and shoving were so common I often did not even write them down. Sometimes these altercations left physical marks. One trader showed me a graphite-stained scar on his hand where a colleague had stabbed him with a pencil. Yet, as Buford observes, outward aggression can be pleasurably coupled with an inner sense of complete presence.

It is this state and the daily engagements with fatefulness that set trading apart from other economic activities and other areas of the financial industry. While engagements with action are defined as outside daily life for most workers who labor in bureaucratic, routinized settings, traders seek them out. This makes them similar to fighter pilots, professional athletes, and others who thrive on the sense of self-determination that comes from being in the action or at risk and whose work involves reactive, disciplined labor, status competitions, injury, and even sometimes death.

A trader's increasing wealth is an outward sign of his ability to perform the alchemy of the risk-taker. Each trade is a chance to prove that he has mastery over himself. He draws on this mastery to read the market, interpret its signals, deftly navigate its peaks and troughs, and skim profit from the global capital markets that circulate through his hands. He is able to determine his own fate while subjecting himself to the whims of the market. The values of self-determination and free will are central to traders' daily engagements with risk in the futures markets. This forges another link between the financial and social stakes of the pit. With every successful trade, the trader accrues an aura of self-determination and success.

Losing money is more complicated and ambiguous. Taking a risk that results in a loss is not necessarily the reverse of gain. Traders take losses every day. Taking losses is a mark of the risk-taker. But over time a trader who is no longer able to make successful trades at the same time that he takes his necessary losses loses his sense of efficacy and his social standing.

With every trade, a local stakes his money and his ability to define himself. Futures trading is a constant test on both levels. One good trade never guarantees the next. Though traders are surrounded by a social order that buttresses those who can prove their risk-taking acumen, other traders are swift to reject those who lose their skill. Even the most successful traders in the bond pit must continually prove their "big dog" status with each trade.

The pit is the place where a trader with ingenuity, appropriate connections, and discipline can climb onto the top step and into the upper echelons of the income bracket. But the promise of the pit hides the pain and desperation that can come from living with constant uncertainty. The pit collectively pays out social rewards; but traders experience the pain of loss as coming from the market itself and as lone individuals.

The physicality of the pit creates a direct connection between the market and the trader's body that plays itself out in stories of self-destructive behavior and sometimes in suicide. Some of these stories are, no doubt, accounts of actual incidents, but they all have the quality of moral tales about the dangers of wealth and hubris. They are tales of the fall, stories of men who had perfected the art of living within the uncertain gap between present and future but could not sustain their mastery and lost all their money as a result. These tales portray the price of linking risk-taking, personal worth, and self-determination. This urban mythology of the pit's dark side expresses the collective fears of the trading floor and the ever-present possibility of failure.

The pit-based tests of speed, skill, and status pump adrenaline into traders' bodies. The adrenaline buzz links the social and financial risks of the pit with physical pleasure and pain. Traders must work to shed the physical feelings of risk-taking and the aggressive affect of trading when they leave the pit. As early as ten o'clock in the morning, traders perch on stools in the lobby bar of the CBOT. They rid themselves of the residue of competition by numbing themselves with alcohol and drugs, releasing energy in the gym, or even through meditation. As Jack commented: "After work I go to the gym and other people will go get wrecked, go get drunk. . . . You have to realize that it is a very physically demanding job and you just have to do something. It's like go out to drink or go home and smoke a lot of dope or go work out, whatever it is."

The physical intensity of risk-taking links body, status, and games of risk. It is not surprising, then, that traders express their fears of loss and humiliation in terms of bodily and social destruction. A trader named Leo told the following story:

> I know guys that killed themselves in this business, put a gun in their mouth. Terrible things. . . . I mean I've seen drugs ruin guys. I saw something happen, it was probably one of the saddest stories of my trading career. I met a young man there, very nice guy. He and I started off at almost the same time. . . . In the three years that I was there and he was there, he probably made three times as much money as I did, or five times. I didn't know him socially, but I heard he got caught up in drugs, and then I heard he got divorced. Then I heard he got remarried and divorced again. . . . He was high on the Board of Trade, and through some other people I sort of heard little bits and pieces, which was basically he was just sinking. And I come to work one morning, and I get to work about a quarter to six in the morning, and I was walking down LaSalle Street, and I looked down in the curb, and there was this guy sleeping. He was homeless, whatever. It just broke me up, broke me

up. And the story doesn't have a happy ending that I know of. I remember I was in his house, and he had a party, and I'll never forget it, it was such a big party. He had two bands. I never was at a party that had two bands. When the first band broke, the other one came on. I mean, it was terrible. But those kinds of things happen.

Joe told a similar story:

[There are] sad stories, suicide-type things. Tim Creighton, somebody who killed himself two years ago. An old timer in his early fifties, because of money. Tim put a gun to his head and killed himself. He had two kids, fifty years old, always a very successful trader. But he went off the floor, traded, for seven years he traded off the floor and lost all his money. He was in debt to a lot of people and killed himself. Another killed himself in the garage. He always used to give people cars. He had a connection to a car dealer. Carbon monoxide. [A third] overdosed on Quaaludes.

These traders could no longer turn risk into profit. Each story describes the collapse of self-management and the loss of the successful speculator's professional identity. These deaths expose the underbelly of the Dionysian qualities of capitalism that attract traders to the action of the pit.[30]

Why would traders subject themselves to these pressures? The action in the pit is a constant test of self-discipline and fortitude. The constant gamble of self demonstrates a trader's particular virtue. Like champion boxers, traders return to the ring even when they can afford to retire.[31] According to Victor, "You have to understand. The U.S. T-bond pit . . . it's just amazing. There's guys there who make so much money and there's guys approaching their fifties now and probably can retire twenty, thirty, forty times over, and they still come in to work every single day." Simple economic logic cannot explain the commitment of traders to their task.

The rewards are more than monetary. Gain is a scorecard. The rewards of trading lie at the nexus of risk and self-definition. The pits—which on the surface seem to be only spaces of crass materialism and economic reductionism—are places where men take pleasure, court danger, and craft risk-taking selves as they create a market. It is significant that traders play the game, not that they play to win. The possibility of defining and redefining the self every day in the eyes of the pit lures the wealthy speculator back day after day. It is not enough for these traders to be at the pinnacle of their professions. They regenerate their character in the eyes of others with each new trade; each new risk is a chance to reassert their discipline in the face of fate, their skill for riding the waves of the market. It is a chance to prove again that they can earn their spot in the pit with every dollar that they pocket.[32] In the matrix of firm decision and swift consequence, a trader rises and falls on his own merits. Anyone can play, but only a few can make their living on the high wire.

Analysts have characterized high-risk activities as ways of escaping the routinized contemporary world. Skydivers and mountain climbers report their attempts to escape social constraint to draw closer to their "true" selves.[33] Traders participate in this Romantic understanding. They take on risks that are generated in modern institutions through the exercise of rationalized control.

The explanation that voluntary risk-taking is a simple rebellion against the limits of modernity is insufficient. Markets create high-stakes situations that have the power to create or destroy a definition of the self. The strength of social and individual rewards and punishments reflect this force. Traders take appropriate economic action by examining the risk-taking self, both in the eyes of other traders and with an internal monitoring gaze. Their responsibility as risk-takers requires active engagement with risk, not simply caution in the face of danger.

Risk-taking is not only a calculated decision but arises in the context of the pit and through techniques of self-formation. The norms of risk-taking in the pits shape the habitus of the traders who work there, creating an embodied reason that is deeply informed by the rules of the interlinked economic and social games of the trading floor. These techniques emerge in traders' engagement with the imminent future. Actors push the possibilities of annihilation of the self through economic risk-taking. This wagering of the self shows how active engagements with risk do more than challenge the daily experience of routinization and the bureaucracy of modern life. These are high-stakes situations where people are made and unmade.

When we define risk as synonymous with danger, the orientation toward hazard occludes theoretical attention to the productive dimensions of risk. Risk shapes the social and physical space of the financial exchange and forms the fulcrum of traders' self-definition. Traders generate strategies of risk-taking that shape the social geographies of the pit and support the circulation of financial goods. We need not see such engagements as critiques of the modern. Active engagements with risk are a locus for the production of contemporary economic selves and social space.

Financial trading floors are dens of incivility. Before a visitor can get her visual bearings, her ears are filled with loud noise, her feet shuffle through the shredded paper that covers the floor, her shoulders are smashed by the flailing bodies of traders in garish attire, and her balance is threatened as traders shove their way into the action. From the din, coherent fragments of language emerge. Curses and raucous laughter flow freely, and dealers trade insults, both hostile and friendly, along with financial contracts. Trading floors are saturated with the metaphorical language of violence, a fitting background for the dispositions, based in self-interest and mutual exploitation, that traders cultivate there. Just as the norms of the trading floor guide conduct, traders' actions, language, and dress also shape the space of the trading room, defining the range of action appropriate to the motives of profit-making.

In the pits, traders bring to life a particular form of economic man—aggressive, competitive, fiercely independent, and often crude—that dramatizes taking profits from the hands of their friends and colleagues. But this unseemly behavior does not come naturally. Traders reflect on and experiment with how to break down the standards of good behavior that hold outside the marketplace. The resulting self-presentations invert the styles of dress and the language of formal business, professional codes of respect and decorum, and standards of constraint—in short, the norms of civility that mark the usual sobriety of calculating economic activity.[1]

The brash actions of traders and the raucous atmosphere of the pits contrast sharply with the sober technicality of the market. In the pit, traders do not express the cool rationality and instrumental calculation that are commonly associated with the market in which they work. Instead, the price-setting function of the market is accomplished through impassioned competition among individuals whose behavior is antagonistic, brash, and frequently outrageous.

Crowds like those on the trading room floor have often been thought to undo reason and unleash passions, and traders' conduct certainly seems to support that claim. Yet dealings with money have been thought to have the opposite effect. The pursuit of wealth, many original philosophers of capitalism thought, would dampen socially destructive passions. These thinkers trusted that the pursuit of wealth would counteract the more violent impulses of competition and channel them toward self-control. Albert O. Hirschman explains that, among Enlightenment philosophers, capitalism was lauded because "it would activate some benign human proclivities at the expense of some malignant ones—because of the expectation that . . . it would repress and perhaps atrophy the more destructive and disastrous components of human nature."[2] Then, as now, believers trusted that capitalism would not only benefit the individual, but also create a hard-working and cooperative society. The discipline of self-interest, according to the hopes of Adam Smith and others, would bring not only a particular kind of calculating action, but a particular type of affect—a calm, but insistent, passion.

Electronic dealing rooms foster more technical modes of conduct. The trading screen encourages a calculating rationality, cooler conduct, and the external trappings of self-control. Under the influence of the screen, traders become instruments of market activity, favoring the technically trained market observers dubbed "symbolic analysts." Electronic traders compete with the market as an entity in itself, removed from the people who make it up. Still, many electronic dealers came from the trading floor, and they bring their aggressive style to the digital dealing room, where the calmer calculations of the screen are only beginning to emerge. In the pits, traders' passionate engagements are now shifting under the new influences of new dealers with college educations, new software with screen-based representations of market movements, and new management techniques.

In contrast with the dispassionate affect that money ideally encourages, humor and hot-blooded behavior mark the trading floor and dealing room. Traders engage ardently with money; they do not perform their economic calculations with detached reason.[3] Their professional conduct creates a brash persona, whose self-interest and competitiveness anchor the market's key activity—finding the price of a commodity.[4] A price is a particular kind of truth—an aggregate of each trader's assessment of the market and attempt to profit from that understanding. A true price is, then, anchored in self-interested action, yet the self-interested person is paradoxically positioned—to create knowledge, on the one hand, and, on the other, to destroy trust in this knowledge by raising the suspicion that it has been manipulated for gain.[5] As Steven Shapin has noted, "The very distrust which social theorists have identified as the most potent way of dissolving social order is said to be the most potent means of constructing knowledge."[6] Traders' behavior plays out this contradiction in dramatic form. Their conduct identifies the market as a space beyond society that is necessary for unbounded competition among men. In turn, this situation creates prices, which are essential to the circulation of commodities. The public's trust in the price of bond futures is predicated on the distrust among traders.[7]

Traders often describe their relationship to the market as one that draws out the fundamental nature of human beings. In this vision, the market reduces the individual trader to his most basic instincts—competitiveness and self-interest—and the stylized performances of the pit reflect this. The competitive, anomic actor of economic life is the product of the financial trade.[8] In traders' vernacular, the market strips away the pretenses and rarified styles of society. Without the social veneer, the economic man can emerge from his cocoon.[9]

On the trading floor, participating in the collective requires contributing to the sentiments and sensations of the space. Conduct in the trading room stands in opposition to the social conventions of politeness and sociality that mediate smooth relationships outside the market. Traders' actions and language in futures markets revolve around competitiveness and individuality, which mark traders as hypercompetitive, masculine actors.[10]

Traders construct selves according to vocational principles, but their performances bear little external resemblance to the abstract economic subjects of capitalism.[11] These principles require what appears to be unsocial behavior, despite the fact that personal connections are a critical component of pit life. In their performances, traders enact an *asocial subject*, conducting themselves in accordance with the competitive, atomistic ideals of self-interest. The "binding ideas" that hold traders together highlight and demand adherence to the principles of a war among economic competitors.[12] Traders subscribe to feral codes of behavior that appear to undermine regulations and restraint.[13]

In daily performance, traders work according to a maverick aesthetic, displaying radical individuality amid the social density of the trading floor. A *maverick* is an unbranded range animal, a beast without the markings of ownership. Traders retain that sense of the unmarked animal that is free to wander. Traders create an aesthetic sphere that reflects their ideal of the self-interested individualist competing for advantage and profit.[14]

The maverick trader does not arise naturally. He is dressed, marked, and molded in his actions and sentiments.[15] The raw emotions that seem to be impulsive expressions of personal feeling are both performances and techniques for engaging the market. The postures, gestures, and displays of physical strength are styles that shape the physical being of economic man. These bodily and emotional methods are part of the "practical reason" of traders, critical parts of their acquired abilities, memory, and routines that establish the habitus of economic action on the trading floor.[16]

The maverick aesthetic seems to undermine the connections and interdependencies among traders, yet they are complimentary. Traders' interdependence and the system of prestige organized around risk-taking do not in themselves contradict the asocial nature of their performance. Maverick aesthetics and asociality both align with the idea of market action based in the autonomous individual.

The individualistic, hypercompetitive character of the trading floor is part of the drama of capital. Demonstrations of individuality separate traders. Their asocial performance reaches beyond them and prepares the space of the trading floor for economic action. The collective life of maverick individuals creates the trading floor as a special space for the cultivation of a risk-taking self and the exercise of "pure" market engagements. The grotesqueries of the dealing room create a space where it is possible to devise economic actions that are disconnected from the influences of the social world.

Ironically, the asocial life of economic man is conducted in the thickly social world of the trading floor of the CBOT, in the London dealing room, and at their after-work hangouts. The sheer physical density of the trading floor creates a counterpoint for this economic man. In his individuality, he thrives in a crowd. Furthermore, he exists through his exchanges with others — those who buy or sell. His performance requires an audience.[17]

On the trading floor, the traders' exaggeration, hyperbole, and excessiveness, marked by laughter, spontaneity, sexual humor, and mocking of official propriety, blend with their sensual nature and strong element of play.[18] In the grotesquery of the trading floor, the traders' bodies and base desires are essential to the composition of the market. By participating in the debasement of the abstract market, the traders become the materials of another sort of market, one that is explicitly embodied, located, and undeniably human.[19]

Traders work hard to fashion themselves into market beings like Freddy, a trader for Perkins Silver and a former pit trader at the London International Financial Futures Exchange. Freddy is a character in two senses of the word. First, he is odd and interesting. Watching him will make you laugh or squirm, turn away in revulsion, or stare riveted into his sneering face. Second, in the dramaturgical sense, Freddy is a character that Chris Smith created and enacts. Freddy is an alter ego with a personality and image all his own.

Chris Smith's creation of Freddy crystallizes the characteristics of the crude market beast. Like any well-made character, Freddy's appearance and demeanor reveal something about his interior landscape. Deep lines frame his face, and his eyes are set well below a protruding brow. When he smiles, his lips draw back to reveal a huge mouth gated with widely spaced teeth. A prickly halo surrounds his head, where a few gray spikes are beginning to show through the black stubble. He wears worn plaid shirts and rotates among two or three pairs of khaki pants. He is particularly fond of a well-worn pair that exposes a large patch of his boxer shorts. His speech is the Essex slang that reigns in dealing rooms all over London. Although he looks like a middle-aged veteran, he is an astonishing thirty-two years old.

Before Freddy settled in the Perkins Silver dealing room, he inhabited the trading floor of the LIFFE. He was a bit of a celebrity there. Everyone knew his habits—his penchants for flashing and for displaying his bodily processes. He leaves little to the imagination. One of his fellow traders on the Perkins Silver floor said admiringly, "He's disgusting; the more you get to know him, the more he disgusts you."

Freddy slouches in a padded desk chair, head and shoulders leaning toward his screen. Sometimes, when the market is slow, he leans back in his chair to let his hands find their way to his nose. He likes to wipe the bounty on office equipment or surprise unsuspecting users of the door handles or the refrigerator. Nigel, a trader from the selective subgroup that trades in Euribor derivatives, cringed as he headed for the nearest washroom, muttering curses at Freddy. "Fucking animal," he griped.

But such complaints do not dampen the spirits of the freewheeling trader. Freddy loves to sing. He often inserts his name, making himself the hero of the lyric. One Freddy standard was, "Who let the Fred out?" The song provided an excuse to bark like a dog, "Woof, Woof, Woof." Like football fans all over America, Freddy put his animal nature on display by aligning himself with canines on the rampage. Other traders in the room often completed the musical phrase for him with their howls.

A commercial for lite beer also caught Freddy's eye. That year a large American brewery released an ad that ran on British television showing a gigantic, self-animated belly, independent of any body, its round hairy mass rippling with fat. The belly chases a terrified looking man through the streets of a British city. The voiceover chants with menace, "Belly is gonna getcha." Freddy appropriated the jingle, alternating between Belly and Freddy.

The man who shares Freddy's desk is named Billy. He keeps a baseball bat by the side of his computer. When he is not doing well in the market, he slaps the bat over and over into his open palm. He relies on Freddy to keep him amused, both during and after work. One Thursday night, the traders ended their after-work drinking rounds at a karaoke bar. Freddy shouted into the microphone and stripped off his pants and shorts. The boxers made an excellent headpiece until the management dragged him from the stage.

Billy, still exhilarated by the evening's mischief, began recounting the story the next morning as he sat down at his station. "Freddy was totally on form last night," Billy reported to Martin, the biggest trader in the room, "And when he's on form he is in a different class." Martin responded with equal parts esteem and amusement, "Yeah, a different class of human."

I was surprised when he reported that Freddy was not his real name. He told me that Freddy came from Freddy Kreuger, the ghoulish protagonist of the slasher series *Nightmare on Elm Street*. "I don't know what that says about your relationship with your neighbors," I said. He smiled, knitting his bushy eyebrows. "Oh, Neighbor" he ominously intoned. He was remarkably convincing.

It is appropriate that Freddy's name would invoke the transgressions of a 1980s horror classic. In the story, vigilante parents burned the villain in a basement furnace for killing neighborhood children. He returned from the dead, scarred and wielding a glove with long, razor-blade fingernails, able to enter teenagers' dreams and murder them in their sleep. Freddy Krueger's gothic transgressions break the codes that make us human.

During the early 1980s, financial futures traders emerged with the transformation and globalization of financial markets. The Chicago exchanges were consolidating their business and spreading their model of financial derivatives trading to exchanges around the world. The LIFFE, Freddy's first home, opened for business in 1982. Freddy and the global financial futures markets grew together. He is a product of that moment, and he is a type that spread with financial derivatives trading.

Freddy's bizarre behavior on the trading floor separates Chris Smith's work and his outside life, which enters into his interactions with other traders only rarely. Chris Smith has an ex-wife, with whom he has a strained relationship, and a son, about six years old, whom he visits on Tuesday evenings. Occasionally, Pat, his sole female peer, will ask about his child, but Chris avoids discussing him in the office. The dealing floor is Freddy's space, where outside attachments and obligations melt away. The focus in the room is on the market, which brings out the absurd and aggressive parts of Freddy the trader, leaving little room for paternal affections.

Freddy's performances epitomize economic man, trader-style. His ratty self-presentation and loutish deeds display the aggressive and naked desires of the debased market creature. Traders like Freddy bring to life the caricatured being of the trader in a typically satirical way. They create characters that shun the manners their mothers taught them and push the envelope on acceptable behavior. They play along the edge of the tolerable, indulging in comically exaggerated savage behavior.

The theatrical aspect of trading is not limited to the dealing rooms of

London. Such economic characters also exist on the trading floor of the Chicago Board of Trade. Traders adopt an aggressive demeanor and express extreme masculine belligerence and overblown competitiveness when they are on the floor and among other traders. Then they discard these mannerisms with equal ease in interview situations and when they are relaxing in their homes after work. These jarring extremes express the dramatic nature of traders' floor personae.

Traders' actions make implicit claims about the connection between the market and human nature. The market, in the traders' view, strips away the social veneer of human decision making to expose an unadulterated economic core. Intimate contact with the raw forces of the market, the sheer power of speculation, of buying and selling, strips the trader of external constraints and unleashes the force of the economic beast. Sean Curley Jr., put it this way: "A pit distills things; . . . the pit boils you down to your essential elements." In the pit where all of these characters gather, traders describe the market as a kind of war of all against all. Traders make a point of displaying their threadbare moral fabric. One London-based manager who has traded for eleven years in the currency and futures markets gleefully stated, "We thrive on other people's pain." There are profits to be made from the economic distress of countries and individuals, and among the asocial, there is no responsibility to any individual or to anything outside of their own goals. Taking advantage of chaos in the economy and of other people's losses to make a profit is the stock-in-trade of speculation. Economic man delights in the carnage. This system of accountability—each trader for himself—is the defining feature of asociality, which allows traders to profit from the ruin of others and escape moral implications.[20] "It's like survival of the fittest," one pit trader who stands on top of the food chain told me. "A dog-eat-dog world," reported another. On a day when groans of defeat were filling the Perkins Silver trading room, Martin, whose ongoing successes were already trumpeted by his Prada outfits, hoisted a dry-erase board onto the dealing room partition. In a taunting display, he mocked other traders in a rhyme drawn from the nicknames of the German debt instruments he trades: "Schatz is red, Bobl is blue, I made shitloads today, Why can't you?" It is not surprising, then, that traders come to think of themselves in animalistic terms. Sean described some of the best traders on the CBOT as "the kind of guys who you wonder what rock they crawled out from under before they came to work this morning."

This stripping away of the social is primarily metaphoric, but at times, such as Freddy's karaoke striptease, the literal and the metaphoric meld. Both on and off the trading floor, pure market action strips man to his most basic elements.[21] Preparations for the Perkins Silver Christmas party began with a trip to the American-style gym on the river a few blocks away, where the women of the office—all ten of us, including support staff and the four female traders—put on our party best. Then we headed out in black cabs to the chic West End restaurant belonging to one of the company's partners.

To restrain the consumption of this hard-drinking bunch, the restaurant offered only beer and wine, and the bar was to close at 11:00, like all other English drinking establishments. The traders did what they could with the watery offerings, bemoaning the absence of their favorite vodka–Red Bull concoction; the sickly sweet taste of Red Bull thoroughly masks the taste of the alcohol, leading to maximum drunkenness and energy.

It took about an hour for the normal after-work conversation to die away and the real festivities to pick up. A DJ played American funk and hip-hop as the lucky traders who could monopolize the few women in the group made their way to the dance floor. Eventually all the traders, with or without female companions, crowded onto the dance floor. After two hours of drinking and sweating in the rising temperature of the teeming space, the traders were ready for a show. The stripping began.

First to go was Tony Healey, the fat, jocular, ex-Essex cop. He pushed his way to the center of the dance floor and began to unbutton himself to the beat of the Commodores' "Brick House." Having rid himself of his confining shirt, he tried to kiss the girls, all of whom recoiled in horror. When the restaurant's owner had retired, Andrew Blair, the company's risk manager and general overseer, allowed himself to relapse into trader behavior. He too lunged to the center of the dance floor, where he stripped off his shirt to expose his hairy chest and backed up into a woman from accounting. Soon the floor was filled with swirling, sweaty, half-naked traders.

Although this scene of holiday cheer took place outside the confines of the Perkins Silver dealing room, this was a moment for the traders to perform for each other. The excesses of the Christmas party are not isolated incidents; they are an integral part of performing the style of economic man. The style has obvious affinities to locker room behavior, but gains symbolic importance when taken as part of the professional ethic of the trader.

These traders turn the Organization Man upside down and shake out the pockets of his suit. At the same time that they undermine conventional visions of methodical economic action, traders' performances have another effect. Their antics work to establish the trading room as a separate space for economic action.[22] It is the work of a modern actor, yet the means for creating this separation do not appear to arise from the rationality of the laboratory or the planning office. Traders' performances decouple their economic action from bureaucratic rationality. They act on an economic impulse rooted in their conception of human nature rather than in the technical skill. Traders' theatrics create a place where economic man, trader-style, can flourish. Their actions construct the marketplace as a place apart from the social world.

The Presentation of the Self in Economic Life

Traders are not dapper, but they put effort into their style, a form of the studied, unstudied fashion that makes a fetish of utterly disregarding professional norms of dress. They demonstrate the masculine economic freedom of the trading floor with their clothes.

The rules of the CBOT require that every trader wear a jacket and tie, and traders interpret this creatively. They follow the letter of the rule while aggressively snubbing its intention—to bring respectability and professionalism to the trading floor. The floor is dotted with human confetti. Each trader's ensemble adds a sprinkling of color. Their clothes also mark their distinct place in the financial world. Some traders choose to wear trading jackets that identify their clearing houses: black with red piping denotes one firm, and white mesh with blue lettering signifies another. Others choose jackets that both catch the eye of other traders and make a statement. A quick scan of the trading floor reveals the tastes of the CBOT traders. A few sport dark blue jackets dotted with American flags. One wears a florescent orange jacket with the black zigzag stripe of Charlie Brown's shirt. Another wears a blinding yellow jacket with black flies swarming all over it. The patently ridiculous figures they cut implicitly critique the regimented masculinity of corporate America. Trading jackets blare forth in shocking colors and clash with the hideous ties slung around their necks.

Traders fix buttons to their lapels emblazoned with messages like "I care" and "I feel like shit," which convey their emotional states with characteristic sarcasm and humor. American flag buttons and patterns are popular, aligning their own rough and tumble style with a specifically American capitalism. Their tags imprinted with three-letter identification codes also adorn their trading coats and have taken on another purpose in addition to their administrative use. Traders use market names on the floor, and often refer to each other by the moniker on their tag. Someone named Michael B. Gwynne might choose the code MBG and be known by those initials on the trading floor. But traders do not have to use their initials. FUN, GUN, and PWR are all characters on the floor, as is SWT, pronounced "Sweaty." Pit names add to the sense of the trading floor as a space apart from outside social conventions, relationships, or consequences.

To compliment their getups, some traders sport novelty ties that only the most oblivious geek would wear with any seriousness. Some of the more creative ones have images of South Park characters; others, of spaghetti and

5.1 Traders do business in the Dow Jones Industrial Average Index Futures pit. EEL contemplates the market, while PIN makes a bid. Photo by Bob Davis.

meatballs, as if the owner had dropped forkfuls of pasta on himself at lunch. Some ties are decorated with money themes—bags of cash tied with strings, an oversized hundred-dollar bill, or the popular navy blue tie with simple dollar signs. One trader satisfied the dress code with a long strip of gauze tape from a First Aid kit tied in a knot. Another declared his inner brute by wearing the Incredible Hulk clenching his teeth, shredding his street clothes, and thrusting out his muscular chest.

Their style mocks the corporate version of manhood by rejecting outright its notions of propriety and by making an overly literal representation of the purpose of business. The moneybags on their ties reduce business to its crudest motive—profit. This performance separates the profit instinct from the social niceties that surround it in other contexts. On the trading floor, economic man lusts only for money.

Traders also enlist what lies beneath their clothes in the service of presenting economic man. A scene from *Liar's Poker*, Michael Lewis's book about the bond markets of the 1980s, describes the foul excesses of the most successful Wall Street traders. He describes exaggerated, insatiable appetites in the chapter "The Fat Men and Their Marvelous Money-Making Machine," in which Lewie Ranieri's mortgage desk in the Solomon Brothers trading floor is the site of astonishing feats of gluttony.

Mortara made enormous cartons of malted milk balls disappear in two gulps. D'Antona sent trainees to buy twenty dollars' worth of candy for him every afternoon. Haupt, Jesselson, and Arnold swallowed small pizzas whole. Each Friday was "Food Frenzy" day, during which all trading ceased, and eating commenced. "We'd order four hundred dollars worth of Mexican food," says a former trader. "You can't buy four hundred dollars of Mexican food. But we'd try—guacamole in five-gallon drums, for a start.". . . They joked how the thin government traders who ran triathlons on weekends still couldn't make any money during the week, which was not entirely accurate. But it was true that no one made as much money as mortgage bond traders.[23]

Lewis's comic exaggerations still capture a truth as the traders he describes strain to display their insatiability in their eating habits. His account embellishes the dramatic qualities of economic man. Each phone thrown at the head of a flunky, the hamburger wrappers left on desks, the screaming and cursing all add up to a virtuoso performance.

Such labor takes its toll. Pit traders are marked by their gravelly voices, their vocal cords stretched and ragged from years of screaming. Victor tried to stave off this effect by drinking ginseng tea with honey. Shouting was not restricted to making trades, but the quick resolution of other outbursts limited their consequences. During one fight that broke out in the Dow pit, one local thought another had cheated him and screamed curses about the other's entire family one by one. A shoving match broke out, but after about twenty minutes, they were standing shoulder to shoulder again. On another day, a broker was toying with an emotionally volatile neighbor who loses control frequently. The other traders, especially brokers, enjoy goading him into losing control. He starts out on one side of the pit flashing and offering like every one else; the broker gives everyone else a cut first, just to watch this trader scream, jump up and down, and turn red. In making the trader lose control, his tormentors show that anger and violence have a place in the traders' expressive repertory. Traders ought to be able to control their emotions, according to the code of the floor. This trader is a fool, because his explosions are controlled by those around him. He spends his temper indiscriminately rather than harnessing it for economic action.

I spent my first few weeks of trading working in the grain room, shuttling orders between the phone desk and the pits. Most orders would go to the soybean, wheat, and corn pits, but once in a while I'd get an order for oats or rice. Each of these smaller pits held about five men. One of the funniest sights in the grain room was a "fast market" in oats, when the five men— who could easily have made their transactions quietly—began screaming at the top of their lungs at each other to get the trade. This was another aesthetic choice. Soft voices are suspect. Transactions between friends that exclude the general market are said to be "done in whispers." Quiet voices are likely to be subverting market ethics.

Traders also indulge in superstition to protect their winning streaks and to stave off losses, and in extreme uncertainty, they appeal to the supernatural to protect them. One antihubris stricture directs traders not to park in the expensive covered garage just west of the exchange. According to one trader, using the pricey convenience could lead to thinking that "you'll continue to make money. Instead, park in the open lot two blocks south." Some traders carry talismans like a lucky tie or assign magical value to different objects. Like professional athletes, some do not change socks when they are on a winning streak. Many obsess over keeping all conditions exactly the same. One superstition that is likely to help clear the area around any trader is "Don't brush your teeth on a winning streak." These methods of ensuring success are used with the same humor that traders bring to the rest of their performances.

Men manage their associations with other men in an idiom of homosocial humor that plays on the paradigms of masculine domination. During my first days on the financial floor, Don, the desk manager, tried to ease me into the trading floor ethos by supervising the desk chatter. Traders often came over to the desk during slow periods to drop off trading cards and to chat. They could sit for a moment on an empty stool and relax. Don told traders to watch their mouths. "There is a young lady working here now," he'd say in a tone of mock gentility. Studiously ignoring me, one trader responded, "This is the boy's club here." Don said, "But it's not the locker room." The guy said, "Yeah, it's more like the showers." Don broke from his chivalrous posture and guffawed at the joke.

The humor and insults that pervade the trading floor comment on the homosocial environment and highlight man-on-man domination. Insults focus on the homosexuality of one's trading neighbor or liken him to a "hard-on." Such seeming invectives slide easily into friendly banter. *Jack off* is a ubiquitous term; inflection directs the listener to the appropriate interpretation. It is frequently used to describe someone, as in, "That guy is a jack off." It is also used to get someone's attention, as in "Hey, jack off," pronounced like "jag off," with a long, nasal Chicago vowel. Other descriptive terms are *fag* and *cocksucker*. *Prick* is a friendly attention getter, as is *homo*. But these words, even when they are used in a jocular way, maintain their aggressiveness; a slip in intonation can slide into real abuse. The pervasive playful use of insults marks the constant threat that symbolic and physical violence may erupt at any moment.

The cursing that colors flare-ups and everyday conversation contributes to the aesthetic of asociality. The market is a place of uninhibited action. Bodies dominate the metaphors of economic competition. Fucking and being fucked are the conventional expressions of financial dominance and ruin. Traders use the full range of sexual words of insult and debasement; *asshole* and *dickhead* are common epithets. The swearing focuses on bodily words, especially organs that penetrate or that can be penetrated. These curses substitute a sexual part for the whole, disarticulating the human body. The violent images of sexual domination destroy the sovereignty of the individual, subjugating his body to the will of a competitor.

Traders describe financial losses in bodily terms of sex and violence: "He really took it in the ass on that one." "I stuffed it in his face." Imagery of sexual violence slips easily into metaphors of physical destruction like "That really blew up in his face." *Blowing out* is the generic term for a trader's losing all his money and being forced to leave the pit. The deeply physical expression of power and competition makes explicit the will to dominate through economic exchange. Each deal parades the speaker's masculine potency in front of other men.

Where fucking is the rule, asociality reigns as a principal of action. Fucking and being fucked, both in sexual and financial terms, are shorthand for the use of one person for the pleasure or profit of another. At the same time, the explicit homosexual allusions of traders' vocabularies parody the single-sex relationships that dominate daily life on the floor, another marker that separates the economic competition of the floor from the world outside.

During a slow period one afternoon, a broker who traded for the firm I worked for brought over photographs from his vacation. One picture showed his head poking above the water of a swimming pool. The hairy arms and wiry legs of a couple of other men jutted into the frame. Another showed him in his trunks on the beach, accompanied by other men in their bathing suits. Making a joke of the continuity between his all-male work life and his male companionship on vacation, he declared, "It's a *gay* tour." Everyone laughed. The joke turns on the fact that the tour is outside the market world, and yet the photographs show only men. Outside the trading floor, this broker should have entered the social world where men desire women and keep their company. But the photographs show that he was apparently unable to return to the social world outside the pits.

Practical jokes, known in British market parlance as "goofs," are a favorite pastime among traders and a staple of workday entertainment. Goofs often engage the theme of homosexual relations between men. My cohort of Perkins Silver traders was initiated with one. After we completed our first two weeks of training, we took our seats in the dealing room. On each of our desks was a memo printed on the Perkins Silver letterhead instructing all of us to call Christof at Leeds and Critchley (Savile Row tailors) to arrange for a fitting of our Perkins Silver trading jackets. Christof would come to the Perkins Silver offices to measure us. Nicholas, one of the graduate trainees, agreed to arrange the appointment. After several phone calls, strangely aborted by Christof, a time was set. Christof told Nicholas to be sure to wear clean underpants because he would have to take his pants off. The briefs needed to be tight for the tailor to take his proper measurements. Nicholas protested, but finally agreed to comply.

When the day of the fitting arrived I was called in first. I approached the conference room but instead met Tony Healey and Billy. "Sorry, love," they said, "we told the other girls, and we thought you already knew. Now go back in there and send in the blokes." The joke was intended to shame the new guys for their inexperience and gullibility by arranging for them to drop their pants voluntarily for the older traders. By conning the new traders into displaying a desire for the natty dress of Savile Row, they also got them to exhibit an effeminate desire for clothing that marks respectability. By excluding the women from the joke, the traders defined us as outside the proper constitution of the trading room.

Traders brought explicit photographs to the trading floor in a kind of sexual show and tell. In the fall of 1998, Viagra was new on the market and was a great source of amusement on the trading floor. One trader brought to the floor a cartoon captioned, "Death by Viagra." A man's erect penis shoots through his head, obliterating his face.

At Perkins Silver, the topless girl on display daily in the *Sun* merited daily public examination and comment. But the Internet provided the easiest access to such amusement. Pornographic photographs of women thrusting their genitalia toward the camera or contorted into unnatural sexual positions frequently made the rounds. Tony Healey kept a picture taped to his terminal of himself mugging for the camera buttressed by two scantily clad strippers. "These are my sisters," he told me with provocative glee. More disturbing was the amusement generated by a picture of a nude, hugely obese woman. Her bulk spread over a divan that could barely contain her. Her arms pushed aside her rolls of flesh in an attempt to find herself with her fingers.

Even when the focus of titillation is on women, traders' performances are about men and for men. This is the locker room, a space apart from the family world where women matter. Men are the appropriate market actors, and women represent society and proper sociability unless explicitly subjugated to men's sexual will.

In the theater of finance the principles of asociality take the form of the exaggerated maverick speculators who inhabit trading floors and dealing rooms of financial futures markets. The construction of economic man does not end with the collective performance of the trading floor. Traders incorporate the principles of asociality into their systems of self-governance. Despite the external performance of excess and recklessness, the internal performance of market action is governed by strict control over the highs and lows of emotion and is devoted to creating a self that is an instrument for reading the market and reacting to its every twitch. The asociality described has its complement in traders' "discipline."

For futures traders who make their living interacting with global financial power, the market is separate from and larger than its individual participants. It is "an object of attachment" that both provides profits and judges their personal worth.[1] Traders consistently describe the market as the highest authority, saying, "The market is always right." Joshua Geller, a manager at Perkins Silver, feels that the market acts as an instrument of the divine. "We don't know value. Only God knows value." Geller sees value as something absolute. Yet every day Geller and his trainees work to find the prosaic value of financial commodities by identifying their price.[2]

Joshua provided a potent description of traders' relationship to the financial domain. The market holds absolute truths. It determines traders' financial fates and acts as the arbiter of the speculators' moral worth. Joshua told me that in the market, "You test yourself every single day. You either made money or you lost money. I'm a good person or I'm a bad person." This common understanding leads traders to respect the norms of speculation that mediate their relationship to the market. To participate in the market and move into the transnational flow of capital, traders submit to the strictures of the "discipline" of speculators.

Traders use religious language to describe their engagement with the market, expressing the commitment they bring to their financial conduct. Yet work in futures markets is consummately secular. Traders make themselves worthy of their profits by practicing a particular form of regimented action before the otherworldly force of the market. The faith, humility, and self-regulation that traders show us in their discipline reveals an economic ethic developed in and for global capital markets.

Traders use techniques of self-formation to create a risk-taking person that can thrive in the action. They call this set of techniques "discipline." In the discourse of traders, discipline is both an idealized state and a concrete set of internal strategies. Managing a trading self requires the artful application of disciplinary methods.[3] There are four core elements of discipline: first, traders separate their actions on the trading floor from their lives outside; second, they control the impact of loss; third, they learn to break down the continuities between past, present, and future trades by dismantling narratives of success or failure; and fourth, they maintain acute alertness in the present moment. Techniques of discipline are at the center of becoming proficient in speculation—of inhabiting the identity and practice of the risk-taker. One trader told me that with discipline, "You can experience the market and become a part of this living thing, intimately connected to it." Traders' sense of vocation is anchored in the practice of discipline. At the heart of the financial system today, traders' ascetic practices of self-discipline create an ethical relationship to the domain of capital circulation. Examining the intricate work of discipline will expand our understanding of the modes of conduct that speculation produces.

Discipline works to remove each trader's concerns and desires from his economic judgments. The central virtue of the responsible trader is acute perception of financial information. Discipline demands that, while engaging with the market, traders purge themselves of affect and individuality, managing investments and reactions with unobstructed perception. According to traders' professional norms, discipline enables them to coast with the uncertainties of the market and judge effectively when to enter and exit the game.

According to the Perkins Silver trainers, "The market doesn't care what you think or who you are." Discipline helps traders temporarily fashion a market actor in harmony with the impersonal and anonymous nature of the market. Philip, the Perkins Silver owner/director, told me that he has spent years trying to figure out a profile that assures that someone will be a good trader, but he does not believe that one exists. Philip's comments reflect the logic of discipline. A good trader must "get rid of [his] ego." The quality of a good trader is located not in personal characteristics but in the talent to transcend individuality.

Traders are proud of their showmanship and seem to enjoy swearing, shoving, and indulging in language of sexual violence. Their performances of self are marked by excess and recklessness. Yet the answer to a standard question, "What makes a good trader?" yields a consistent response: discipline. Although discipline does not appear to have a place in their trading strategies, traders govern themselves with strict control.

Discipline separates traders from the guiding principles of the outside world by differentiating the time and space of the market and creating a specific market being. It breaks down the continuities that enforce obligations to people outside the financial arena. If a trader breaks from his internal codes, the market "punishes" him by causing losses. This discipline from above imposes norms of behavior on those who lack the resolve to do it themselves. Traders work to internalize this mode of control and avoid the consequences of a lapse.[4]

Speculators like those at the CBOT and Perkins Silver work on a second-by-second basis. They fill their accounts with skimmings from the vast flow of financial capital that circulates through futures markets. The demands of discipline are most visible in the actions of a subset of traders who practice a particularly risky style of trading. Scalpers buy and sell futures contracts outright; without hedging their positions, they buy in anticipation of a quick rise in price or sell in expectation of a rapid fall. In the language of finance, they do not "offset" any risk by buying or selling products that will limit their losses. The financial consequences of scalping are immediate and stark, win or lose. In an ideal trade, the scalper observes the market and its motions, makes a judgment, and executes a sale or purchase. He monitors each price change and its effect on his stake, looking for the best moment to complete the trade and reap his profit or take his loss. If he gauges that the market is going to turn against his position he may "scratch" the trade, getting in and out of the market at the same price, only to reenter it seconds later.[5] This uncomplicated technique allows the scalper the flexibility to move in and out of the market in an instant, taking advantage of every rise and fall of a commodity's price. According to the ideals of discipline, the speculator should never look back, whatever the outcome. An effective scalper must maintain acute attention and responsiveness every moment he is in the market. He must move on to the next trade with a clear mind to evaluate market conditions as they present themselves.

Traders learn this discipline in formalized and informal settings. On the floor of the CBOT, new traders learn it as part of the apprenticeship process, absorbing norms from the older members who sponsor them. In electronic dealing rooms like the one at Perkins Silver, such opportunities are limited. The Perkins Silver trainers knew that in London the new traders would not yet have learned the lessons central to the practice of trading. Teaching the constraints of discipline was the key to creating a cohort of reliable risk-takers, and they created a formal training program to drive home these lessons. The managers claimed that they didn't care if money was made or lost as long as each trader practiced obedience to the discipline. The trader's responsibility was to his technique of self-regulation, not to the profit and loss figure at the end of the day. With adherence to discipline, the managers believed that traders would prove themselves responsible and profits would follow.

The two-week training at Perkins Silver focused a part of each session on creating a population of responsible risk-takers. This was a difficult task. Andrew and Joshua used many techniques to ensure that their traders were developing discipline. They monitored the traders' activities through the on-line risk-management system that allowed manager Andrew Blair to oversee every computer on the trading floor in both London and Chicago. In the patterns of a trader's profits and losses, the managers discerned marks of self-management. The easiest thing to see was a weakening of discipline. When traders are unable to maintain the division between their market and out-side lives, their trainers believed their trading suffered. Adam Berger, a Perkins Silver manager, told me, "I can tell by watching trades come across my screen when someone has had a fight with his wife." According to the strictures of discipline, dissolving those ties while inside the market is es-sential to making oneself into an instrument that can receive market signals, act on them spontaneously, and take advantage of every opportunity.

Perkins Silver traders dreaded early afternoon phone calls from Adam. He arrived at his Chicago office at 7:00 a.m. (1:00 p.m. London time), looked over the trading records for the day, saw who was letting his losses run, and dialed the offending trader's extension. To train traders to internalize their techniques, the managers required them to turn in weekly journals in which they analyzed their trading, giving reasons behind trades and confessing lapses in discipline or exulting in successes in maintaining a regulated trad-ing practice.

A Separate Space

Traders use specific measurements to account for gains and losses. They segregate market currency from the money exchangeable for goods and ser-vices outside the market, a practice that separates action in the market from consequences in their lives outside of it. Market money is specific to the time and space of trade. It is not exchangeable for food, mortgages, tuition, cars, and vacations that draw the trader into a web of relationships outside the market arena.

Discipline redefines the trading object. Traders transform the dollar bal-ances in their accounts into the abstract market measurement of "ticks." A tick is the generic term for the price intervals of any market. The market moves up and down by ticks. In the futures market on the Dow Jones In-dustrial Average (DJIA), ticks are measured in 1/100 increments in the price. If the price of one contract moves from 110.80 to 110.81, the .01 increase in the price is a tick. In the DJIA, each tick equals $10 on one contract, but discipline directs traders not to calculate the sums of money at stake. They count their gains and losses in ticks. Because traders gain and lose ticks while they are trading, they separate their market actions from the space of monetary exchange outside the market. Distinguishing money from ticks allows traders to separate the consequences of good and bad trades from the necessities of everyday life outside the market.

Dividing ticks and dollars also segments space. The space of money and the space of ticks are physically and socially separated by their assigned currencies. Maintaining different names and accounting strategies for each currency divides the space of the market from the world outside the trading floor. An underlying tenet of discipline is that market and emotional matters are irreconcilable. Traders who bring family financial concerns to the domain of trading impair their ability to act and react in the temporal and physical space of the market. Accounting practices that separate market and social space allow traders to purify market calculations from outside considerations.

Ticks are the currency of the market. Classically, from Simmel and Weber forward, money has been thought of as the ultimate tool of exchangeability. Assigning a price makes all things equal and exchangeable for money. Viviana Zelizer has written, in contrast, about the ways in which people assign specific functions and significance to money.[6] Yet Zelizer's examples involve actors who are outside a formal market context. It deepens her insight to see how traders, whose sole professional task is to create a market, decommensurate the money *in* the market *in order to enter the market.*

Traders must work consciously to strip money of its social connotations. It takes orchestrated effort to maintain the segregation of market and "outside" currencies. The market, where money should appear as most abstracted and depersonalized, does not obey a pure quantitative logic. Traders invent their own market currency to remove it from the realm of outside social relations. Money's ability to foster and sustain social relationships and commitments such as those between a trader and his family is so strong that it overrides its ability to add to the market state of the trading pits. Money must be transformed to serve the abstract context of traders' market decisions.

Taking Loss

Discipline manages the emotional effects of financial risk-taking while maintaining an intense concentration and focus on the present moment. One of a trader's greatest vocational challenges is to suppress his individual reactions, desires, and concerns in order to make himself into an instrument for reading and reacting to the market. This is especially difficult when taking losses.

Even the best traders take losses repeatedly during the day. As Joshua Geller explained, "We are wrong all the time." Losing ticks is an inevitable part of speculation, but the emotional impact can be devastating. Joe Rose told me, "If you are losing money on a regular basis, it hurts. You feel like you can't trade. I feel like I never even knew what I was doing. When I lost money a couple of days in a row, I felt like I was just a fake." The repercussions of losses can invade the trader's confidence and self-assurance, both of which are crucial in their rapid-fire work.

Ideally traders are able to forget about the consequences of each trade. Adam Berger told Perkins Silver trainees, "You can't ever make your money back. If you've lost money have a funeral for it. You have to have closure. It is gone . . . you have to look at the next trade." But in a one-on-one interview he admitted the difficulties of containing the effects of financial loss. "You can't make that money back. It's gone. . . . And believe me, it is a lot like having a death. You go through that." Scalpers may take a hundred losses in a day.

Discipline as a principle covers all types of speculation, but each trader must come to understand his own personal limits. This requires a special kind of self-knowledge. The trader must assess how many ticks he can lose before he loses his composure. The disciplined trader commits himself to take his loss after the market has gone a certain number of ticks against his position. After, say, three ticks, he will complete the trade and take the loss. He will not allow himself to get to the point where he loses his cool and clouds his judgment.

Traders use discipline to control the emotional impact of losing ticks. Everett Klipp, an old-timer at the CBOT, was famous for his techniques for training young traders. He was utterly devoted to trading. Even after he retired, he would walk the halls wearing his signature bow tie and a trading jacket that draped from his aging frame. One friend of his told me, "He'd say, 'You'll never become a millionaire if you don't learn how to take small losses.'. . . He didn't teach [new traders] how to win. He taught them how to lose." Klipp's belief in the salutary effects of discipline was unshakable. He would stand behind the neophyte trader under his care and force him to take small losses, a critical skill to learn. Discipline directs traders to exit the trade before the position moves against him more gravely. Klipp's theory was that taking small losses teaches traders to become familiar with losing and to gain control over the impact of a loss. In May 1999, *Futures* magazine quoted him saying, "You have to love to lose money . . . to be successful."

Taking losses is so significant for traders' discipline that traders often claim that their "best" trades were the ones where they cut their losses before a situation became dire. They insisted on a distinction between the "best" trade and the trade that made them the most money. The responses below show the premium placed on applying discipline and taking the loss that the market has doled out.[7]

The most important thing . . . is you have to be able to take your loss. . . . If you don't take your losses then you're just going to get killed. . . . And oftentimes at the end of the day you'll remember the best trade you had was a loser, and you took your loss right away, and if you hadn't, you'd have gotten killed.

As far as great trades, the best trade that I can recall was scratching [getting out of a trade with no gain or loss] and then seeing [the market] go just totally against [the position I just left]. And had I stayed in it [I would have lost a lot of money], like wow, that was great. So I used the discipline, I stuck to my guns, and it just totally worked out. . . . So I was trying to become really aware of just doing the right thing, making the right trade, . . . following the rules. And that's very tough.

Breaking Down Narratives of Success and Failure

Isolating events in time—separating past and present—helps traders to form and sustain economic judgments in the maelstrom of the market and reinforces the boundaries between market and outside space.[8] To observe the quick movements of the market and maintain discipline, traders must immerse themselves in the market and block out external influences. They treat each trade as if it has no effect on the next. Traders deconstruct the ongoing narratives of success and failure that might accrue to them by breaking time into small segments that bear little relation to one another. A disciplined trader leaves every trade in the past, isolating one decision from the next. He reacts to the market and leaves his own judgments quickly behind when the market proves him wrong. He does not build stories about his successes or failures that would provide a sense of weakness or invincibility that could affect his decisions and timing in the market.

One good trade never guarantees the next. Developing a sense of ongoing success or failure is a trader's Achilles heel. Traders segment time in the market to accentuate the constant regression to the mean that is a necessary part of discipline.[9] In the trade, there is no past and no projection ahead: the present moment takes precedence. One veteran trader lectured me, "Once the trade is done, it is history." Part of discipline is learning how to separate the consequences of each trade from the next to limit the psychological effects of success or failure.

Dissociation from each decision is accompanied by dissociation from the circumstances of the individual decision maker—that is, whether profits are up or down for the day, week, or year. Traders must work to break down any narrative that might arise from a series of successive losses and gains. It takes active effort to ignore the sense of continuity that comes with repeated success or failure.

When traders are unable to separate the consequences inside the market from the potentials for wealth and possibilities of devastation outside the market, they may bring their personal desires into their economic decisions. Traders whose discipline has lapsed may also invest themselves in a given position, personalizing the success or failure of that single decision. Joshua Geller warned against what he considers to be one of the greatest dangers of trading. On the days when Geller would wander the Perkins Silver trading floor, he would stand at a trader's shoulder and watch the rhythms of his trades. If a trader increased a position that was already posting losses or hung on minute after minute in a trade that was running against him, Joshua would hiss into his ear, "Wishing, hoping, and praying."

Wishing, hoping, and praying break discipline's cardinal rule, bringing personal desires and convictions into market judgments and clouding a trader's view of the market's objective movements. These desires then mediate between the trader's actions and his reactions to the constantly changing information before him. To structure the self as an instrument of perception and reaction, traders must give up their desires.

Scalpers' ability to skim a profit from market fluctuations relies on a constant clarity of vision. In their second-by-second time frame, they must maintain a reactive sense of what is happening in the market. With every extra moment spent on a losing trade, opportunity for reevaluating and taking a profitable position is lost. For a self that is disciplined to be an instrument for reading the market, taking the loss removes a constraint that would block a quick move into the next opportunity. Joshua Geller warned us, "If you are hoping for something to change or come back you are missing an opportunity. You are not taking advantage of opportunities." Traders discipline themselves to push away their own judgments, desires, opinions, and concerns to absorb the rapidly changing information that the market conveys.

Successful discipline allows traders to act instantly. Wishing, hoping, and praying undermine the ability to react quickly, extending the present moment forward in time. A trader who attaches hope to an individual trade is no longer responding to the information available at the moment. When a trader breaks his discipline, the consequences of an individual trade begin to matter. Wishing, hoping, and praying can easily slide into an attachment to an individual decision.

After a few minutes in the same position, watching the gains or losses tick up and down with the market, a trader's neighbors may begin to heckle him, "Are you married to it yet? Hey, I think Charles has gotten married." The unlucky groom may elicit a spontaneous recital of the wedding march from the other traders. "Marriage" betrays a trader's weakness. He has formed a connection with his position that goes beyond the moment and the explicit purpose of making money, investing himself in the object. When a trade has gained some value in its own right, it loses the status of pure instrument. "Getting married" to a trade is a way to say that a trader has abandoned his senses. The inability to separate market reason from personal attachments has undermined his craft.

Entering the Zone

From the point of view of the scalper, the market resides in the present, in the agreement between a buyer and a seller that is in the process of closing. By the time a price has been made and a trade settled, the market has moved. On the floor of the CBOT, the market is the agreement that is being made between traders in the pit at this very moment. In online markets, it is the trade that is now matching buyer and seller. As the CBOT traders explained to me, once the clerks record a trade and the result is printed on the electronic screens that hang in red, yellow, and green lights above the trading floor, the market that they represent is history. And history is gone. Scalpers constantly attempt to grasp the direction of the market. Because it is always moving forward in time, it always remains uncertain. Scalpers exist in a flexible relationship to the just-emerging future.

On the CBOT trading floor, the space and time of the market are localized in the pit. Anything outside the pit is outside of the market. While "outside events" (as traders refer to them) affect the flow of orders into the pit and the price of the contracts, attention remains focused on the time and space of the present. For floor traders, the sense of being "inside" the market can happen in only one place. The action in the pit links the time and the space of the market and creates the feeling that the market is a living thing.

This bias for the present lends itself to Zen-like aphorisms. Joshua Geller advised, "Accept the market as it is and try to be with it." A popular book that outlines the path to success counsels traders to follow its title, *The Tao of Trading*.[10] Traders speak of their best trading moments in ways that make them sound like mystical engagements. They need to abandon self-consciousness to gain full access to the market's interior and use discipline to block outside contexts from their conscious thoughts and to enhance their abilities to read, interpret, and ultimately merge with the market. Traders often speak of being "in the zone" or of a "flow" experience.[11] In the zone, economic judgments and actions seem to come without effort from the instincts of the trader. The market and the trader merge, giving him special access to the natural rhythms of financial fluctuations.

Traders most value a sense of total absorption in the market. In the "zone" conscious thought disappears and an ultimate sense of presence takes over. They are able to act without explicit thought. Their senses are heightened to the rhythms and sounds of the market and the flow of trades. Achieving oneness with the market can wipe away thoughts beyond the moment. As Joe Rose, said, "The only time in my life when I am not anxious is when I'm trading. I am just out there making money, losing money. And it absolutely wipes out all anxiety. I live in the moment when I trade."

This absorption in the present echoes descriptions of the athlete's and musician's crafts. Joshua Geller attributed the success of one of his traders to his musician's access to the rhythmic flow of the market; the man had been a drummer in a jazz band. "He sways with the market," Geller said. He followed the market cadence, switching his positions with the changing tempo of trading, moving his positions in and out with an improvisational technique.

A disciplined scalper always remains in the moment. He is flexible and reacts to the market situation immediately at hand. He cannot put too much confidence in his own judgment, or have a sense of weakness. This paring down of the self leaves only the part that can become absorbed in the market with no outside commitments. The technique allows a feral sense for market action to develop that bears little resemblance to strict calculation. Scalpers react to each move of price regardless of their own judgments and desires about what the market "should" do according to their individual estimates.

Pit traders speak of living within the heart of the market. They must have the physical discipline to remain in the market through the adrenaline spurts of active markets and the deadened tempo of trading lulls. In the pit, this means standing shoulder to shoulder with hundreds of other men, hour upon hour, without sitting. Physical aches and pains cannot distract a trader from focusing on the market and its movements. The physical immersion in the market is both a challenge to his focus and a powerful force for drawing him in. On the CBOT floor, the collective excitement of the trading pits, the rousing noise, and the jostling bodies draw traders into the market. They are surrounded by and soaked in the sweat of exchange.

The CBOT traders had the advantage of this physical immersion in the market, but the Perkins Silver traders were distanced from their dealing partners by electronic networks and trading screens. The need for discipline, both of body and spirit, is heightened in online exchange. In the electronic dealing room, the market does not surround the trader. He trains his attention on the numbers on his screen that represent the market. Online traders do not have much visceral stimulation to spur them into action and to reinforce the norms of financial action. Joshua Geller stressed the importance of constant physical readiness in our training. He demonstrated the disciplined crouch that brought his eyes inches from the screen. His index and middle fingers rested lightly on the right and left buttons on his mouse. "Have your cursor over the relevant hot button so that when the opportunities happen you are there to act on them immediately." Mustapha, the most profitable scalper at Perkins Silver, visited the hospital because the tendons in his hands were throbbing. The physical therapist there told him that clicking the mouse (indicating the frequency of his trades) was not to blame for his injury. Rather, the damage came from the holding his index finger slightly above the mouse, poised to click. Hours of hovering each day damaged his hand.

A trader must react neither to boredom nor excitement. One of the greatest challenges, especially for online traders, are periods when very little is happening. These "flat" markets can be deadly. They tempt speculators to "over trade," to take a position for the sheer stimulation of being in the game. Discipline is equally important for deciding to enter or stay out of the market. Each day, a flurry of activity surrounds the market opening, but that burst soon wanes. Depending on external events, or other market activity, there may be more spurts of activity or simply a steady drone of trades that carries the traders into the second period of concentrated action around the closing bell. The temporal rhythms of the market try the patience of speculators. Discipline supports a trader as he stands in the pit or keeps his eyes glued to his screen, resisting the quicksand of boredom, which dulls the senses and tempts the trader into chatting, taking long lunches, and making telephone calls. Traders thrive on the high-stakes game. Dead periods challenge the disciplined trader to resist his desire for action. Josh Geller held up a coworker in the five-year pit as the greatest example of this aspect of discipline:

> The guy was a trading machine. He would make one, maybe two trades a day. He would just stand there waiting to pick off a perfect trade. Put the entire stake on one moment where he was sure. He never left the pit. He didn't eat. He didn't go to the bathroom. I don't think he even blinked. He was an awful human being but he was a great trader.

Despite his own inaction, this trader was able to stay totally focused on the market. In Josh's portrait, his successful neighbor was able to excise the human urges that lead others into trading traps. The neighbor's machinelike quality reverses the usual notion of mechanistic motion. To be a trading machine in this case was to follow the dictates of discipline to inhuman extremes of inaction. In his role as a Perkins Silver trainer, Joshua's goal was to produce such human machines.

The immediacy of the market forces traders to focus on each price movement. Traders act as if they are tracking an animal. Calculations or elaborate strategies that take them out of market time are seen as an impediment. Traders ultimately value reactive speed and perceptive clarity rather than complex calculative skill. Sean Curley Jr., who was trained as a lawyer, explained how his legal training sometimes impedes his trading abilities:

> Sometimes I think [my legal education] hurts me. Because I'm more prone to get set in my ways. I'll reason to a particular conclusion based on assumptions that I've got built into the market, whether it's based on fundamentals or it's based on some technical thing. You know, just like I'd craft an argument . . . There are a lot of guys who may never look at a chart, they never read a newsletter, they don't care. They just want to know what's bid and what's offered. And they just trade . . . A lot of those characters aren't the kind of guys who went to dental school or have a law degree. Maybe they didn't get out of high school but they're damn good traders because they trade the market. They know the market. The market has been their education.

Tom Walsh, who holds an MBA in finance from MIT, agrees. He believes that his university education makes him consider situations too closely. Neil Marks, a veteran trader, acquired the nickname "Don't tell me anything" Marks early in his career because of his belief that knowledge of events or analyses outside the immediate market are a distraction. When he began trading at the CBOT, he canceled his subscription to the *Wall Street Journal.* He said that the minute he started listening to the information, he started losing money. Marks believes the traders' advantage lies in their presence in the heart of the market. He says that "traders have the pulse of the market. They are on top of it every second." For him the adrenaline rush of trading and the feeling of being in the zone come with the gut-level immediacy of being directly inside and surrounded by the market.

Discipline checks the instinct to out-think the market. One danger for traders is having too much conviction in their own assessments of the market because their second-by-second time frame scalpers continuously assess and reassess their positions. The Perkins Silver trainers instructed us, "Don't think." Traders must remain flexible and ready to react immediately to changes in the market. As one trader told me, "It doesn't pay to have too much of a view." A trader with too much confidence in his judgment may come to see a losing position as a temporary problem. He may decide that his original judgment is correct, that the market will soon turn around and go in his favor. Discipline places a limit on the role of explicit calculation. If a trader persuades himself that he has "figured out" the market rather than sticking to his discipline, he risks becoming tied to his decision and exposing himself to further losses. Setting limits for losses helps a trader to separate himself from the fear of losses and from calculations that place his intellect above objective movements of the market.

The Ethical Practice of Discipline

Most important, discipline requires traders to acknowledge that the market itself is the only authority. The movements of the market represent financial truth. It is not surprising that traders' attitudes to the market take on a quasi-religious aura. Their discipline is, in a way, a technique of the sacred.[12] Practicing discipline allows traders to attain the proper state for engaging the force of the market, a state that parallels the asocial ideals of the market. Traders speak about the market in religious ways that make this analogy appropriate. "The market is always right," assigns ultimate truth to the market. Men must fit themselves to its requirements.

The market is the traders' moral authority, and it monitors their discipline. It judges their worthiness for profit. It is both the single truth and the arbiter of a trader's work. In many of my discussions at the CBOT, traders returned often to the idea that the market disciplined them. When a trader becomes too confident from recent successes, he says that the market "knocks [him] down." Traders' action is based on a belief that "you can never be smarter than the market," an assertion that the market is a mysterious and powerful force that can be apprehended only if approached with the correct humility.

Discipline is an ethical system and a profit-making strategy. It is a method both for engaging the market and being accountable to it. Maintaining discipline allows traders to allay the dangers of acting in the market. Overconfidence brings punishment.

> You become very opinionated on the market, instead of just trading it and scalping in and out. I go in with a set feeling that I'm right. Sometimes I just don't want to give up. And that is when it happens, after I'm doing really well and I'm feeling omnipotent. You think you're bigger than the market and then you just ask for it . . . You get killed whenever you start thinking like that.

Humility in relation to the market demands recognizing that success can be perilous. A trader's claim to special knowledge or access to the mysteries of the market invites retribution. There is a fine distinction between maintaining a basic confidence in one's ability to interact with the market and an arrogance that will draw its wrath. A disciplined trader knows that the market takes away the earnings of the arrogant trader: loss is the penalty for the breakdown of discipline. The trading journal of one Perkins Silver trader stated bluntly, "Just when you think you're starting to figure these markets out, they come back and squash your ego like a peanut." The market seems to insist on the complete remaking of the trader in accordance with its requirements. It does not give out subtle hints. As Adam Berger said, "Any crack or psychological weakness, the market will find it . . . and will put a chisel in there and bang, bang, rip it apart."

When discipline breaks down and the trader's mastery of the game is called into question, he begins to use the language of death. Common descriptions of losing money include "getting killed" and "getting burned." These physical metaphors draw attention to the danger of close contact with the market. The break from discipline lends these losses moral meaning. One trader, David, described to me the unraveling of his proper trading technique:

> There have been [trades] that I just got killed . . . just everything goes against you. You sell it when you shouldn't, you buy it when you shouldn't, all day long and it's a busy market, you're trading numbers you shouldn't, value down, trying to get it back, so you're trading bigger. When you have a profit, normally you'd get out, but because you're down money, you're trying to squeeze it, get more out of it. [You] turn it into a loser. Hate yourself. Hate yourself. Consumed with self-hatred. I'd still be down money but instead I tried to squeeze it for another five hundred and now I lost seven hundred. Hate myself, threw my pen. Oftentimes I'll throw my pen. Just hate yourself.

When he cannot manage his profit-making strategies and emotions with discipline, David's downward spiral of loss gathers force. The more losses he incurs, the greater his self-loathing, and the more losses he takes on. He is consumed by emotion and unable to divest himself with techniques of discipline.

Discipline is an ideal that traders work to enact. Yet even those who can successfully lose themselves in the market encounter significant obstacles to maintaining discipline over time. The greatest challenges to practicing disciplined trading are the pressures that impose themselves on traders from beyond the market frame. The strains of money and family tempt traders to allow their thoughts to wander beyond the market present and, therefore, to break the ethical imperative to separate economic and social spheres. Shaping the self into an instrument that can read and trade in the market is a vocational practice that is difficult and painful to maintain. Adherence to discipline waxes and wanes. Traders operate under the constant threat of losing their discipline and with it their focus and trading skills.

LIFFE's open-outcry markets opened in 1982. The wild behavior and spending practices of the mostly working-class traders became legendary as these "barrow boys" stormed the City of London.[1] In the pits the traders would scream out orders, cut deals with their buddies, scribble out completed trades on note pads, and verbally abuse the clerks who checked their trades. The clerks, knowing that many successful traders had begun on the lowest echelons of the hierarchy, hoped that someday they too would have the connections or the capital to climb into the pits. The trading pit was more than the social world of these rough-and-tumble traders. It shaped how traders perceived the market and, in turn, conditioned how they took action within it. The pit, in this sense, was a "means of perception" that structured how traders did their daily work to create circulation in financial commodities.[2]

Information technologies, like the pit, underpin traders' daily practice of economic judgment by shaping the available informational resources. Yet these foundations of financial knowledge and action are rapidly changing. New electronic trading technologies and all-digital exchanges are supplanting the traditional open outcry pits where traders meet to exchange contracts in financial futures. For traders, this shift from face-to-face to screen technologies has transformed the relationship between trading skill and exchange technology.[3] The screen changes how traders apprehend and interact with the market. Specifically, it reconfigures the embodied work, techniques for understanding the market, and material context of trading. In doing so, trading screens create new kinds of market actors. In the pits, the traders lived the markets in their bodies and voices. On the screen, traders *observe* the market and work *on* it.

This technological shift in financial futures markets displays the tensions between the technological creation of rational market players and the existing norms and practices of contemporary financial capitalism.[4] Futures traders using both technologies enact a specific form of modern economic rationality that combines technological acumen with financial interpretation. Their actions are based on a form of reasoning that is far from strict calculation. Futures traders act under highly uncertain and rapidly changing conditions. Their techniques focus on creating fragile scenarios that account for constant shifts in the market. These scenarios identify the specific social information—the identities and patterns of their competitors—within the bid and offer numbers for financial contracts.[5]

Traders base their interpretations of financial conditions on the numbers that represent the market. Numbers are a cornerstone of economic calculation, the essential tools of rationalized action. Yet the practice of economic judgment in futures markets challenges this representation of economic action and requires a shift in the way we think about numbers. Numbers have often been considered elements of knowledge production that increase objectivity and certainty. The fluid numbers of futures markets invite us to examine the use of numbers more closely. Traders look for clues to the direction of the market by observing the numbers. At the same time, the short time frame of futures trading introduces a fundamental instability and uncertainty into economic judgments based on these numbers. The provisional nature of market numbers and the approximate character of traders' conclusions suggest that their practices are best characterized as interpretation rather than calculation. But scholarly theories of numbers and quantitative representation are insufficient to provide a full reading of the power of numbers in financial futures markets.

Numbers acquire the status of definitive statements through a process of "firming up," becoming, in their ideal form, stable in time and meaning and adding to a transparent presentation of knowledge.[6] These "firm" numbers that scholars point to as a foundation for accounting and scientific knowledge contrast with the fluid numbers of the pit and screen. Firm numbers work in the service of accountability and objectivity as tools of standardization and commensuration, establishing expertise and authority, making knowledge impersonal, portraying certainty and universality, and contributing to resolving situations of doubt, conflict, and mistrust.[7] In Mary Poovey's words, numbers perform ideally as representations of "non-interpretive facts." As stable objects, numerical units resist conjecture or theory and serve in the production of systematic knowledge.

The pace of trading in futures markets undermines this stability. Traders at the CBOT and Perkins Silver practice scalping and spreading that focus on the profits to be made within the daily fluctuation of futures markets. In these trading styles, numbers that represent bids and offers for financial contracts are the material traders use to interpret market conditions and orient their profit-making strategies. A bid is a price at which a trader is willing to buy a financial commodity, and an offer, or "ask," is the price at which he is willing to sell. In the CBOT's own account, these numbers represent the "needs and expectations of hedgers and speculators."[8] They are not established price facts. Rather, they are temporary assessments of market conditions, momentary markers of approximate valuation.

Bid and offer numbers surge into the market and fade away in instants. The tempo of the market speeds and slows as the number of contracts on bid or offer increases or diminishes and one set of possible trades slides into the next. The trader will not always "get 'em," or be able to turn his evaluation into a completed purchase or sale. He may add to or withdraw his bids and offers as time alters market conditions. Traders develop styles of interpretation that incorporate the fluidity of numbers at the same time that they construct explanations for market fluctuations.

The technological transition from open-outcry pit to trading screen reconfigures the foundations of market knowledge by changing the representation of the bid and offer numbers and how traders read them. Each technology represents the market in numbers, but the numbers are not all alike. The structure and design of the pits and the screen influence how traders apprehend and act within the market, shaping their techniques for managing quantitative information, for fashioning their calculations, and for understanding the dynamics of competition and emotion that are central to financial action.

Informational Transparency

Open outcry pits and electronic trading screens are information technologies shaped and constructed in accordance with particular ideals of economic information. The representation of market action—whether in the pit or on the screen—relies heavily on the capacity of numbers to convey abstract and objective information. Both trading technologies are based on highly rationalized techniques of exchange and information delivery. Modern financial markets build toward an ideal of informational transparency that presents market information as facts free from the distortions of social information. The numerical foundations of financial markets reveal a desire for "correct representations" of economic information.[9] By supplying these economic truths, market technologies lay the foundations for traders' calculations. In 1869 the CBOT introduced the pit to create a unified market space where all participants could see each other and hear all the bids and offers available.[10] About a century and a half later, designers of online trading systems have used technology as a tool to reshape traders' knowledge context. These architects of financial exchange deliberately distilled the economic content of the market by removing the social information so readily available in the pits.[11]

The designers and the market managers who hire them rely on a narrative of rationalization that rests on a particular idea of the way that market data is constructed, transmitted, and received. In an ideal competitive arena, market information must have self-evident meaning. To achieve such "informational transparency," all information must be visible for interpretation. In the pit, this information is transmitted through the bodies of traders and received by their colleagues, who challenge and help them in face-to-face competition. The numbers shouted in the pit have this claim to "clean" representation. The designers of electronic dealing systems seek simply to "purify" the transparent representation that already exists in open outcry.[12] Alan Lind, an ex-official at the German-Swiss Eurex exchange and the designer of the Perkins Silver graphic user interface, championed the connection between technological rationalization and democratizing access to information. "The truth comes out in the electronic world. There are no physical crutches required." On the screen, a trader needs only eyes to read the market and a finger to click.

The presentation of the market as a set of numbers is critical to the production of informational transparency. But the visual and auditory contexts of open outcry pits create opportunities and ambiguities that are not present in the graphic user interface of a digital exchange offer. In the transition from the pit to the screen, the contrasting representations of "the market" demand that traders develop new strategies for using numbers to understand it.

In both technological contexts traders undermine the rationalizing effects of technology. The tensions between the rationalized technology and situated action emerge on the trading floor and in the dealing room as the social is displaced and reconfigured.[13] Traders search out social information contained in the bid and ask prices that anchor their knowledge of the market. They interpret the market numbers through the particular framing of each technology and thereby unearth the specific social dimensions of market conditions. Traders bring questions about the social content of the market to their calculations. Who are the competitors? What are their individual styles? Are they scared, stolid, eager, or anxious? Traders avidly pursue this information, and when it is not apparent, they often fabricate it. Social contextualization and interpretation are critical parts of a trader's calculations.

What constitutes "social" differs in the pit and on the screen. The technological context influences the scope and content of the social in economic life. In the pits, social information is founded in deep knowledge of the local environment. Traders organize trading strategies with the situations and motivations of their particular competitors and compatriots in mind. On the screen, social information arises from the landscape of competitors that traders imagine and identify within the changing digital numbers. These competitors are cloaked in the abstracted numbers of the market, but traders assign personalities and motivations to the characters behind them. In the London dealing room where I worked, traders did not construct these visions alone; they reached out to their co-workers to help them interpret the social dimensions of the electronic marketplace. Software designers may attempt to excise such information from their technologies, but traders create new social contexts to replace the ones they have lost.

The profit-making strategies of traders are based on the many-sided nature of market information. Through their particular technological framings, quantitative objects that seem straightforward gain a complexity that conveys information far beyond what they apparently describe.[14] Located in the interaction between the presentation of market data and the technology of exchange, the layered information of market numbers inspires each trader to interpret its meaning.

What Traders Know about Numbers

Traders in both open outcry and online markets exploit the informational ambiguities of numerical information.[15] The changing bids and offers of futures markets demand interpretive agility. Traders learn that numbers have contradictory roles in the market. Between the representation of the market and the decision to buy and sell futures contracts lies what traders "know" about numbers.

The first thing they learn is that numbers tell very little. Although the full number of a bond futures price is five digits long, traders use only the last one or sometimes two digits, playing the differences between fractions of a point in the price of a bond. Numbers, in this sense, are simply placeholders in a sequence leading from 1 to 9. Once the last digit of a price passes 0, traders refer to their bids and offers as 1s or 9s again without specifying the larger change. The number is only a symbol in a sequence that stands apart from its mathematical significance.

For short-term traders, larger numbers do not indicate potential for profits. Rather than always "going long," or buying contracts anticipating that the price will rise, futures traders play both the rise and fall of daily volatility. They can also profit by "shorting" the market, selling contracts in advance of a drop in price. If their predictions prove correct, they can then buy them back at a lower cost and pocket the difference. Traders have the opportunity for profit as prices ascend and descend the scale.

Traders know that numbers stand on their own without reference to events outside the immediate bids and offers. Events external to the immediate market, such as rate cuts, election news, economic reports, or the intervention of a large buyer, can storm the market unexpectedly. The immediacy of the market dictates that attention remain on the bid/ask figures that represent the position of the market at that second. Outside news is supplemental to the information available in the bid/ask numbers. Traders can act with little information or understanding of the instruments they trade or the economic conditions of the countries that issue them. Government announcements are some of the most powerful forces that alter market conditions. A surprise intervention that occurred at Perkins Silver shows the attenuated connection between trading in second-by-second markets and the fundamentals of their underlying assets.

On November 3, 2000, the Perkins Silver dealing room was relatively calm. The market was steadily ticking up and down. Suddenly, shouts erupted from behind computer terminals as routine patterns snapped and the market for all European products spiked upwards. Traders who had bought contracts rode the move upward. Traders holding short positions cursed as the market pummeled their bearish expectations and forced them to take losses. The market move took only about thirty seconds but reversed the downward trend in bond prices denominated in the ailing Euro, which had dropped toward .80 to the U.S. dollar. Once the action ebbed and the traders had regained their composure, they leaned toward their neighbors and asked each other what had caused the move. The first trader to lift himself from his seat and find a terminal with a Reuters wire scrolled down the screen until a headline appeared on the electronic tickertape. It read, "C-bank intervenes in Euro." The traders buzzed about Citibank until an older trader pointed out, nonchalantly, that "c" bank meant Central bank. Although such a basic mistake would make any economist squirm, to these traders, it is immaterial if it is Citibank or the European Central Bank that takes action. The market prints the result before the news comes through the wires. Knowing the cause is more important for satiating an after-the-fact curiosity than for organizing market action. The news wire can supply the reason, but it does not necessarily cause the reaction or even precede it. All the necessary information for these second-by-second traders is in the bid/ask numbers.

Traders also learn that numbers have particular personalities and effects on the human mind. This is especially so for traders who practice "technical analysis." This interpretive strategy bases predictions of future market movements on historical trading patterns. Technical analysts are also known as "chartists" for their use of graphs and other visual tools that describe the past movements of the market. In technical analysis individual numbers gain strength or weakness, positive or negative potential, as points of support and resistance to the overall trend of the market. Numbers that halt a decline in the market are called "support levels" and numbers that "turn back a price advance" are attributed to powers of resistance. The numbers themselves in these statements are agents.

According to the book considered to be the bible of chartists, John J. Murphy's *Technical Analysis of the Financial Markets*, numbers gain further significance for technical analysts because "traders tend to think in terms of important round numbers, such as 10, 20, 25, 50, 75, 100 (and multiples of 1,000), as price objectives and act accordingly."[16] Traders invest these numbers with their own psychological significance and the expectation that these numbers are significant to other traders.[17] Numbers develop greater solidity as signs of support or resistance as more traders invest in a particular price area. According to Murphy, "The more trading that takes place in that support area, the more significant it becomes because more participants have a vested interest in the area."[18] The limited variation around a price defines a "trading range." Trades build up around the fair value, or modal price. When the market sharply departs from oscillation around the mode, or between points of support and resistance, technical traders call it a "range break" and seize the opportunity to buy into or sell that swing.

It is not only by watching investments at certain prices that traders assess the quality of a number. Traders identify the significance of an individual number as the depth of bids or offers builds up around a price. The larger the number of offers, the greater the expectation that the market will begin to decline in price. And the greater the number of bids, the more likely it seems that the price will go upward. Weighty numbers create an informational gravity attracting other traders to the price. For short-term traders, the perceived judgments of other market participants contained in the bid/ask hold an opportunity for making money. As critics of technical analysis point out, this continuous evaluation of others' perceptions of the weight of the bid/ask creates a self-fulfilling effect that validates the circular judgment of traders in relation to the numbers they trade.

Numerical information and technological presentation are intimately connected. Because the meaning of these numbers is flexible, traders use the context of the technology to tell them more about the numbers than they represent on their own.

In the Pit and on the Screen

Standing on the trading floor of the CBOT, a roar from inside the raised octagonal pits follows the opening bell. Traders stand in the tiered pits, each dedicated to a single contract—some based on the American Treasury bond complex, others on the Dow Jones Industrial Average or other indexes. Individual voices pierce the din shouting "Fifty at three," or "Five for a hundred," indicating the quantity and price they are selling "at" or paying "for" futures contracts. Each call indicates how many contracts a trader is willing to buy or sell at their price.

These shouts—which represent a key technology of the open-outcry system—are the main mechanism for conveying bids and offers in the pit. The tiered steps of the pits organize the physical space of open outcry trading. Most important, the stepped structures create a unified space of financial competition where each trader can see and hear all the bids and offers in the market.[19] Every bid or offer is legally required to be shouted to the competitive market. In this regime of exchange, shouts are most often accompanied by hand signals. Hands turned toward the body, palms possessively pulling inward, show a desire to buy, and hands thrust forward, palms out, indicate an offer to sell. Numbers from 1 to 5 are shown predictably with the fingers on each hand extended upward and turned sideways to show the numbers 6–9. Zero is indicated with a closed fist.

In a simple transaction, a trader makes an agreement with another trader by meeting his eye in response to a bid or offer. The selling partner in the operation yells, "Sold." The two jot down the price, quantity, and three-letter code of their trading partner on a card, and each trader hands the card to his clerk, who will hunt down his counterpart and confirm that each party agrees that the trade took place.

By design and by regulation, all trades must enter into the space of competitive bidding and offering. Rules 332.01A and 332.00 of the CBOT handbook state that

> Bidding and offering practices on the Floor of the Exchange must at all times be conducive to competitive execution of orders. . . . All orders received by any member of this Association, firm or corporation, doing business on Change, to buy or sell for future delivery any of the commodities dealt in upon the floor of the Exchange must be executed competitively by open outcry in the open market in the Exchange Hall during the hours of regular trading.[20]

The accountability and competitiveness of the market reside in these shouted quotations. Any trades that happen beyond this arena, either outside of trading time or through whispers of trading neighbors, are illegal. Each bid and offer in the market must be outwardly presented for all participants to see and hear.

Physical strategies for delivering and receiving bids and offers in the pits are part of the traders' financial strategies. Delivering and receiving the bids and offers of the pits are full bodily experiences that require stamina and strength. While there is only one ex–Chicago Bears player on the floor, many traders compete with him in size. Those who lack the natural stature of a professional athlete can visit the cobbler in the basement of the CBOT, who will add lifts to their shoes. Traders from the CBOT and the nearby Chicago Mercantile Exchange can be identified in the streets of the western Loop not only by the loud oranges, blues, reds, and yellows of their trading coats, but also by the extra inches of black foam affixed to the soles of their shoes.

A trader's physical location in the pit can limit or expand his access to other traders' bids and offers. Being seen or heard when they deliver their bids and offers to the market may be difficult or easy. Their sightlines may be obstructed by other traders or limited by their position in the pit, or they may have wide angles of vision, enabling transactions with a large area of the trading arena.

Because of the physical and emotional information conveyed along with the numbers, not all bids and offers are equal. Every bid or offer in the pits is transmitted through the voice and bulk of another trader. The numerical information cannot be divorced from the bodies through which it is conveyed and received. The tone of voice, the body language of the trader, who may be steadily and confidently holding his hands forward in engagement with the market, or who may be yelling his bids, spittle flying and eyes wide in desperation to get out of a trade, are crucial inflections that traders draw on to form market judgments.

In a pit bursting with six hundred screaming traders, a trader's skills and calculative repertoire require physical and emotional techniques for transmitting and receiving market information in the pit. Leo described training himself for the vocal and emotional demands of open outcry trading: "When I first got in the business, I had to go in front of a full-length mirror every night and practice screaming, looking at myself."

The intricacy of physical strategy in the pit becomes particularly clear when smaller traders must compensate for their stature by manipulating other resources to get the attention of potential trading partners. It is not enough to be on the right side of the market; each trader needs to attract the others' attention—to have another trader *receive* the numbers they shout into the market. Victor, an ambitious young broker who is physically short and narrow, described how he creates a presence in the pit that will attract attention to his bids and offers:

> Voice is number one. . . . You have to be a controlled loud. You can't be like a panic loud because once the panic comes out of your mouth, you're pretty

much admitting to whoever wants to assume the other side of the trade with you that that's not a good trade. . . . Tones of your voice are very important. A lot of guys have higher voices, . . . and they can really be heard throughout the pit. . . . A lot of it is hand gestures, being able to kind of like offer your hands out at just the right pace to catch people's attention. . . . Sometimes it's jumping up. People watch me sometimes when I start to catch air, and they go, hey, there's Victor, you know, bidding them.

In addition to orchestrating the presentation of bids and offers, timing the delivery is key. Victor described how he attracted the attention of one of the "big dog" traders:

> Just at the right time, I mean literally it was within a second, a split second. I literally caught a little pause in his offer where he was just kind of looking in all directions. I just happened to jump and bid and scream at him at literally— I mean I'm not even going to say tenths of a second—I'm going to say hundredths. . . . If I didn't jump and jump a foot and a half off the ground and bid fours at that guy just as I did and the way I did it, he wouldn't have seen me.

The presentation of market numbers in voice forces traders to cope with the immateriality of the bid or offer. A number is rarely shouted once. Because each bid or offer hangs in the air for only a second, the trader barks the number into the pit repeatedly to make sure he is identified with it. At the same time he holds out his hands, fingers extended into numerical signals, to bring a concrete visual presence to his bid or offer. The sounds of repeated numbers form the cadence of the market and can convey urgency or boredom. In receiving the numbers that others bring to the market, traders appeal to "feeling." This word, encompassing all sensory information, is one traders use to characterize their knowledge of the market.

The body is a key interpretive instrument for the pit trader. Listening to rhythms of the numbers as they run in the pits leads traders to judge the market as "heavy" or "light," likely to rise or fall according to their sensory estimations. Beyond creating the basis for individual traders' economic judgments, the ambient noise of the pit affects the market as a whole. Economists studying the CBOT pits found that increased sound levels lead to higher trading volumes and foreshadow periods of high volatility in the pits.[21] But just as numbers cannot be divorced from the bodies that deliver them, noise cannot be divorced from the numerical content that it conveys. Traders monitor the changing bids and offers of the pits through their eyes and ears. Numbers, in the context of the dense arena of exchange, produce emotional states in the traders that shape their predictions. Rather than functioning as obstacles to rational decision making, these signals work on an intuitive level as a central trading tool. Traders see formal calculation as a hindrance to their job and to their ability to react. In training their bodies to be both receiving and delivery instruments for the underlying information of market numbers, the first step is learning not to calculate.

Sean Curley Jr. assessed the effects of his legal education on his habits of mind and trading practice: "I am prone to get set in my ways. I'll reason to a particular conclusion based on assumptions that I've got built into the market. . . . Just like I'd craft an argument. I'm crafting a plan, and then all of the sudden my plan is this, and, boy, the market had better listen." It rarely did. Sean's deliberative skills led him to conclusions that may have been theoretically correct according to the system he had established, but in formulating arguments, he lost the ability to play on the indeterminacy of market movements. Explicit construction of logical systems inhibited his ability to adapt his positions to rapidly changing market conditions. Leo says, "If you start thinking too much during the course of the day when the battle is on, it is really a disadvantage." Jack added, "It's just like you're in there and, you know—like, sometimes you just don't want to be buying or you don't want to be selling. I presume, like, you could figure [some things] out after trading off the floor for a long time and really watching things and charting—but nothing like knowing—nothing like standing there and having that feeling." The immediacy of the market requires traders to interpret every present moment. Perceiving and interpreting sensory cues in both delivering and receiving numerical information in the pit requires all a trader's wits and physical skill.

In contrast to the overpowering sensory information in the pits, screen-based technologies actually narrow the scope of information available to traders. The representation of the market as a set of changing numbers on the screen is the primary source of information for traders in electronic markets. At the same time, traders try to gain contextual clues from other traders by calling across the dividers that separate them, offering interpretations of market movements. In addition to drawing contextualizing interpretations from their co-workers, traders search within the numbers to find social reasons for the movement of the market. They craft identities for their competitors and construct motivations for these illusory actors in the online arena. Fashioning a social narrative for abstract information helps traders create understandings of market fluctuations that direct their decisions to enter and exit the market. Traders create stories around the shifting direction of numbers that many economists consider a "random walk."[22]

The E-trader graphic user interface is the point of contact between Perkins Silver screen traders and the market. The interface refines the representation of the market in numbers. In his design, Alan Lind, the creator of E-trader, framed a numerical and visual representation of the market.[23] Fulfilling his role as a "pragmatic technician" of economic rationality, Lind's design cleaves to the dictates of informational transparency.[24] The interface design presents all market action and information as if available in plain sight, introducing the closest thing to a noninterpretive format possible. It pares market data down to a minimum—boldface numbers in rectangular boxes. Lind's central concern was to use the design to reduce the distance between the trader and the market. For him this meant assembling the simplest visual cues to represent market action. The outward simplicity of the user interface illustrates its numerically rationalized representation of the market.

7.1 In a private office in the CBOT building, a floor trader examines the market on screen. Photo by Bob Davis.

The interface organizes the market for each financial product into a vertical or horizontal strip. The trader can drag each block to drop it where he likes it on the screen next to a record of his filled orders, a record of all the orders he has placed in the market, and the box that displays profit and loss (P&L). A casual glance at a trader's screen can show if he has made or lost money that day. If the numbers in the P&L box are a profitable green, then he is up for the day. If the numbers are red, the trader often slides the box off to the right of the screen so the numbers are invisible to him and any curious bystanders. The most important information, the bids and offers and the "depth" of the market, that is, the number and the price levels of bids and offers, are shown in black lettering against blue and red backgrounds.

This spare visual depiction embodies a commitment to reducing the intermediation between trader and market and to providing a simple and unadorned numerical representation of the market. The use of numbers as a means of transparency draws the trader toward a distilled idea of the market where disembodied actors display supply and demand for futures contracts.

This attempt to reduce the interface to bare, numerical representation shapes the traders' informational environment by elevating numbers to the status of the market itself. Numbers gain a synecdochical power in their relationship—the price stands for the market as a whole. On the interface, numbers that represent the bids and offers are supposed to raise all hidden information to the surface and deliver the total market information. In a sharp break from the complex information system in the pit, where fathers and sons, friends and allies passed information through tightly controlled networks, the interface displays the market in terms available to the eyes of any trader with access to the screen. In addition to overcoming social and physical distance between actors in a global network of exchange, numbers are, in Lind's design, a technology of proximity drawing traders toward the market.[25] Lind's strategy endeavors to cast aside the intermediation of the social information of the pits to present "pure" information, based on a representation of the market in numbers.[26]

Lind created direct contact between traders and market information through the numbers of his interface. As he explains, his plan was to "strip down the chassis" of the exchange technology.

> [Traders] don't care about German economic status or European economic status. What they're looking at typically are numbers. They're trading numbers, using numbers to make decisions all day long. I would say that it's like a motor racing driver that doesn't look at the scenery as he's doing two hundred miles an hour going down the track. He's looking at the hazy outline of the road. He's looking at the numbers on his dial. That's it. He's focused.

The organization of the trading industry places many intermediaries between participating traders. The mechanisms of exchange are located in the clearing firm, the material technology itself, the CBOT and Eurex, and their programs for completing trades. However, in the technological framing of E-trader, these intermediaries become virtually invisible, producing an experience of direct connection between the trader and the market.[27]

The technology of E-trader holds the informational frame steady while it delivers the constantly changing bids and offers to the trader's eyes, fixed inches from his screen. Using this data to form interpretations, the electronic trader can leap into the market with a click of his mouse. Understood in terms of informational transparency, the design works to eliminate not only institutional intermediaries but also intervening tools of evaluation. As Lind explains,

> [I want to communicate] ultrafast prices. In other words, I want to show you the real market quicker than anyone else so that you can make the decision to trade. I'm not going to give you analytics, fancy recommendations, because my recommendations may need some explanation, or they may need to be mathematically complex. . . . The Spartan approach with technology today is still the best one. Keep it down to the absolute minimum; get rid of the stuff you don't ever look at. . . . Only observe the market that you want to.

Lind created a system of information delivery that provides austere data about bids and offers. While reducing the market to a few printed numbers, he also opened the possibility of interpretation based on the very simplicity of the interface.

In the dealing room, Alan Lind's design becomes part of the training methods of the Perkins Silver managers and the daily practices of Perkins Silver traders. To enter the dealing room floor, traders pass through three doors leading from the elevator bank. At each door they swipe their key cards through a security lock. Swaths of gray dividers partition the trading space. Each bank of trading desks is split again into four workstations, personalized by bits of decoration that are pinned to the fabric walls. Light filters through the cloudy London sky, supplementing the blue-tinted glow of the computer screens. A beige, plastic-encased terminal sits at the center of each trader's desk. A thin layer of glass screwed to the monitor shields the trader from the screen's radiation.

A walk down the left-hand corridor of the dealing room reveals images of soccer-club posters, hot cars, babies, and girly pix. Traders program their computers to make a noise when Eurex, the German-Swiss futures exchange, has filled their trades. During busy markets, tinny computer speakers fill the room with the simulated sounds of breaking glass and ricocheting bullets.

Here, the Perkins Silver traders and managers brought Alan Lind's spare, silent numbers into social context of competition both inside the dealing room and beyond it. The managers tried to supplement the weak sensory information available through the interface with a program called Market Sound that augments the visual data of the screen. This software replicates the aural dimensions of the pit by recreating ambient noise levels linked to the size of bids and offers in the market. A trader can hook into the program by plugging an earpiece into the speakers on his computer. Hardly any of the traders used it. The algorithm that replicates the noise of open outcry trading recreates only a sliver of the total body experience of the pits. Although there are demonstrated effects of noise on trading activity in the pits, without the context of face-to-face interaction, the noise of Market Sound was more distracting than illuminating to the screen traders. The sort of sensory information helpful to pit traders' interpretations was inappropriate to the context of the screen.

Despite the raucous atmosphere, the Perkins Silver managers insisted on discipline from their new recruits. In our logs, we kept an abbreviated record of our trades. Some excerpts from my own trading journal, which documents part of a morning's trading activity, show the focus on the patterns and rhythms and the problem of learning to make sense of the numbers.[28]

> Trying to go long the spread at 7 or 8.
> Long at 8.
> Very slow moving—trying to sell 9 now 0 after shift in Bobl.
> Back to 9s, out at 9.
> Looks like the spread is moving down. Bobl moving up again. A steady
>   Schatz.
> Bought 62s
> Going 1/2/3 seems like upward pressure.
> Scratched.
> Buying the Spread at 61, Spread 0/1/2
> Bought 9s trying to scratch
> Bought 0s

These spare representations show the trader's focus on numbers.

Some other cues were available that oriented us to the direction of the market. For example, at the same time that the other new traders and I were developing our basic trading skills, we were learning to develop a narrative around the patterns of the market by listening to the calls and responses of the more experienced traders. Market chatter is an important device for interpreting market fluctuations, despite the ephemeral nature of the conclusions that arise from it.[29] The importance of market chatter lies in the collective construction of unstable interpretations. These weak narratives supply interpretive logics for the market's movements.

Jason and Paul were the most prolific chatterers in my cohort. In a process that was at once competitive and cooperative, they exchanged commentary and tips back and forth across the aisle that separated them. They assessed and reassessed the market's movements in relation to their positions. "I'd get out of there, the bid's about to disappear." "The offer is weak." "The Bund is moving, watch out in the Schatz." They commented on the pace and depth of the numbers, trying to evaluate the forces shaping the rise and fall of the digits. Market chatter could not produce a definitive explanation of the action on the screen; the uncertainty and instability of the commentary paralleled the constant fluctuation of the market.

Traders compare positions with each other, or simply tell other traders their positions to confirm their decisions or seek help in recalibrating their interpretations. This information is not usually shouted across the room, but shared between traders at the same desk. At the desk across the aisle from me, Freddy was flailing through the transition to screen-based trading. The three traders who shared his desk were helping him sharpen his skills at interpreting the market. They identified actors and significant changes in the market. They showed Freddy how to spot big traders by watching how the bid/ask increased or decreased. If a big trader changed his opinion of the market's direction and moved his orders, the bid number would drop by a large, round amount, such as 500 contracts. The more experienced traders encouraged Freddy to accumulate knowledge of the strategies of other players in the market by watching the changing quantities. Jason and Paul picked up on their remarks and discussed them between themselves. The chatter at the desk helped Freddy, Jason, and Paul to form their own interpretative strategies.

Market chatter does not always help the traders who listen to it. It can be used as a tactic to undermine others' confidence. The confinement of an individual to his own screen and the faceless nature of screen-based trading create opportunities for savvy traders to supply misinformation to the room. A trader can misrepresent his interpretations in chatter to gain information about the others' positions and opinions. Martin, the object of envy for most Perkins Silver traders, fed his co-workers his own exaggerated reactions. He would gasp as if his gains had been decimated by a market move only to reveal minutes later, as he headed triumphantly out the door for the day, that he'd pocketed enormous profits. He faked panicked reactions to market events, hoping to fluster the other traders into chattering about their own positions. His status in the room meant that his opinions could confirm or cast doubt on the others' abilities to read market action.

Despite hints available in the environment of the dealing room, the information on the screen was the focus of traders' interpretive energies. This absorption is pronounced in Perkins Silver's Chicago dealing room. Joshua Geller called me in, worried that the London room had given me a distorted picture of the market chatter and the social nature of online dealing. When I arrived at the Chicago office, he led me to the trading floor, where about thirty traders sat in silence staring at their screens. "I try to get them to make some noise," he told me, but their attention was concentrated on their screens. During my visit, Alan Greenspan was scheduled to talk to Congress, and Geller turned on the trading room television set. The traders shrieked at him to turn it off and then compromised on a lower volume.

For both the London and Chicago screen traders, the majority of players with whom they exchanged were outside the Perkins Silver room. Online traders' individual actions are represented in the aggregate numbers of the bids and offers, which narrow the opportunity to understand the intentions of particular traders. There is no access to individuals' strategies that traders can leverage for their own profits. Yet the social context of competition is crucial to traders as they form narratives of market action that offer an explanation for the market's behavior. When denied the social information of competition and strategy so easily available in the pits, the Perkins Silver traders constructed social scenarios to explain the movements of the market.

The Perkins Silver traders learned to look for signs of key players hidden in the rhythms and sizes of the changing bids and offers. The traders at Freddy's desk were trying to help him notice and collect this kind of information about the social content of the market. These characters are usually types constructed on the basis of trading styles and risk-taking strategies. Traders locate these characters in the swiftly moving bid and offer numbers, creating a conceptual sketch of the market as a field of specific competitors. Drawing this field establishes a narrative space of competition into which they can insert their own strategies.

The most persistent character was called the Spoofer. The Spoofer used large quantities of bids or offers to create the illusion that there was more demand to buy or pressure to sell than the "true" bids and offers represented. The Spoofer manipulated the weight of the numbers to force the market to go in his favor. Traders learned to identify a spoofer by watching changes in the aggregate number of bids or offers on the screen, creating a novel strategy for profit. By riding the tail of a spoofer, a small trader can make money on market direction. Traders who dealt in large contract sizes aspired to "take out" the Spoofer by calling his bluff, selling into his bid and waiting for him to balk. There was great symbolic capital attached to "taking out" a Spoofer by matching wits with this high-risk player. It showed the prowess of a trader in one-on-one combat.

Eliminating the Spoofer has the effect of enforcing the informational transparency of the bid/ask numbers. Although there was nothing illegal about a Spoofer's maneuver of supplementing the numbers with the weight of his bid or offer, he undermines the verisimilitude of the bid/ask representation. The Spoofer attempts to post bids and offers to manipulate the market, an intention that disrupts the abilities of other traders to interpret market numbers with their usual tools. The trader who takes out the Spoofer returns the market to the "true" bid and offer by eliminating the distortion. With the Spoofer eliminated, traders can once again use their interpretive techniques with confidence.

The social information that traders construct is not limited to identifying individual actors and their strategies. Traders considered the market as a whole to have convictions and sentiments. They searched within the numbers to understand these states of market affect. For Perkins Silver traders, the first task of the morning was trying to understand the mood of the market. Traders approached this understanding by "testing" the market. They sold into the bid to see how easily the market would absorb their trades. A market with strong conviction could absorb the pressure from the sale without a shift in the bid/ask, supporting their conviction that their interpretation of the market was correct. They were willing to ignore a signal that another trader believed the market would fall. If the test did not change the composition of the bid/ask, the trader sensed confidence that the market would rise. He would likely buy contracts in anticipation of this climb. If the other traders immediately withdrew from the bid, the Perkins Silver trader would have less confidence in his interpretation that the market would rise.

Traders took short-term losses to make these tests. But the managers of Perkins Silver valued gaining information about market sentiment with this method. They trusted it would help traders make correct interpretations of the market's direction and, therefore, secure profits. Andrew Blair said that he was always nervous if he saw that the company was making money in the early hours of any market. Traders must "pay the price of admission" to understand what lies beyond the surface representation of the bid/ask.

Losing money to gain information was not unique to the morning test. A trader who bought a large number of contracts in expectation of a market rise was said to "get run over" when the market reversed its direction. But such losses were not entirely negative. A loss produced by a strong trend could signal the market's sentiment that the contract was overpriced. The trader might then find an opportunity to take advantage of this information. Joshua Geller believed that losing money to the market provided a "free look" at dimensions of the market that were not visible in the numbers. The market might be skittish or stolid, immediately giving in to pressure to sell or standing firm. Such metaphors expose the contradictions within the ideal of informational transparency. In the methods Joshua taught, traders used the numbers presented on their screens to unearth information about the strategies and characters that populate the market. Although their interface reduces the market to a set of visual cues, traders can use the patterns of the market and strategies for gathering social information to understand more about the bids and offers than the numbers alone can show.

The ideals of information systems designers and financial exchange managers fit neatly with familiar narratives of progressive rationalization. Yet there is reason to be suspicious of this neat fit. Traders' uses of information technologies can break down the analytical complicity with economic discourses of standardization, depersonalization, and technological rationality. As users of numerical representations, traders combine abstract information with social narratives. In other words, they search out other individuals to compete with, both in the numbers and in their trading room. At the same time, discourses and strategies of rationalization are fundamental elements for the design and implementation of information systems and financial markets. Numbers operate as critical materials for rationalization, but they are not always used as the system designers intended. Traders who use financial technologies do not perceive numbers as objective descriptions of supply and demand. In both pit and screen formats, traders find a patterned logic in the movements of market numbers by identifying competitors around whom they generate specific strategies.

The meaning of numbers must be understood within the specific context of their simultaneous production and consumption in financial markets, and within the technologies that present them. In the context of both open outcry and screen-based technologies, traders seek out nonquantitative information in the market numbers. In the new digital context, the social dimension is a market element to exploit for profit, and traders search it out where there seem to be only non-interpretive facts. Traders prosper from understanding the layers of meaning that lie between market numbers and their material presentation. The transition from pit to electronic trading creates a new informational matrix, and each technology demands competence in different skills of interpretation.

Flexible interpretation rather than formal calculation characterizes the styles of reasoning common in financial futures markets, both in the pits and on the screen. In contemporary trading rooms, sentiments, actors, and market numbers are always in flux. The technological presentation of the market provides a context and establishes the parameters of financial knowledge. Searching for the hidden values and phantom figures that lurk behind the numbers is the anchoring activity in a global marketplace where the only certainty is instability.

During my last visit to the trading floor, the bond futures pits stood half empty. The thirty-year T-bond is sleepy compared to the days when I began my fieldwork in 1998. Many traders had moved to the busy ten-year pit, and many others had left the floor altogether. The traders who continue to work in the pits, whether ten-year or thirty-year, suspend computer notepads from their waists to work both the online and pit markets simultaneously. Traders no longer have to compete for spots, and they leave their thick-soled shoes at home in their closets. David, who first introduced me to the CBOT, told me flatly, "The physicality of the pits is gone. You can't trade in here without a computer." David still works in the pit, but he rarely lifts his head from his monitor. With ears open, he can glean a certain amount of "feel" and the important information that the pit has to offer: who, exactly, is buying and selling. But for David, simultaneous trading in the pit and on the screen has caused problems. He pulls two trading cards out of his pocket and points to a number, 159, that he has labeled "pit." The number is matched by what he has traded on the screen. He is flat, with no outstanding trades for the day, but he is uncomfortable with the arrangement. "One-fifty-nine is kind of a weird number," he tells me. It is not a round number, and he sees it as evidence of the disorientation produced by trying to work across technologies and different visions of the market: "I sold three in the pit and bought one on the screen. Then I sold eleven in the pit, so I was short fourteen in the pit and long one on the screen. It's hard to keep track."

Today, the market exists somewhere between the pit and electronic space. The traders' hand-held devices provide a window into the online world, even as they stand in the pit, but the shift to the screen is almost complete — only about 5 percent of ten-year contracts change hands on the trading floor. Many locals have left the pits to trade in offices or in boutique firms established to house the ex–pit traders. Echoing the logic of technological rationalization, David says that there is no longer any advantage to being in the building at all.

The shift to the screen was not the first time that CBOT had been through the process of rationalization. As we have seen, the organization has a long history of aligning technology and market practice in an effort to remove social connections and cultural life from markets. During the construction of the 1930 building, as well as in the transition to electronic trading, managers and transnational trading firms worked to extricate the market from the web of personal relationships. Although social ties create the basis among traders for understanding and analyzing the market, the effort to create spaces, technologies, individuals, and representations that express pure market reason is a key part of the rationalization process. Whenever market designers

C.1 A pit trader watches the online market on a monitor
hung around his neck. Photo by Bob Davis.

C.2 The pits, once teeming, now stand half empty. Photo by Bob Davis.

move to rationalize the marketplace, traders work to resituate rationalized information within their distinctive ways of understanding, interpreting, and calculating.

The interplay between these two sets of economic rationalities and professional sensibilities drives a process of creative destruction in market forms. The shift to the trading screen, however, was the first technological change to threaten the existence of the Chicago nexus. Online technologies created the possibility of a decentralized marketplace that stretched the institutional fabric between cities and forced managers and designers to reinvent local trading styles for the increasingly global exchange. The CBOT, like so many institutions of capitalism before it, is now endangered by the dynamic system that it has worked so hard to produce.

To managers, designers, and traders in the financial arena, the contemporary markets pose the question of how to create fields in which competitive individuals can operate with what Max Weber might have called a "thorough market freedom," a space where autonomy in judgment and action facilitates competitive struggle. For Weber, as for contemporary market champions, autonomy means that the participants orient themselves only to the thing being traded—the commodity—without "obligations of brotherliness or reverence, and none of those personal human relationships that are sustained by personal unions."[1] Creating autonomous market spaces depends on a commitment to separating the trader from the ties of family, friendship, place, and work; it is, therefore, a political as well as an economic process. An individual is to be measured solely in terms of personal achievement, not by the conditions of collective work life. However, there is no clear way to establish the conditions in which economic competition and individual action are possible. The "rational, purposeful pursuit of interests" that marks the autonomous economic sphere is not a natural tendency, but a project that requires strategic construction, constant vigilance, maintenance, and repair.

The everyday work of rationalization in financial markets takes the form of "practical experiments," projects in which the goals of economic rationality are brought into line with the existing and evolving social forms of market action. The experimenters—architects, CBOT managers, software designers, online dealing-room managers—work to align ideals and material realities. In particular, the experimenters align the technological and social infrastructure of the market to create conditions in which traders can become more detached observers, providing distance from the heat of exchange that facilitates calculation based on pure economic information. The experimenters conjure images of an observable market, the conditions of observation, and the individuals who will conduct rational evaluation.

These experiments are never binding and rarely durable; they remain provisional, often ad hoc, and constantly under revision. Yet market designers remain devoted to the challenge of creating institutional conditions and fostering professional habits that promote virtuous economic action. They manipulate the materials of market rationalization—space, technology, social composition, the self, and the representational order—because the success of the exchange or firm hinges on how well all these components are organized. The challenge, though, is that it is never clear exactly how the designers can bring market spaces, whether physical or digital, in line with economic norms. Consider some of the projects we have seen: the new trading floor of the 1930 building; the practice of seeding the London trading pits with Chicago traders; the Perkins Silver dealing room, built around the principles of multiculturalism. These are all practical experiments in market rationalization.

In these projects, managers and designers work with unstated notions about how individuals make decisions and take action in market environments. This everyday labor of rationalization is one of the key elements of contemporary economic life that departs from the economic and political engineering of financial systems.[2] Weber had a label for experiments like these: they are attempts to produce the "substantive conditions of formal rationality," intended to create a material and social form in which individual calculation and competition can operate as fully as possible and autonomous economic action can flourish. Yet if, on the one hand, this form of market rationalization seeks to eliminate the social from the market, on the other hand, it manipulates the social to fashion what managers hope will be an autonomous market. In this sense, the materials of rationalization are both human and technological, shaped by social labor and the culturally organized preferences and practices of the same actors they are designed to constrain. Moreover, such work is never quite finished: there is no end to the process of producing the conditions of formal rationality.

Nonetheless, the long-standing and ever-changing project of creating purely economic spaces is not merely a fantasy. The drive to improve the conditions of economic action leads to the making and remaking of new technologies, reformed rules, creative calculative practices, and emergent classes of professionals who bring the market into being. Design is central to establishing a formal order that can influence economic action. The transformation of futures trading from the pit to the screen and the extension of Chicago-style trading practices to London markets demonstrate that there is nothing self-evident about how professionals create the conditions in which calculative actors can emerge, even in domains that we think of as the most formally rational. The labor of creating a market takes unexpected forms, from constructing bridges in Chicago and planning the architecture of a trading floor to the rationalizing of personal conduct through discipline.

Ultimately, financial markets are social and technical fields—groupings of actors, both collective and individual—held together by material technologies, the problems of risk and circulation that they address, and by competition for profit.[3] In financial markets, the overarching problem is circulation—how to produce consistent circulation in markets that professionals call "liquid," while arranging a field of action designed with regard to economic norms—particularly, how to make profits from individual competition. Within these markets, organizational arrangements and collective expectations about individuals' behavior, or norms, work in tandem with exchange.

Financial markets pose a series of problems to designers and practitioners. Focusing on these problems highlights how markets work in practice, how traders and managers think they *should* work, and what kinds of new arrangements exchange managers, traders, and the technology professionals they hire generate in the interplay between practice and normative ideas about markets.[4] These problems are not simply economic; they are, in important ways, frames for political engagement as well. Once a problem is defined, it creates needs, attracts resources, and draws attention, as we have seen with the struggles of the CBOT over electronic trading. The world's financial exchanges are organized around a constant and evolving series of problems that market managers must solve. Formal economic theories often inform solutions to these issues, shaping the financial field in their image.[5] However, the executives in charge of managing these markets are not often academic economists; rather, they are technicians who translate general ideas into practice, tweaking economic ideas as intentions come into conflict with existing techniques, technologies, and forms of exchange.[6] Theirs is a stripped-down approach to making things work, concerned with theory or system only when those are essential to its operation. This approach is itself meaningful, driven by constant calculation, judgment, and assessment of profits and people—it constitutes the cultural life of contemporary economies.

At both the CBOT and Perkins Silver, managers and traders attempt to solve problems in market action by shaping five elementary forms of financial life: space, technology, social composition, selves, and representation.[7] To conclude, then, I return to these elements and consider what an anthropology of finance and exchange helps us learn about them and, in turn, about the culture of markets.

Space

The problems of arranging and profiting from financial circulation immediately raise the question of geography. The rhetoric of globalization has taught us to think about financial markets as generators of flows that cross national boundaries. The spatial arrangements of global capital exchange involve both the possibility of and conflict over practical experimentation. Historically, the city has been the site of capital markets, and the work of rationalization has focused on drawing commercial space together through the development of a central place, or urban nexus.[8] In the nineteenth century, Chicago grew to be America's primary capitalist city as it drew together western agriculture and the eastern market with railroad tracks and shipments of grain and meat.[9] The CBOT was instrumental in developing the hub city by orchestrating the physical development of the harbor and roads that channeled Chicago's commerce. Ultimately, however, the CBOT's major innovation was to replace the movement of goods with the movement of money, drawing participants and information together in the trading pit that its managers designed and redesigned to create better conditions for competition. By creating open sightlines and good sound conditions in the space of the trading floor, designers engineered a physical field that minimized the benefits of cliques and heightened the importance of an individual's speed and acumen. The plan was to atomize traders and generate autonomous, rational, calculative actors. Immersed in the crowd, each speculator was to operate alone.

Within the pit, however, the whirl of speculation remains entangled in the social network of traders. The stepped rings of the pit defined a space where relationships of obligation and reciprocity between traders were put to work and where information about financial commodities was evaluated and solidified into a price. The social organization of the marketplace became a central feature in traders' strategies, and deciphering the cultural life of the pit was a necessary first step for anyone who wanted to work in the exchange. The pit structured traders' daily economic actions by reliably producing liquidity. As a trading technology, it was successful enough to command the allegiance of the CBOT's membership when electronic trading appeared. Over time, as we see now, CBOT traders defined themselves through their relationship to open outcry and the physical space of the pit. It became their symbol, the official icon of their organization, and many of its participants fought to maintain the pit when electronic systems transformed other exchanges.

Now that futures markets are electronic, they continue to be based in cities, yet traders who work together in digital dealing rooms and encounter global markets through a screen have developed new techniques of calculation and new understandings of the market. For market designers, the rise of digital dealing has renewed the challenge of organizing the space of the trading room, which is focused now on the screen rather than on face-to-face interaction. For market managers and city officials, the transformation of the market poses a new question: How can they retain their protected marketplaces and sustain the presence of financial organizations in their cities when new centers are competing for a slice of the action?

In electronic markets, a new sense of space emerges that unites locations that share digital circuits rather than adjacent land.[10] Up-to-the-minute technologies, the newest financial products, and the sharpest economic talent intersect in productive and sometimes reckless ways.[11] Circulation happens as capital moves from place to place, but some cities have greater roles than others. Especially in New York, London, and Tokyo, highly educated workers produce, analyze, and trade on information that drives the global economy.[12] These are capitals of finance and producer services, like law and accounting. But other cities, like Chicago, have more specialized roles.[13] Clusters of urban centers emerge as significant sites for some interests.[14] Futures markets bind Chicago, London, and Frankfurt together through ties of technology and trade. These cities house both major exchanges and traders who deal in the others' markets. The exchanges wrangle over if and how they should engineer these connections. For instance, members of the CBOT and LIFFE have direct access to all of each others' markets, a deal that they struck after a similar alliance between the CBOT and the German-Swiss exchange, Eurex, fell apart. Each alliance is forged through a complex process of political negotiation between exchange officials and the regulatory bodies that coordinate economic activity across national borders. In the case of the connection with Eurex, the exchanges fought over the technologies for connecting the two exchanges. Although technology provides the infrastructure that makes these alliances possible, it is the struggle over potential alliances and the arguments over the use of new equipment and techniques that ultimately shapes the network.

But even as markets move online, traders continue to do business from their desks in the world's financial centers. The global network does not end the importance of the city; rather, it raises new questions about how cities influence online action. Most important for our story, the trading techniques developed in Chicago now form a common reference for understandings of risk and norms of conduct in the global futures market. The members of Chicago derivatives markets have worked with their counterparts in other financial centers to spread Chicago-style trading. But the Chicago forms are not simply reproduced elsewhere. They are taken up and transformed as they are refracted through local styles. These transformations have serious consequences for cities. Chicago has long been the leader in derivatives markets, but since electronic trading has threatened to circumvent the Chicago nexus, its exchanges are fighting to retain their city's place among the global players.

Socio-Technical Arrangements

Markets are arrangements of technical devices, such as the trading pit and telephone; techniques, such as the bodily postures that traders master; and institutional arrangements, such as the design of the Perkins Silver trading room or agreements for trading and payment with the German-Swiss exchange Eurex. Technical devices such as computer screens, which may seem freestanding, always operate in relation to human skills and institutional contexts, giving managers and designers the opportunity to organize their use.[15] Through a messy set of cultural and political processes, the managers and designers plan and orchestrate the elements of socio-technical arrangements that encourage individual calculation and competition.

Fierce debates over the prospects of Chicago's futures markets involve two socio-technical arrangements: open outcry and digital dealing. The particular arrangement of the open outcry system features many diverse elements: the architecture of the trading pits, the bodies and voices of traders, traders' social hierarchies and the skill of exploiting them for profit, the structure of the CBOT building, and the structure of the Chicago Board of Trade itself as a membership organization. The elements of digital dealing, however, are more difficult to delineate. Although the material connections provided by fiber-optic cables that channel the electronic impulses of individual trades are important, I have concentrated on the trading room, where speculators act. The view from the dealing floor amplifies several elements: the social composition of the trading room, the skill of reading a social field from a computer representation, and techniques for constructing information among traders in the dealing room.

The shift from face-to-face to online markets requires that managers, designers, and traders answer questions about who should be included in the collective constitution of the market and what kinds of faculties those individuals should have—both at the level of their trading rooms and on the scale of the global marketplace. With the transition from pit to screen, traders could no longer embody the market. In digital dealing, the market develops a material reality on a computer screen that traders can observe. Each trader's relationship to the market requires social, personal, and calculative capacities, some of which are incommensurable across technological contexts. As the new cultures of trading evolve, some speculators will be able to make the leap and some will not.

Today managers of trading firms are redefining their criteria for who will make a good trader with the trading screen in mind—a decision that leads to redefining who will be included and excluded in the field. New technologies thus provide opportunities for social experimentation at the levels of organization, trading room, and individual. Debates about who should enter the marketplace and how—as in the Perkins Silver strategy for replacing the working-class futures traders who began in the 1980s with university graduates—make those technologies political.[16]

The practical experiments designed to shape electronic trading in new institutional contexts leave little question that market-makers recognize the importance of the physical and social architecture of finance. The history of the Chicago Board of Trade shows that earlier market makers had these same concerns when they designed the trading pit. The famous CBOT building in the downtown Loop is a "walk-through machine," a structure that both shapes the markets that operate inside its walls and is shaped by them.[17] But the edifice is also a symbol of the organization's place in the city. The trading pits that the building houses are themselves architectural technologies; the ringed steps shape competition as they arrange bodies and channel communication among traders. Electronic markets take on a different form. Telecommunications networks, electronic trading systems, and highly developed information networks create global interconnections among actors in real time. Financial markets would not have their contemporary form without them. This is the form of technology that Castells describes as the "material support for the space of flows [which is] actually constituted by a circuit of electronic impulses."[18] Yet these material devices of inter-connection are important because they channel traders' deals, which them-selves depend on traders' techniques for gathering and deploying informa-tion, their strategies of profit-making, and the legal arrangements between exchanges. The materiality of technological devices seems to crystallize the possibilities of interconnection and speed, two prospects that make them hard to ignore for institutions that value rationalization. However, material equipment simply marks the beginning of the inquiry.

The first level at which technology matters is that of the material infra-structure of markets, but it is equally critical at a second level. Information devices shape the way traders work—how they understand and interpret the market and how they take action in it. Technologies shape economic ra-tionality by establishing common frameworks for the evaluation of knowl-edge and a common trust in the contracts that constitute the objects of transaction.[19] In electronic markets, actors with no physical contact and no personal knowledge of each other are integrated through their trading screens into the global social system of financial exchange.[20]

Socio-technical arrangements establish common ways of understanding and interpreting the market and, in doing so, set the basis for understanding how other actors will receive the information. Technological objects on the trading floor and in the dealing room carry information to traders and pro-vide frames for interpreting it. For the rapid work of traders, the goal is not firm knowledge but the creation of fragile interpretations that allow traders to draw profit from uncertain economic conditions.[21] Unlike scientists, whose goal is to establish truth, traders regard their technologies and their under-standings of the market simply as tools for producing profit. They do not strive for stable knowledge; instead, their technologies enable profitable im-provisation. As Niklas Luhmann has explained, such forms of understand-ing are built on "a 'provisional' foresight," in which "value lies not in the certainty that it provides but in the quick and specific adjustment to a real-ity that comes to be other than what was expected."[22]

These common styles of reasoning form a kind of community based on shared approaches to knowing and acting in the market.[23] Technical devices are powerful agents for bringing these communities into being. The archi-tecture of the trading pit and the visual technology of the trading screen are inseparable from how financial traders ply their business. The tools condi-tion how traders think and work every day.

Because technology in the second sense is such a powerful force in the operation of markets, exchange executives meticulously design and manage both the technical and social composition of the market. They examine how traders use technologies and constantly reform them to bring them more closely in line with market ideals such as impersonal competition, complete information, and direct contact between individuals and markets. But traders do not blindly accept the tools they are given. In their daily use of them, they manipulate these technological devices to their advantage, and this often means discerning in technologies the social content that designers have worked so hard to extract.

Although technology is crucial in creating the material conditions for formal economic rationality, the conduct that financial exchanges and managers promote and that traders teach, learn, and transform in their everyday work is equally important. In other words, we need not only to understand how machines and humans are tied together into a financial system, but to focus on the relationship between technologies and practices—ways of thinking about and acting in the market—that are linked through practical experiments in rationalization.

Social Composition

Rationalizers work not only to purge the market of social influences but also to use the social characteristics of traders to engineer efficiency. This was most apparent in the efforts of the Perkins Silver managers to create a team that would bring their firm greater profit. The managers used American notions of multicultural individualism to engineer their trading room, recruiting and developing a cohort of traders that included Asians, blacks, and women. Their goal was to increase profits by expanding the ways their traders would perceive the market and strategize in it. They assumed that including individuals who were under-represented in the overwhelmingly white occupation of futures trading would extend their profit by multiplying perspectives, an idea that dovetails with notions of standpoint epistemology. These managers believed that each trader's ethnic or racial background and gender would shape his or her approach to the market. Profitability would come from aggregating these diverse reasoning processes. Ideally, such a mixed group would create a new kind of instrument for perceiving and acting on the market. The multiple points of view stemming from varied social categories would add different facets to the lens, creating a new mechanism for profit-making.

This use of perspective to build a dealing room ties ethnicity to a postnational discourse of market inclusion. These traders worked from particular points of view, born in the history of British migration and gendered labor. The managers wanted the Perkins Silver trading room to be a collection of their social vantage points, from which would emerge a new way of seeing the market that would help the firm draw greater profit from it. The Runnymede Trust's report on multi-ethnic Britain uses a parallel form of multiculturalism, which marks an economic as well as a cultural transition. The report replaces a common notion that links Britain's class-based society and industrialism with a multicultural vision that fits neatly with the vision of the global marketplace expressed in places like the Perkins Silver trading room. In this emergent vision of global markets, individuals, regardless of location, social position, or personal characteristics, can seek profits through competition. This is not a race-blind strategy. Rather than denying the importance of ascriptive characteristics, it elevates them to useful tools in the search for profits. Instead of understanding the operation of race in markets as "possessive investment in whiteness" or as discrimination,[24] this strategy prompts us to see how firms work with race in the pursuit of profits and also how they use race and gender to buttress collectivities (like trading rooms) that are spaces of neither racial solidarity nor conflict. The Perkins Silver managers treated race, gender, and ethnicity as resources, finding in the politics of the trading room an approach to the social and economic uncertainties of the new online markets.

Although not explicitly, the markets of the CBOT were also produced through social orchestration. Access to the market was informally granted and restricted along social lines. Through the networks of family and friendship that granted access to membership at the CBOT, the city's African American population was excluded. So when Pat Arbor declared that "Chicago breeds futures traders," the breeding grounds were limited primarily to the white neighborhoods of the city and its suburbs. The Chicago trader in whose blood trading runs is almost certainly white and male. The legendary liquidity of the futures markets and the city's claim of prowess at creating traders are products of white ethnic networks of trade.

The recruitment of traders through networks of family and friends restricted the composition of the trading floor. Ethnic networks and racial exclusion shaped the basic function of the market.[25] Recruiters appealed to the skills of the local population and to the ties of obligation in local relationships in order to create liquidity. Supporting and extending those ties determined the social composition of the market. The networks of white, Irish, German, and Jewish men made the market work.

As the technologies and spaces of the market change, new forms undermine the networks that gave whites the advantages of exchange membership. In England, however, in the moment of technological change, the exclusion of others from the market field began to appear as a hindrance to liquidity. The Perkins Silver managers took advantage of this social dislocation to realign the relation of race and profit. They harnessed the perspectives of their newly hired traders to their profit-making strategies. The shift away from the CBOT trading floor and the anonymity of the new trading screen assisted them in their project. It hid race and gender from the eyes of competitors, creating rationalized conditions in which an individual's skills could emerge.

Paradoxically, at the same time that the Perkins Silver managers sought the new perspectives of diverse young people, they also worked to teach each trader a particular relation to the market. In the Perkins Silver trading room, managers blended multiculturalism and the notion of the self-regulating individual. Although each trader brought a perspective, the managers trained them all to develop an ethical relation to the market by developing an interior space dedicated to market action and to regulating affect.

Self

Becoming a finely tuned market instrument required each trader to develop a particular relationship between self and market that severs certain capacities and connections and builds up others. Speculation requires temporarily giving up part of the self to enter into the space of economic action. Specifically, daily self-discipline requires separating the world of social responsibilities from the world of speculation. Despite the outwardly raucous atmosphere of a trading floor, there is an ascetic component to the way traders manage themselves to become risk-takers. These practices enable a trader to focus on the movement of the market alone and to act as a purely economic individual. To achieve this state of reason on the trading floor, traders use discipline to temporarily reject the responsibilities of social connections, especially the connections to their families. Traders discipline themselves to be responsible only to the market, which determines their success or failure and reveals whether they have acted with virtue—that is, with economic acumen alone, not from their responsibilities outside the market or from an arrogance derived from success. Separating his market self from his social self, a trader refashions himself as a machine for trading, immune to the physical discomforts of standing for hours in the trading pit or hovering over a computer screen—an actor who ignores the future consequences of success or failure and whose sole aim is to draw profit from the market.

Speculation positions traders at the edge of the present moment, a location of high uncertainty where the authority of knowledge fades as traders try to anticipate slight market movements.[26] With this murky view of the future, traders orient themselves with charts and social knowledge, but the material that they shape the most assiduously is the self. The discipline of speculators unites techniques of profit-making with continuous formation and re-formation of self. Shedding outside responsibilities and working to disconnect from desires for continuity, the trader makes himself into an economic man. Speculation places money and self-definition on the line simultaneously.

For the managers at Perkins Silver, nothing was as critical to convey to the London traders as self-discipline. In the Chicago pits, their friends, financial backers, and trading neighbors had instructed them in these techniques as markets rose and fell around them. The conditions of the electronic dealing room and the distance from the Chicago pits forced them to examine these techniques explicitly and plan how to train the London traders. First, online dealing separates traders, assigning them to their own neat spaces. No other trader can see or hear the positions a new trader takes on or the panic or elation in his voice on a winning or losing streak. Online traders act alone. In the absence of the informal training of the pits, the Perkins Silver managers improvised new techniques to develop self-discipline. First, they required traders to maintain trading diaries to record their deals and give reasons for their them; second, they watched traders' deals through the online surveillance system. As the managers formalized these techniques, they trained their traders to be rationalized observers of the self.

Representation

As we have seen, economic rationality is also aesthetically patterned. Whether through the architecture of buildings, the garish ties of traders, or even through technologies that have symbolic aspects in addition to their rationalizing functions, the representational order defines the spaces of purified economic activity and shapes the affect and self-image of those engaged in trading.

These representations are part of the practical experiments that separate economic activities from the social. The architecture and screen design at the CBOT and Perkins Silver create distance between the technological order, social interaction, and even nature. In contrast, a trader's self-presentation and style of interaction mark the trading space as asocial, where human nature is stripped of the manners that smooth social interaction and reduced to brutal competition. Markets are places where technological rationalization combined with the natural competitiveness of economic men establishes an autonomous space of economy.

Holabird and Root's design for the 1930 CBOT building was an image of machine-honed nature. The new building committee and the CBOT membership preferred the symbolism of nature transformed over the neo-Gothic spires and the neoclassical columns of the competing designs. Neat limestone ribs run like railroad tracks from the building's base to the tower's peak. Interior details show ships and grain chutes but not the human hands that operate them. These modern images represent the order that technology can impose on nature and create a feeling of control over the matrix of price and weather that futures contracts themselves accomplish.

As the CBOT worked with architects to hone its modern image, it also designed the trading floor to establish the conditions of calculation and economic competition. The arrangement of the trading floor and the invention of the trading pit structured traders' sightlines. The pit's steps elevated traders so that they could see all of the bids and offers, bringing each trader into contact with the full market. Engineering the acoustics of the trading floor was equally important to creating a centralized market. Designers and managers considered what materials would allow sound to travel without producing disorienting noise and created an arena in which each trader could clearly perceive information—a level informational playing field where traders could compete primarily on the basis of their understanding of the market and their speed at executing trades.

This marking of space at the CBOT is not the first example of Chicago's elite using the architecture of order to counterpoint the chaos of capitalism. At the famous Chicago World's Fair, the White City—a literally purified image—created an idealized Chicago that banished the muck of capitalism, replacing it with the rhythmic and regular display of neoclassical architecture. Architecture's reflection of capitalism's operation continued in the construction of the glass tower extension of the CBOT, where the constructed abstraction of capital matched the structured abstraction of the building.

The screens of E-trader extended the project of establishing aesthetic distance between the image of the market and the human elements that compose it. In representing the market in a set of bid and ask numbers simply presented in the columns of a trading screen, designers composed visual elements to achieve a shift in calculative practice.[27] The numerical representation of the market resonated with the principles of *disintermediation*, a term that came into vogue in the 1980s as companies began to use securities like junk bonds to raise money from investors rather than banks, eliminating intermediaries between the borrowers and their market.[28] The design of the trading screen was intended to achieve a similar direct contact between market actors, creating disintermediation in the manipulation of visual information. Of course, from an analytic perspective, there are always agents, whether human, linguistic, mechanical, or electronic, between traders. However, technological rationalization supports the idea that eliminating human intermediaries provides greater contact with "true" market forces. The numbers consolidate the image of the market on a trading screen; in those numbers, traders confront only the aggregate market they receive through their computers, not an image of their human competitors.

The architectural environment and the picture of the market presented on trading screens give a particular look and feel to the market. The architecture of the 1930 CBOT building marks the transformation of nature through technology that is the foundation of the circulation in futures contracts. It also marks the CBOT as a space of modern action, where men not only work to integrate the city with the market but also create circulation well beyond its boundaries.

The aesthetic rationalizations of the trading screen heighten this effect. They create the image of a complete market apart from the human actors who comprise it and require that traders on the system become observers of this distanced entity. By changing what it looks and feels like, disintermediation shapes a trader's interactions. Secluded in front of the screen, he measures his skills directly against the market as a whole. The tranquil and measured quality of the screen leaves behind many of the habits of the trading pit, but it retains others. In particular, it replicates the dispassionate aesthetic of discipline. However, like the techniques for teaching discipline that the Perkins Silver managers employed, the new screen imposes a quiet intensity that the ex-floor traders who import their raucous work habits resist.

Whether they remain in the pits or work in the new confines of the dealing room, traders display their commitment to competition as the primary mode of human interaction in their dress, language, and aggressive demeanor—conduct that undoes, at the representational level, the social ties between people and aims to dissolve any collectivity that might emerge. This image of competitive human nature, which links competition and profit to the vitality of both men and the market, obscures the continuous use of social information to make decisions. Traders say that being in the market brings them closer to the maverick, uncompromising spirit they associate with human nature, as if the market strips away the pretenses of society. The one-upmanship, crass jokes, and the insults that traders hurl mark the trading room as a place for war between men over money and status. These games of dominance and defeat help to create an asocial space. When the Perkins Silver managers tried to control the obscene language of the London traders, requesting that they stop using the word *cunt* to mitigate the brutality of the trading room for their new female recruits, the traders revolted. The new, seemingly feminized trading room threatened the connection between masculinity and market rationality that gave these men special access to the market. The cosmopolitan order of the American directors abstracted reason from masculine play. Yet the traders clung to the crass characters that reflected the asocial economic actor, persisting in their intense competitiveness. In the digital dealing room, however, the new recruits submitted to the newer affective order of the market observer—more distant from direct competition, more reflective, and quieter. The new conditions of electronic trading create a new economic aesthetic form, and with it is emerging a new variant of economic man.

The processes that produce abstract information in financial markets are not themselves abstract. Managers and designers integrate people, technologies, places, and aesthetics into a zone of autonomous economic action. The move from the pits to the electronic screen realigns human abilities and technologies, just as the transition from the crowded old Chicago Board of Trade building to the new, more spacious trading floors did in 1930. In their quest to make perfect markets, designers attempt to evade the social world. Shifting the market from its location in the bodies and voices of traders to the quiet blinking of a trading screen creates a new order of formal rationality based on digital representations. Yet traders inevitably develop profit-making strategies that bring social and cultural materials back into the rationalized market, producing a cultured structure that organizes everyday life and labor in the futures markets. Today, at the dawn of the digital age, market makers are inspired by the enticing possibilities of electronic exchange. Soon these technologies will appear insufficient, and a new generation of designers will begin their own practical experiments, convinced that they can improve on modern markets.

Introduction

1. Peter Galassi, Andreas Gursky, and Museum of Modern Art, *Andreas Gursky* (New York: Museum of Modern Art, 2001), 40–41.

2. David Harvey, *The Condition of Postmodernity* (New York: Blackwell, 1989), 164.

3. These depictions of financial capital can be read as fetishism in the classic, Marxian sense in which the object itself (here immaterial, but no less an object) seemingly imbued with powers to organize human action, obscures the conditions of its own production. But these new critics of capitalism take a very different approach. They do not examine the intricate relations of production. Instead, their analysis focuses on the feelings and confusion that the movement of capital generates. This positions capitalism as a producer of affect as much as a producer of goods.

4. Jean Comaroff, "Occult Economies and the Violence of Abstraction: Notes from the South African Postcolony," *American Ethnologist* 26, no. 2 (1999): 279–303; Jean Comaroff and John Comaroff, "Millennial Capitalism: First Thoughts on a Second Coming," *Public Culture* 12, no. 2 (2000): 291–343.

5. Harrison White, "Where Do Markets Come From?" *American Journal of Sociology* 87 (1981):517–47; Neil Fligstein, *The Architecture of Markets : An Economic Sociology of Twenty-first-Century Capitalist Societies* (Princeton, NJ: Princeton University Press, 2001); Mark Granovetter, "Economic Action and Social Structure: The Problem of Embeddedness," *American Journal of Sociology* 91, no. 3 (1985): 481–510; Mitchell Abolafia, *Making Markets: Opportunism and Restraint on Wall Street* (Cambridge, MA: Harvard University Press, 1996); Michel Callon, "Introduction: The Embeddedness of Economic Markets in Economics," in *The Laws of the Markets*, ed. Michel Callon, 1–57 (Malden, MA: Blackwell, 1998); Donald MacKenzie, "Physics and Finance: S-Terms and Modern Finance as a Topic for Science Studies," *Science, Technology and Human Values* 26, no. 2 (2001): 115–44.

6. For clear explanations of financial markets and instruments, see Doug Henwood, *Wall Street* (New York: Verso, 1997); Burton Gordon Malkiel, *A Random Walk Down Wall Street* (New York: W. W. Norton, 1996); and Roy Smith and Walter Ingo, *Global Banking* (New York: Oxford University Press, 2003).

7. Benjamin Lee and Edward LiPuma, "Cultures of Circulation: The Imaginations of Modernity," *Public Culture* 14, no. 1 (2002): 191–213.

8. Ash Amin and Nigel Thrift, "Introduction," in *Cultural Economy Reader*, ed. Ash Amin and Nigel Thrift (New York: Blackwell, 2004), xiv.

9. Max Weber, *The Protestant Ethic and the Spirit of Capitalism*, trans. T. Parsons (New York: Routledge, 1992); Georg Simmel, *The Philosophy of Money* (New York: Routledge, 1990), and "Domination," in *Georg Simmel on Individuality and Social Forms*, ed. D. Levine (Chicago: University of Chicago Press, 1971).

10. Stephen Gudeman, *The Anthropology of Economy* (New York: Blackwell, 2001); Bill Maurer, "Complex Subjects: Offshore Finance, Complexity Theory, and the Dispersion of the Modern," *Socialist Review* 25, nos. 3–4 (2005): 113–45; Daniel Miller, "Conclusion: A Theory of Virtualism," in *Virtualism: A New Political Economy*, ed. J. G. Carrier and D. Miller (New York: Berg, 1998), 187–217; Hirokazu Miyazaki, "The Temporalities of the Market," *American Anthropologist* 105, no. 2 (2004): 255–65; Annelise Riles, "Property as Legal Knowledge: Means and Ends," *Journal of the Royal Anthropological Institute* 10, no. 4 (2004): 755–976.

11. James G. Frazier, preface to Bronislaw Malinowski, *The Argonauts of the Western Pacific* (1922; repr., Prospect Heights, IL: Waveland Press, 1984), vii–xiv.

12. Clifford Geertz, "Suq: The Bazaar Economy in Sefrou," in *Meaning and Order in Moroccan Society*, ed. C. Geertz, H. Geertz, and L. Rosen (New York: Cambridge University Press, 1979), 123–313. Geertz saw his essay as working *with* the then-recent economic theories (e.g., those of Kenneth Arrow and George Akerlof) that stressed the roles of information, communication, and knowledge.

13. Marshall Sahlins, *Stone Age Economics* (Chicago: Aldine Atherton, 1972), xii. Today, economists like Gary Becker have taken up problems of economy and culture, claiming that processes considered to be cultural are, in fact, economic. For instance, by describing even family relationships and romantic love in terms of rational-choice theory he overcomes the dichotomy between economics and culture by obliterating culture. His analysis assumes that individuals always maximize welfare. Although he challenges economists by expanding the range of human motivations, the individual and his or her desire to maximize are at the core of his method. See Gary Becker, "Nobel Lecture: The Economic Way of Looking at Behavior," *Journal of Political Economy* 101, no. 3 (1993): 385–409. This approach takes economic logic to its extreme conclusion, but it should also hold a warning for anthropologists. Economy cannot be reduced to culture, nor can culture be reduced to economy. This position challenges us to hold economy and culture both together and apart as we redraw the object of inquiry to overcome such analytic dichotomies.

14. Anthropologists have pursued a different trajectory, focusing on the problem of exchange, questions of value, and the chains of commodity production that link distant locations in equations of production and consumption. Together these have led to a burgeoning and productive interest in "cultures of circulation" (see Lee and LiPuma, "Cultures of Circulation"; and Greg Urban, *Metaculture: How Culture Moves Through the World* [Minneapolis: University of Minnesota Press, 2001]). But the current neglect of Mauss's other mission, analyzing the cultural nature of economics and offering alternatives, is mysterious.

15. Paul Rabinow, *French Modern: Norms and Forms of the Social Environment* (Chicago: University of Chicago Press, 1995); James Holston, *The Modernist City: An Anthropological Critique of Brasília* (Chicago: University of Chicago Press, 1989).

16. Clifford Geertz, *Available Light: Anthropological Reflections on Philosophical Topics* (Princeton, NJ: Princeton University Press, 2000), 110.

17. Michael M. Fischer, *Emergent Forms of Life and the Anthropological Voice* (Durham, NC: Duke University Press, 2003); Douglas R. Holmes and George E. Marcus, "Cultures of Expertise and the Management of Globalization: The Refunctioning of Ethnography," in *Global Assemblages: Technology, Politics, and Ethics as Anthropological Problems*, ed. A. Ong and S. Collier (New York: Blackwell, 2005), 235–52; Aihwa Ong, *Buddha Is Hiding: Refugees, Citizenship, the New America* (Berkeley and Los Angeles: University of California Press, 2003); Paul Rabinow, "Midst Anthropology's Problems," *Cultural Anthropology* 17, no. 2 (2002): 135–50.

Chapter One

1. Upton Sinclair, *The Jungle* (New York: Penguin, 1985), 32–33.

2. William Cronon, *Nature's Metropolis: Chicago and the Great West* (New York: W. W. Norton, 1991), 230.

3. David A. Hounshell, *From the American System to Mass Production, 1800–1932: The Development of Manufacturing Technology in the United States* (Baltimore, MD: Johns Hopkins University Press, 1984).

4. Cronon, *Nature's Metropolis*, 250.

5. The CBOT leaders translated the abstract ideals of the market into the physical and social forms of the marketplace. These "specific intellectuals" worked with the space of the city and architects to build and experiment with how the market could and should work. Their approach to finding practical ways to overcome impediments to economic circulation and competition is similar to the work of modernist urban planners that Paul Rabinow examines in *French Modern: Norms and Forms of the Social Environment* (Chicago: University of Chicago Press, 1995). Both groups used the newest technologies to shape both human behavior and the environment. However, their projects differed in two key respects. First, the CBOT was concerned with creating a marketplace and conditions in which traders could flourish; "society" was not their object. Another key distinction is in the role of experts. The member-managers of the CBOT did not draw on formalized knowledge in the way that Rabinow's designers did. Their approach to markets included unarticulated assumptions that were far from the measured certainties of science, and they did not use their organization as a case that would augment scientific discourse. Their goal was practical in both ends and means: to create a working market in which its members could profit.

6. James Carrier notes that separating marketplaces from the general life of the city is a "practical abstraction" supporting the notion that markets operate with their own sphere and with their own laws ("Abstraction in Western Economic Practice," in *Virtualism: A New Political Economy*, ed. J. G. Carrier and D. Miller [New York: Berg, 1998]). However, in Chicago, the whole city was material for the practical abstraction of the market. City and market rose together and supported the idea that economic arrangements undergird the social life of the city.

7. Creating an autonomous, "disembedded" market depended, paradoxically, on building infrastructure for smooth circulation. The work of Richard Sennett and Carl Schorske on key urban streets shows how the values of movement take form in

the city. In *Flesh and Stone* (Boston: Faber and Faber, 1994), Richard Sennett argues that an individual's ability to move freely is a key condition of the capitalist city. The free circulation of bodies in the city parallels the circulation of the individual within the specialized marketplace for labor. Without attachments, economic man could move, selling his skills where and when the market offered a price. One effect of this free movement, epitomized by the circular that bends around Regent Park in London, is a diminished sensory awareness. I agree that sensory awareness is a key to urban space devoted to trade and exchange. To bring the city in line with the dominant value of circulation, Sennett depicts an urban space of flat affect and rapid, smooth movement. But the infrastructure of city streets and sewer systems *channels* those senses and affects, rather than deadening them. In both the bleak scenes of meatpacking and the brutish competition of the financial exchanges, another use of affect in the service of circulation operates. There, disgust, greed, and, surprisingly, self-abnegation play key roles in supporting smooth circulation. Chapters 5 and 6 elaborate these themes.

Carl Schorske analyzes Vienna's Ringstrasse as a key architectural element of the value of circulation. On the Ringstrasse, "The public buildings float unorganized in a spatial medium whose only stabilizing element is an artery of men in motion" (*Fin-de-siècle Vienna: Politics and Culture* [New York: Vintage Books, 1981], 36). The key difference between Schorske's Vienna and Sennett's London and Chicago is the medium in which the planners work. The Ringstrasse and Regent's Park circular each smooth the physical movement of human bodies. In Chicago, planners worked specifically to move commodity goods and financial products through the city. The CBOT employs individuals to create that motion. They are not its subject.

8. Information about the founders comes from William D. Faloon, *Market Maker: A Sesquicentennial Look at the Chicago Board of Trade* (Chicago: Board of Trade of the City of Chicago, 1998).

9. The futures markets allowed not only easy circulation but also fixity. The grain did not have to travel to market to gain a price. The physical absence of the grain allowed futures contracts to circulate freely, creating value separate from the exchange of physical goods. In Annette Weiner's explanation, value is based in part on objects that are withheld from circulation; see her "Inalienable Wealth," *American Ethnologist* 12, no. 2 (1985): 210–27. The value of these inalienable goods arises from the object's ability to bring past time into the present, allowing for histories of ancestors to become part of contemporary identity. Futures contracts also keep objects out of circulation and create value by manipulating time. They bring the future under the control of present planning and also link the present and the future by giving value to things not yet in existence.

10. Mary Poovey calls the remaining connection between abstract tokens of value, such as futures contracts, and their material underpinnings "residual materialities," showing both the financial world's constant push to extend value through abstraction and the impossibility of completely separating value from the material world ("Residual Materialities," unpublished ms., 2004).

11. Charles Henry Taylor, *History of the Board of Trade of the City of Chicago* (Chicago: Robert O. Law, 1917), 167.

12. Ibid., 161.

13. Donald L. Miller, *City of the Century: The Epic of Chicago and the Making of America* (New York: Touchstone, 1996), 91.

14. Cronon, *Nature's Metropolis*, 295–309.

15. A. T. Andreas, *History of Chicago: From the Earliest Period to the Present Time* (Chicago: A. T. Andreas, 1884), 263.

16. Ibid., 582.

17. Ibid., 583.

18. James Carey describes how the telegraph enabled a "redefinition from physical or geographic markets to spiritual ones. In a sense they were made more mysterious; they became everywhere markets and every time markets and thus less apprehensible at the very moment they become more powerful." See his "Technology and Ideology: The Case of the Telegraph," in *Communication as Culture: Essays on Media and Society* (New York: Routledge, 1992), 220.

19. Andreas, *History of Chicago*, 585.

20. Ibid., 583.

21. The inspiration for this section on standardization and much of the specific detail about the early grain market comes from William Cronon's chapter "Pricing the Future: Grain" in *Nature's Metropolis*.

22. A redefined "bushel" of winter wheat weighed sixty pounds; a bushel of oats, thirty-two pounds (Taylor, *History of the Board of Trade*, 189).

23. Cronon, *Nature's Metropolis*, 416.

24. Taylor, *History of the Board of Trade*, 189–90.

25. The architectural form does not foster the experiments with use and meaning that surround the development of consumer technologies. Pinch and Bijker's example of the bicycle shows the flexibility involved in designing such an artifact; see Trevor Pinch and Wiebe E. Bijker, "The Social Construction of Facts and Artifacts; or How the Sociology of Science and the Sociology of Technology Might Benefit Each Other," in *The Social Construction of Technological Systems: New Directions in the Sociology and History of Technology*, ed. Wiebe Bijker, Thomas P. Hughes, and Trevor Pinch (Cambridge, MA: MIT Press, 1989). The design of markets is less flexible because of the capital investment involved in trying out new physical forms.

26. Designers consciously assessed what kinds of human behaviors the market required and arranged the trading floor to encourage open competition between individuals. From this perspective, we can see buildings as tools that "configure users"; see Steve Woolgar, "Configuring the User: The Case of Usability Trials," in *A Sociology of Monsters: Essays on Power, Technology and Domination*, ed. J. Law (1902: repr., New York: Routledge, 1991), 58–97.

27. The CBOT buildings are technological artifacts that give "structures to social institutions, durability to social networks, persistence to behavior patterns," as Thomas Gieryn has argued in "What Buildings Do," *Theory and Society* 31, no. 1 (2002): 35–74.

28. Frank Norris, *The Pit: A Story of Chicago* (New York: Doubleday Page, 1994), 39.

29. Norris gave his novel about the dangers of speculation and the passions of trade the subtitle *A Story of Chicago*. For Norris, Chicago and the speculation at the CBOT are one.

30. Thomas Bender and William Taylor argue that the vertical and horizontal symbolisms of architecture align them with commercial and civic purposes respectively ("Culture and Architecture: Some Aesthetic Tensions in the Shaping of Modern New York City," in *Visions of the Modern City: Essays in History, Art, and Literature,* ed. W. Sharpe and L. Wallock [Baltimore: Johns Hopkins University Press, 1987], 189–219). They also note that skyscrapers' horizontal cornices and creation of "business blocks" lent a civic significance to New York's early tall buildings. Chicago's urban project of greatness through commerce complicates the opposition of civic concern and profit-driven motives in architecture. Since its founding, the CBOT has been dedicated to both the city's development and the profits of its members. The collective civic ideal that Bender and Taylor describe in New York architecture did not have the same power in Chicago, where a monument to profit could be also a monument to the city's civic life.

31. Carol Willis argues in *Form Follows Finance* (New York: Princeton Architectural Press, 1995) that the imperative to generate rents dominates the architectural form of the skyscraper. The CBOT saw its building as a place in which to lease office space as well as to create markets in financial instruments, but this did not deprive architects of flexibility in shaping the symbolism of the building.

32. Granger to Building Committee, August 25, 1925. Richard J. Daley Special Collections, Chicago Board of Trade Archive, University of Illinois at Chicago. Hereafter referred to as CBOT Archive.

33. The contract for the building was originally given to Holabird and Roche. The firm changed its name in 1929, and all correspondence between the CBOT and the architects after that date was addressed to Holabird and Root. I follow the convention of using the name Holabird and Root for the architects for the 1930 building.

34. The skyscraper as an architectural form highlights the project of the CBOT, linking the design values of the "clean tower" to functionalism, efficiency, speed, and the "iron reason" of the modern age (Cecelia Tichi, *Shifting Gears: Technology, Literature, Culture in Modernist America* [Chapel Hill: University of North Carolina Press, 1987], 289–93).

35. In Marilyn Strathern's formulation, the building is a place where the network is cut; see "Cutting the Network," *Journal of the Royal Anthropological Institute* 2, no. 3 (1996): 517–35. The relationships between an organization like the CBOT, its individual constituents, and the firms that seek to influence it seem to multiply endlessly. The concept of actor-networks, developed in science and technology studies, amplifies the quality of the limitless extension of networks. Strathern turns our attention to how nodes in a network can *stop* (as well as carry) flows. The CBOT building is just such a site: certain relationships are continued, others are established, and still others are discarded as the network is given a solid form in architecture.

36. This established the building as a "black box" of network connections; see Bruno Latour, *Science in Action: How to Follow Scientists and Engineers Through Society* (Cambridge, MA: Harvard University Press, 1987).

37. Rumsey to Dennis & Co., November 25, 1927, CBOT Archive.

38. Rumsey to E. P. Peck of the Omaha Grain Exchange, November 25, 1927, CBOT Archive.

39. Holabird and Root to Rumsey, October 31, 1927, CBOT Archive.

40. Ithiel de Sola Pool, ed., *The Social Impact of the Telephone* (Cambridge, MA: MIT Press, 1977), 140–41.

41. Christopher Paschen to Rumsey, March 15, 1929, CBOT Archive.

42. Rumsey to Clutton, April 19, 1930, CBOT Archive.

43. This "heterogeneous design" process resolves conflicts among competing interests—builders, managers, and city planners—at the same time that it creates a building (Gieryn, "What Buildings Do"). See Michel Callon, "Introduction: The Embeddedness of Economic Markets in Economics," in *The Laws of the Markets*, ed. Michel Callon (Malden, MA: Blackwell, 1998), 1–57; and John Law, "Technology and Heterogeneous Engineering: The Case of Portuguese Expansion," in Bijker, Hughes, and Pinch, eds., *Social Construction of Technological Systems*, among others, for further discussion.

44. Building Committee to CBOT Directors, April 5, 1930, quoting a 1927 memo from Holabird and Root. CBOT Archive.

45. Holabird and Root to Rumsey, October 4, 1928, CBOT Archive.

46. John Holabird from the Secretary of the New Building Committee, Dean Rankin, February 15, 1929, CBOT Archive.

47. Ibid.

48. Arthur Lindley to John Bunnell, January 5, 1926; Rumsey to Lindley, January 18, 1926, CBOT Archive.

49. Rumsey to the President of the Board of Directors, April 5, 1930, CBOT Archive.

50. Ibid.

51. *Chicago Daily Times*, November 13, 1931.

52. John Fisher to Rumsey, December 3, 1927, CBOT Archive.

53. Karin Knorr Cetina has argued that scientific practice is built on a "detachment of objects" from their natural environment; see *Epistemic Cultures: How the Sciences Make Knowledge* (Cambridge, MA: Harvard University Press, 1999). The laboratory creates a space of science apart from nature in a way similar to the way the CBOT buildings and trading floors create a purified market environment. Once inside laboratories, objects gain the ability to circulate among laboratories. Likewise, the creation of a market space distinct and apart from the locations of commercial transactions (where actual grain is inspected and changes hands) detaches the market from the space of physical transaction.

54. The CBOT's addition in the 1980s corresponded with a "particularly important period of landscape reconstruction" in the City, London's financial district. As Linda McDowell points out, the revolution in communications technology supported a reorganization of financial trading. Open-plan trading rooms replaced the small, individual offices of older buildings and often required banks and exchanges to construct completely new buildings, filling in the existing urban space with contemporary constructions that lent new meaning to the city's space. The same clash of financial forms, made concrete in architecture, constitutes the contemporary significance of the CBOT buildings for Chicago's landscape; see Linda McDowell, *Capital Culture: Gender at Work in the City* (Malden, MA: Blackwell, 1997), 57.

55. Anthony Giddens associates "disembedding" with the expansion of "symbolic tokens" and "expert systems," and futures markets include both of these elements

(*The Consequences of Modernity* [Stanford, CA: Stanford University Press, 1991]). Giddens's concepts of disembedding and time-space "distanciation" obscure the manipulation of the physical and urban environment to achieve these effects. The CBOT's involvement in shaping the city of Chicago and its manipulation of its trading environment show how "disembedding" is not simply a negation of an older relationship of time and space but rests on creating a new set of physical relations that may create the *appearance* of disembedding for symbolic purposes.

56. Blair Kamin, "A New Fortress for Financial Wars," *Chicago Tribune*, February 19, 1997.

57. Mike Davis writes of the fortress architecture of contemporary Los Angeles that "the privatization of the architectural public realm . . . is shadowed by parallel restructurings of electronic space" (*City of Quartz : Excavating the Future in Los Angeles* [New York: Verso, 1990], 226). The 1997 trading floor combines these designs—the CBOT employed fortress architecture to produce and contain the human infrastructure and electronic information of financial space. Unlike the 1930 building's integration of Chicago and the region's agricultural economy, the new stone pod walls off financial space from its urban surroundings, physically cordoning off a section of the city for producing financial circulation.

Chapter Two

1. The pit shapes traders' actions at the same time that traders' practices over time configure the norms of economic competition within the space of the pit. The interaction of the defined physical space and the conventions of trading work together to define the norms of the pit. Only certain kinds of problems can be considered and solved in the pit; others must be left at the trading room door.

2. The modern has always had such elements; the conflict at the CBOT simply exposed these repressed aspects.

3. Of course personal relationships can facilitate as well as hinder criminal activity, as David Greising and Laurie Morse describe in detail in *Brokers, Bagmen, and Moles: Fraud and Corruption in the Chicago Futures Markets* (New York: Wiley, 1991).

4. Michel Foucault, quoted in Paul Rabinow, *Anthropos Today: Reflections on Modern Equipment* (Princeton, NJ: Princeton University Press, 2003), 47.

5. Janet Abu-Lughod, *New York, Chicago, Los Angeles: America's Global Cities* (Minneapolis: University of Minnesota Press, 1999); Saskia Sassen, *The Global City* (Princeton, NJ: Princeton University Press, 2001).

6. The CBOT's struggle with technology was fought on a very public stage. This chapter combines fieldwork with an analysis of the official documents and professional reports that the exchange members used to substantiate their positions. The upheavals in the futures industry were frequently covered in the *Wall Street Journal* and *Financial Times* as well as in industry magazines and the city's newspapers. These records demonstrate both the content of the arguments for and against new technologies and the public nature of these disputes.

7. Sassen argues that "[u]nderstanding the actual work that needs to be executed in Chicago captures the specialized functions of the city's markets" (*Global City*, 161).

8. The analysis presented here owes obvious debts to Thomas Hughes's approach to the study of technical systems. He stresses the importance of relationships between organizations, technological artifacts, and political maneuvering. See his *Networks of Power: Electrification in Western Society, 1880–1930* (Baltimore, MD: Johns Hopkins University Press, 1983), and "The Evolution of Large Technological Systems," in *The Social Construction of Technological Systems: New Directions in the Sociology and History of Technology*, ed. W. Bijker, T. P. Hughes, and T. Pinch (Cambridge: MIT Press, 1989), 51–82. Hughes directs us to look at technologies as "problem-solving systems," an approach that lends itself to teleological thinking, as John Law has recently pointed out. Law prefers thinking of technical objects in terms of "fractional coherence," avoiding the idea of a technological march toward problem solving (*Aircraft Stories: Decentering the Object in Technoscience* [Durham, NC: Duke University Press, 2002]). Instead of beginning with the technological object, I raise the question, How does the form of exchange within one organization shape the reaction to new technologies and their development? How do the debates over the methods of economics mold arguments about technological systems? The object of the analysis is not technology itself but the fertile interaction between technologies and economic life that directs the arguments and decisions of the CBOT members and directors. Their actions in turn define the course for one of Chicago's key global organizations by directing their problem-solving efforts.

9. The CBOT has recently stopped using the term *open outcry* in favor of the term *open auction*. The new phrase abandons the role of voice in the dealing process. Losing this mark of the shouting trader reframes the trading-floor auction as indistinct from online markets. The phrase *open auction* marks the discursive triumph of online exchange.

10. William Faloon, *Market Maker: A Sesquicentennial Look at the Chicago Board of Trade* (Chicago: Board of Trade of the City of Chicago, 1998).

11. Traders cannot legally use inside information to "front run" the customers. But occasionally a broker may illegally expose his deck, doling out coveted information to a favored trader. Social loyalties and exchange of favors exist alongside brokers' responsibilities to act as the agents of outside buyers and sellers. The market is not simply a meeting place of outside forces but a social world of its own where relations take shape and are cultivated. The pit is not only a place of trade but also a realm of social interactions and exchanges.

12. The founders of the CBOT often had commercial stakes in the grain business as well as the ability to profit from price changes. The traders who work in the open outcry pits for financial futures do not have this same dual interest. Most are speculators who trade in and out of the market for profit. In the market's own terms, these speculators provide liquidity, the ability for any number of contracts to trade at any time. They are the switchmen of the exchange, and the market comes alive in their bodies and voices.

13. In contrast to the usually white and male runners who have connections in the pits, there is also a coterie of "career" runners, whose minimum-wage and outsider status mean that they navigate the packed channels between the pits with no possibility of moving into the pits as traders.

14. Paul Solman, "Chicago May Consider End to Open Outcry," *Financial Times*, June 20, 1998.

15. At that time there were 573 Project A workstations in use, including 18 in London and 42 in New York.

Chapter Three

1. In the language of Daniel Beunza and David Stark, the managers set out to engineer "an ecology of evaluative principles" ("Tools of the Trade: The Socio-technology of Arbitrage in a Wall Street Trading Room," *Industrial and Corporate Change* 13, no. 2 [2004]: 369–400).

2. David Kynaston *LIFFE: A Market and Its Makers* (Cambridge: Grant Editions, 1997).

3. Michael Useem "Business and Politics in the United States and the United Kingdom," in *Structures of Capital*, ed. S. Skin and P. DiMaggio (New York: Cambridge University Press, 1989); Linda McDowell, *Capital Culture: Gender at Work in the City* (Malden, MA: Blackwell, 1997); Will Hutton, *The State We're In* (London: Vintage, 1996).

4. Hutton, *State We're In.*

5. John Edwards, quoted in Kynaston, *LIFFE*, 10.

6. Kynaston, *LIFFE*, 72.

7. Ibid., 94. By stating that the new City brokers did not have "an O-level to [their] name[s]," the *Mail on Sunday* was suggesting that they had completed only a very low level of education and had dropped out of school before the ordinary level exams were administered (at around age sixteen).

8. Nick Leeson, *Rogue Trader* (London: Little, Brown, 1996).

9. M. Pryke, "An International City Going 'Global': Spatial Change in the City of London," *Environment and Planning D: Society and Space* 9 (1991): 197.

10. Micaela di Leonardo has described how class becomes ethnicized for whites; see "White Ethnicities, Identity Politics and Baby Bear's Chair," *Social Text* 41 (1994): 165–89. In the case of Essex Man, the class distinction, embodied in consumption styles, is inscribed on an evolutionary scale of difference. Essex Man is distinguished not on the basis of race but by allusion to earlier forms of humans—although race differences are easily coded in this way as well.

11. In *The Accursed Share*, vol. 1 (New York: Zone Books, 1989), Georges Bataille developed an idea of economy whose organizing principle was the consumption of wealth. This idea shifts the perspective on the spending habits of traders. Instead of seeing spending habits as a moral failure, it reframes them as necessary expenditures of energy.

12. Paul E. Willis, *Learning to Labor: How Working-Class Kids Get Working-Class Jobs* (New York: Columbia University Press, 1981); Robert W. Connell, *Masculinities* (Berkeley and Los Angeles: University of California Press, 1995).

13. In *Family and Kinship in East London* (1957; repr., Berkeley and Los Angeles: University of California Press, 1992), sociologists Michael Young and Peter Willmott state the stereotypes that they intended to fight. "Manual workers are said to be shiftless, lazy, improvident, rascally, uncultured, acting for themselves alone." They assert with earnest indignation, "We could not, on the basis of what we found, subscribe to any such condemnation." In fact, they claim, the way of life in London's East End neighborhood, Bethnal Green, "could in some respects be regarded as a

model for those who were (and still are) doing the denigrating" (xv). In their mid-century text, Young and Willmott struggled against the stereotypes of East Enders. By the time Perkins Silver began recruiting, London traders had appropriated pieces of these stereotypes for their own use as they constructed roguish personae that fit the autonomous and competitive economic man of foreign exchange and futures markets.

14. Under the leadership of Brian Williamson, LIFFE "demutualized" in 1998, switching from being a membership organization like the CBOT to a corporate structure, citing the demands for swift action required under an electronic regime.

15. Andrew Leyshon and Nigel Thrift, *Money/Space* (New York: Routledge, 1997), 147.

16. Fat fingering was a critical mistake not only because of its economic consequences, but for the trader's engagement with the market. It precluded the trader's plans and disrupted his immersion in the market's fluctuations, throwing him out of the screen-world and back into the physical environment of the trading room and his own noncompliant body. The games would, the managers believed, train our bodies to operate as uninterrupted conduits between the dealing room and the online world, allowing our fingers to become seamless extensions of our economic intentions. Fat fingering, the failure of this training, showed that the body could not be trained to be a perfect instrument as it, at times, impeded the smooth transfer of strategy to economic action. At the same time, fat fingering severed the space of the dealing room from the space of the market by shattering the trader's absorption, a key element of his profit-making abilities. The managers prescribed the arbitrage and video games not only to discipline attention and action, but also to train the body to become an "intention extension," to maintain the union of physical and online action, and provide a medium for economic reason. In the fast-paced work of futures trading, such an alignment could not be taken for granted.

17. Linda McDowell, "Body Work: Heterosexual Gender Performances in City Workplaces," in *Mapping Desire*, ed. D. Bell and G. Valentine, 77. London: Routledge, 1995.

18. James G. Carrier and Daniel Miller, eds. *Virtualism: A New Political Economy* (New York: Berg, 1998).

19. In *The Stranger* (in *Individuality and Social Forms*, ed. D. N. Levine [Chicago: University of Chicago Press, 1971], 143–49), Georg Simmel states that the synthesis of nearness and remoteness "is to be found in the objectivity of the stranger. Because he is not bound by roots to the particular constituents and partisan dispositions of the group, he confronts all of these with a distinctly 'objective' attitude . . . a distinct structure composed of remoteness and nearness, indifference and involvement" (145). The power of electronic trading and the possibilities of export placed the Perkins Silver managers in the position of the stranger with regard to their own practices. Chapter 1 described the problems of the CBOT members in finding this balance of nearness and remoteness in relation to their constituencies and their partisan dispositions with regard to technology and their norms of economic action.

20. I agree with James Clifford's understanding that "practices of displacement" are "constitutive of cultural meanings" and are not "simple transfer or extension."

See his *Routes: Travel and Translation in the Late Twentieth Century* (Cambridge, MA: Harvard University Press, 1997), 3.

Chapter Four

1. Both historical policy debates and contemporary social theory have drawn analogies between financial markets and casinos in their orientations to risk; see, for example, Susan Strange, *Casino Capitalism* (New York: Manchester University Press, 1984); David Harvey, *The Condition of Postmodernity* (New York: Blackwell, 1993); and Frederic Jameson, "Culture and Finance Capital," *Critical Inquiry* 24 (1997): 246–65. In the nineteenth century Chicago futures exchanges worked to distinguish themselves from "bucket shops," establishments typically close to the exchanges that offered betting on the direction of futures prices. The exchanges established their legitimacy by denying the resemblance between trading and gambling. They claimed that their contracts could be used in the service of production as "hedging" tools; see William D. Faloon, *Market Maker: A Sesquicentennial Look at the Chicago Board of Trade* (Chicago: Board of Trade of the City of Chicago, 1998); and Cedric B. Cowing, *Populists, Plungers, and Progressives: A Social History of Stock and Commodity Speculation, 1890–1936* (Princeton, NJ: Princeton University Press, 1965). The analogy points to the critical role of risk and risk-taking in financial markets, but this obscures the specificities of risk-taking in financial markets and the special relationship between financial markets and capitalism. The suggestion of illegitimacy denies us a more nuanced understanding of the significance of risk and risk-taking in this high-modernist institution.

2. Sociocultural examinations of risk have focused on two major themes. The first is the theme of anticipation and avoidance of loss. Risk is most often examined in the ways that groups or organizations classify, mobilize, and intervene against the threat of loss or vulnerability to loss; see Ulrich Beck, *Risk Society: Towards a New Modernity* (London: Sage, 1992); Robert Castel, "From Dangerousness to Risk," in *The Foucault Effect: Studies in Governmentality*, ed. Graham Burchell, Colin Gordon, and Peter Miller (Chicago: University of Chicago Press, 1991), 281–98; Mary Douglas and Aaron Wildavsky, *Risk and Culture* (Berkeley and Los Angeles: University of California Press, 1982); Ron Levy, "The Mutuality of Risk and Community: The Adjudication of Community Notification Statutes," *Economy and Society* 29, no. 4 (2000): 578–601; Pat O'Malley, "Risk and Responsibility," In *Foucault and Political Reason*, ed. Andrew Barry, Thomas Osborne, and Nikolas S. Rose (London: University of Chicago Press, 1996), 189–209. The focus on ecological and technological peril to exemplify the concept of risk in the two most widely cited theories, those of Ulrich Beck (*Risk Society*) and Mary Douglas and Aaron Wildavsky (*Risk and Culture*), narrows their sense of the concept. Particularly for Douglas and Wildavsky, risk is synonymous with danger, a focus that fits their concern with the sociocultural selection of risks. Although, unlike Beck, Douglas and Wildavsky do not see risk itself as a particularly modern problem, their claim that the concern with technological hazards is a modern trait fits with Ulrich Beck's definition of a "risk society" that poses reflexivity as a central contemporary problem. Both of these studies closely associate risk with the potential for loss and, even more specifically, the potential for physical harm.

3. From this perspective, futures contracts and markets work as a type of insurance—technologies for distributing risk. This focus on the distribution of risk unites Schumpeter's figure of the entrepreneur (who takes voluntary risks for economic profit) with recent writing on governmentality. Connecting risk and the political rationality of neoliberalism, work on governmentality identifies several manifestations of risk, focusing especially on risk-avoidance rationalities and self-governance as critical parts of neoliberal subjectivities; see Andrew Barry, Thomas Osborne, and Nikolas S. Rose, *Foucault and Political Reason: Liberalism, Neo-liberalism and Rationalities of Government* (London: University of Chicago Press, 1996). Drawing the analysis into the economic sphere, François Ewald argues that insurance is a way to protect financial well-being that encourages individuals to conduct their lives in market terms; see "Insurance and Risk," in *Foucault Effect* (see note 2). The existing literature, however, focuses less on *generating* wealth, even though wealth is critical to satisfying needs. In the economic arena, the creation and conservation of economic goods must be considered together.

One important distinction between insurance and financial trading is the widely different contexts engaged by each. Insurance bridges the gap between social and economic domains, importing a logic of risk and financial calculation into spheres less fully penetrated by market logic. The neoliberal subjects forged under these conditions project the odds of harm and financial compensation far into the future, even potentially to the end of their own existence in the case of life insurance.

4. See Niklas Luhmann, *Risk, a Sociological Theory* (New York: A. de Gruyter, 1993), and "Describing the Future," in *Observations on Modernity* (Stanford, CA: Stanford University Press, 1998), 63–74; and Anthony Giddens, *The Consequences of Modernity* (Stanford, CA: Stanford University Press, 1991). Niklas Luhmann's work moves a step closer to a concept that illuminates voluntary risk. He understands risk as a condition of decisions, and places the responsibility for the loss (or gain) in the act of anticipating a future that is still undetermined (see Luhmann, *Risk*). Risk is, therefore, a problem of acting at the limit of knowledge. In the work of speculation, traders make hundreds of predictive decisions in a day, placing a stake on the future direction of the market. Luhmann focuses attention on the problem of making decisions at the border between present and future, a problem central to economic action. Even though Luhmann's conceptual approach does not incorporate the *work* of risk-taking, his framework can help us to understand the practices of risk.

5. See Stephen Lyng, "Edgework: A Social Psychological Analysis of Voluntary Risk Taking," *American Journal of Sociology* 95, no. 4 (1990): 851–86; Richard G. Mitchell, *Mountain Experience: The Psychology and Sociology of Adventure* (Chicago: University of Chicago Press, 1983); Catherine Palmer, "'Shit Happens': The Selling of Risk in Extreme Sports," *Australian Journal of Anthropology* 13, no. 3 (2000): 323–36; and Jonathan Simon, "Taking Risks: Extreme Sports and the Embrace of Risk in Advanced Liberal Societies," in *Embracing Risk: The Changing Culture of Insurance and Responsibility*, ed. Tom Baker and Jonathan Simon (Chicago: University of Chicago Press, 2002), 177–207.

6. I use the concept of productivity here to describe the formation of risk-taking selves and active marketplaces. The concept of market productivity usually refers to the manufacture of objects. However, in an economy based on the circulation of signs, the concept of productivity and the importance of work are still central.

7. We can apply an analysis of risk as a productive force equally to Douglas and Wildavsky's (*Risk and Culture*) and Beck's (*Risk Society*) arguments and also to the work on risk as a component of governmentality (e.g., O'Malley, "Risk and Responsibility"). The negative side of risk in all three of these perspectives emphasizes protection rather than productivity.

8. In recent decades risk has emerged as a key concept across the social sciences, particularly in studies of contemporary modes of governance, self-formation, political responsibility, and reflexivity; see Beck, *Risk Society*; Graham Burchell, "Liberal Government and Techniques of the Self," in Barry, Osborne, and Rose, *Foucault and Political Reason*, 19–36; Douglas and Wildavsky, *Risk and Culture*; Anthony Giddens, *Modernity and Self-Identity: Self and Society in the Late Modern Age* (Cambridge: Polity Press, 1991); Colin Gordon, "Governmental Rationality: An Introduction," in *Foucault Effect*, 1–54 (see note 2); O'Malley, "Risk and Responsibility"). I agree with Asa Boholm and Pat Caplan that the metatheories of Beck and Giddens and the individualized, choice-based perspectives of psychology and economics leave the anthropological arena of risk untouched; see Asa Boholm, "The Cultural Nature of Risk: Can There Be an Anthropology of Uncertainty?" *Ethnos* 68, no. 2 (2003): 159–78; and Pat Caplan, "Introduction: Risk Revisited," in *Risk Revisited*, ed. P. Caplan (London: Pluto Press, 2000), 1–28. Explorations of active, intentional engagements with risk are particularly underdeveloped, and here anthropology can intervene productively; see David Garland, "Rise of Risk," in *Risk and Morality*, ed. R. Ericson and A. Doyle (Toronto: University of Toronto Press. 2003), 48–86; and Deborah Lupton, *Risk* (New York: Routledge, 1999). A close investigation of the way financial speculators work can yield new perspectives on both the concept of risk and the relationship between markets and risk-takers. Economics has long recognized the importance of taking risks in making profits, both for individuals and for the dynamism of capitalism; see Joseph Schumpeter, *Capitalism, Socialism and Democracy* (New York: Harper and Row, 1950). Drawing on the foundational work of Frank Knight (*Risk, Uncertainty and Profit* [Chicago: University of Chicago Press, 1971]), economics maintains a rigid distinction between the probabilities of risk and the haze of uncertainty, the domain of profit for the entrepreneur. As Pat O'Malley has observed, the positive human sciences have sought to subjugate the creative role of risk to rationally calculable plans. Weberian analyses of rationalization have also banished activities that have uncertainty at their center; see Pat O'Malley, "Moral Uncertainties: Contract Law and Distinctions between Speculation, Gambling and Insurance," in *Risk and Morality*, ed. R. V. Ericson and A. Doyle (Toronto: University of Toronto Press, 2003), 231–57. However, speculation is now receiving the kind of attention that it lost at the end of the nineteenth century. The analytic distinction between risk and uncertainty does not hold up when we consider the practice of speculation. Yet anthropology and the other human sciences, where competition is a subject of keen attention, have largely neglected to account for the actions and potentials of risk-taking that are most visible in the economic sphere.

9. Michael Burawoy and Leslie Salzinger have shown how social games work in the service of manufacturing; see Michael Burawoy, *Manufacturing Consent: Changes in the Labor Process under Monopoly Capitalism* (Chicago: University of Chicago Press, 1979); and Leslie Salzinger, *Genders in Production: Making Workers in Mexico's Global Factories* (Berkeley and Los Angeles: University of California

Press, 2003). These games are equally important in the postindustrial economy, where the circulation of information and the exchange of signs is crucial. At the CBOT, the circulation of financial commodities fosters the daily re-creation of risk-taking subjects. In this sense the trading pit is an important example of a culture of circulation where norms of evaluation, constraint, and action develop around the act of exchange (Benjamin Lee and Edward LiPuma, "Cultures of Circulation: The Imaginations of Modernity," *Public Culture* 14, no. 1 [2002]: 191–213). Like the rivalry of the cockfight, the wagering of the self and status that takes place in the pit is central to the action (Clifford Geertz, "Deep Play: Notes on the Balinese Cockfight," in *Interpretation of Cultures* [New York: Basic Books, 1973], 412–53). At the CBOT, the action is simultaneously the creation of a market and the constitution of a social field and the individuals that comprise it.

10. See Goffman, *Where the Action Is*, 237, for a discussion of the wagering of the self under conditions of "action."

11. In *Where the Action Is*, Goffman describes how in moments of action, "The individual . . . display[s] to himself and sometimes to others his style of conduct when the chips are down. . . . To display or express character, weak or strong, is to generate character. The self, in brief, can be voluntarily subjected to re-creation" (237).

12. The practice of trading is strikingly similar to Goffman's moments of meaningful action and Foucault's idea of the "limit experience," performances that transcend the subject and create something new. For Foucault, playing beyond the limits of reason is a powerful way to remake the self. In economic action, the future is that site of unreason. We can imagine and plan for possible futures, but we can never know them. This territory at the edge of the present is both fertile and potentially destructive for the financial managers and traders who make up capital markets. The traders at the CBOT are financial specialists whose labor is handling the risk and uncertainty generated by the transactions of others. Yet they are not the rational, scientific classifiers who define and discipline objects of unreason. Traders manipulate social situations, tacit knowledge, and corporeal strategies, all of which they do to extract profit from the market. Their forms of reason, as Pierre Bourdieu would say, are practical, not scholastic (*Practical Reason* [Cambridge: Polity Press, 1998]). Profit and loss figures are the measures of successful action—not institutions or theories.

13. Michel Foucault, "A Preface to Transgression," in *Foucault: Aesthetics, Method, and Epistemology*, ed. J. Faubion (New York: New Press, 1998), 241.

14. Futures contracts are examples of the way that "the future is continually drawn into the present by means of reflexive organization of knowledge environments" (Giddens, *Consequences of Modernity*, 3).

15. As with the work of Niklas Luhmann, Ulrich Beck, and Anthony Giddens, the work on governmentality argues that efforts to manage risk and control uncertainty are central to modernist projects.

16. Understood this way, financial exchanges are hubs in "the market for security" (Ewald, "Insurance and Risk," 198).

17. Bruce Carruthers and Arthur L. Stinchcombe ("The Social Structure of Liquidity: Flexibility, Markets, and States," *Theory and Society* 28 [1999]: 353–82), William Cronon (*Nature's Metropolis: Chicago and the Great West* [New York:

W. W. Norton, 1991]), and Wendy Espeland and Mitchell L. Stevens ("Commensuration as a Social Process" *Annual Review of Sociology* 24 [1998]: 313–43) have all shown the importance and complexity of creating common measurements and the "necessary fiction" (Cronon, *Nature's Metropolis*) of homogeneity within products for commercial circulation. These processes establish tradable commodities, the necessary first step for creating liquid markets. Economists claim that liquidity mitigates risk. If traders or managers doubt their positions in the market, a liquid market allows them to close out the positions quickly rather than spending time (and thus incurring additional risk) searching for buyers.

18. Ira O. Glick, "A Social Psychological Study of Futures Trading," PhD diss., Department of Sociology, University of Chicago, 1957.

19. In this sense, futures markets are exemplary sites of "cultivated risk" for speculators (Giddens, *Modernity and Self-Identity*, 133).

20. Looking at risk as part of the traders' self-presentation in the market draws on Avner Offner's essay on economic life as the pursuit of regard and Harrison White's observation that producers' scrutiny of their competitors constitutes markets; see Avner Offner, "Between the Gift and the Market: The Economy of Regard," *Economic History Review* 50 (1997): 450–76. What Harrison White claims for the level of the firm is also true for individual traders in the pit. He claims that "what a firm does in a market is to watch the competition in terms of observables" ("Where Do Markets Come From?" *American Journal of Sociology* 87 [1981]: 518). What traders watch are their competitors' patterns of buying, selling, and risk-taking. This mutual observation, imitation, and judgment of risk-taking is a fundamental way that market makers learn successful techniques of trading and self-display and contribute to the structuring of market transactions; see Christina Garsten and Anna Hasselstrom, "Risky Business: Discourses of Risk and (Ir)responsibility in Globalizing Markets," *Ethnos* 68, no. 2 (2003): 249–70; and Donald MacKenzie, "Social Connectivities in Global Financial Markets," *Environment and Planning D: Society and Space* 22 (2004): 83–101.

21. The gendered aspects of the pit deserve a full-length treatment of their own. I thank Ann Anagnost for reminding me of Bourdieu's essay, "The Sense of Honor" (in *Algeria 1960* [New York: Cambridge University Press, 1979], 93–123), that informs this analysis.

22. In addition to structuring the social landscape of the pit, the creation of trading neighborhoods affects the price of CBOT products. The neighborhoods create small markets within the larger market, a fragmentation that exaggerates price volatility; see Wayne Baker, "The Social Structure of a National Securities Market," *American Journal of Sociology* 89, no. 4 (1984): 775–811. The social organization of the pit has a direct impact on the overall market as well as the individual strategies of traders.

23. Risk-taking among traders is not "compensatory" in the way that Richard Mitchell describes for mountaineers who seek risks in the mountains that are absent in the rationalized, controlled workplace (see Mitchell, *Mountain Experience*). This perspective opposes "daily life" and risk-taking, whereas in the futures markets, these are one and the same. For traders, risk-taking is the central activity of their occupation.

24. Risk-taking in futures markets thus resembles Erving Goffman's observation about the affective state central to "the action," where intensity and fatefulness are combined (Goffman, *Where the Action Is*).

25. This state is very similar to the flow experience that Mihaly Csikszentmihalyi describes in *Flow: The Psychology of Optimal Experience* (New York: Harper & Row, 1990).

26. Goffman, *Where the Action Is*, 185.

27. Goffman noted that working with risk differs from playing with risk as a leisure activity. He claims that in occupations where people take risks, a special relationship to the work world emerges—one that makes a virtue out of voluntary engagements with fate (*Where the Action Is*, 188). Goffman's distinction between working and playing with risk is important for seeing speculation as an ethical field rather than as just another expression of gambling. However, his argument reduces the attractions of risk to a necessary evil. Those that work with risk in his description must rationalize their risk-taking. These occupations *reinvent* risk as a virtue. Goffman still begins from the assumption that positions of risk are undesirable—a notion that leads him to underestimate the pleasurable side of risk in work.

28. Goffman, *Where the Action Is*, 185.

29. Bill Buford, *Among the Thugs* (New York: Vintage, 1990), 205. Mobs, violence, and speculation have been associated in social theorizing at least since the time when Gustave Le Bon (*The Crowd: A Study of the Popular Mind* [New York: Penguin Books, 1977]) and Charles Mackay (*Extraordinary Popular Delusions and the Madness of Crowds* [Boston: L. C. Page, 1974]) trained their Victorian eyes on the irrationalities of crowds. Both observed the dangers of succumbing to unreason, especially the loss of individuality and the predisposition of crowds to violence. The unreason of crowds links speculative manias such as the tulip mania in seventeenth-century Holland, when tulip bulbs cost as much as real estate along Amsterdam canals, with the murderous nature of witch-hunts. For in-depth treatment of speculative manias, see Charles Kindleberger, *Manias, Panics and Crashes: A History of Financial Crises* (New York: Basic Books, 1989) and Edward Chancellor, *Devil Take the Hindmost: A History of Financial Speculation* (New York: Plume, 1999).

30. See Nigel Thrift, *Knowing Capitalism* (London: Sage, 2005) for a discussion of the Dionysian qualities of capitalism.

31. In "The Prize Fighter's Three Bodies," (*Ethnos* 63, no. 3 [1998]: 325–52) Loïc Wacquant shows how, for poor African-American men on Chicago's South Side, boxing is more about bodily and spiritual transformation than about the dream of getting rich. Wacquant's skepticism about economic explanations is as applicable in the CBOT pits, where money is central to traders' labor, as it is in the ghetto gymnasium.

32. This quality is not unique to trading, yet it is not the central concern of all jobs. As Gerald Suttles observes, "Most people reach the top of their profession or occupation relatively early in life, and if they are to continue to find interest in what they are doing, they must play with their stratification system. . . . Indeed, one might advance the hypothesis that the person who is a grind, someone who adheres to accepted practice with unfailing devotion, is unlikely to win the long-term acclaim that he is said to be heading for. He will expire of boredom beforehand. Style and

self-esteem, then, are as essential as the incentive of ultimate social acclaim" ("Introduction," in Mitchell, *Mountain Experience*, xi).

33. See, for instance, Joe Simpson, *Touching the Void* (New York: HarperCollins, 1988).

Chapter Five

1. A first look at the trading floor might support Georg Simmel's comments on crowd behavior: "There develops a great nervous excitement at the expense of clear and consistent intellectual activity; it arouses the darkest and most primitive instincts of the individual which are ordinarily under control" ("Domination," in *Georg Simmel on Individuality and Social Forms*, ed. D. Levine, [Chicago: University of Chicago Press, 1971], 112).

2. Albert O. Hirschman, *The Passions and the Interests: Political Arguments for Capitalism before Its Triumph* (Princeton, N.J.: Princeton University Press, 1997), 66.

3. This elaborates Simmel's insights into the passionate potential of economic activity from his essay "The Miser and the Spendthrift," a classic essay about economic affect, even if Simmel did not conceive it that way; see Georg Simmel, *The Philosophy of Money* (New York: Routledge, 1990), 326–31.

4. David Noble has pointed out the connection between celibacy and reason that emerged from medieval European monasteries; see *A World without Women: The Christian Clerical Culture of Western Science* (New York: Oxford University Press, 1993). Traders' use of metaphors of sexual violence to establish dealing rooms as spaces of base instinct is striking.

5. Often, modern forms of trust are understood as situated in systems rather than people; see Anthony Giddens, *The Consequences of Modernity* (Stanford, CA: Stanford University Press, 1991). But at the CBOT, trust in the price-making system relies on the conduct of the human beings that make it up. The organization presents itself as constituted by competitive individuals and assigns itself the role of applying the limited constraints that allow trust in the prices arrived at through competition.

6. Steven Shapin, *A Social History of Truth: Civility and Science in Seventeenth-Century England* (Chicago: University of Chicago Press, 1994), 17.

7. There is yet another twist to this paradox. In the pits, traders must trust their dealing partners to accurately record and honor the commitment to the agreed price and quantity of a trade. But this essential obligation is the only acknowledged and legal commitment to a social bond. The screen eliminates this piece of the paradox by replacing the human system of honor and trust with a machine, allowing traders to pursue their self-interest more fully, free from the constraints of interpersonal trust.

8. Incorporating this perspective into approaches to economic life requires a critique of some previous approaches. Economic sociologists have approached the problem of economic man by trying to resituate "undersocialized" ideas of action within the "embedded" social world; see Mark Granovetter, "Economic Action and Social Structure: The Problem of Embeddedness," *American Journal of Sociology* 91, no. 3 (1985): 481–510. This approach engages economists on their theoretical biases. However, if an anthropology of finance is to move beyond reforming the practice of economists, analysis of economic man must move beyond a simple debunking or amending of economists' constructions. Revising the economists' models

can do little to illuminate anthropologists' and sociologists' understandings of economic action because we already assume, as economists themselves do, that their models of economic man are socially impoverished.

Inspired by Michel Callon's introduction to *The Laws of the Markets* (Malden, MA: Blackwell, 1998), social studies of finance have developed a set of inquiries into the sources of rational economic calculations based in the performative logic of economics and framed by calculative technologies. This approach attempts to understand how the ideals of rational economic man enter the calculative apparatus: "He is formatted, framed and equipped with prostheses which help him in his calculations and which are, for the most part, produced by economics" (51). This addresses the operational problem for calculative actors, but obscures the practices and set of affects that create an always emergent figure of economic man. Callon's approach risks reducing traders to the slaves of financial modelers.

9. Traders' claims that they enact a form of "natural" behavior call for investigation of the embodied practices, performances, and emotions that make up this "natural man."

10. This analysis draws on the uses of emotion and affect in service work; see Arlie Russell Hochschild, *Managed Heart : Commercialization of Human Feeling* (Berkeley and Los Angeles: University of California Press, 1983); Robin Leidner, *Fast Food, Fast Talk: Service Work and the Routinization of Everyday Life* (Berkeley and Los Angeles: University of California Press, 1993); Andrew Ross, *No-Collar: The Humane Workplace and Its Hidden Costs* (New York: Basic Books, 2003). Hochschild and Leidner focus on the production and exploitation of emotion in work. Corporate interests exploit the workers' presentation of affect in the production and consumption of service-based labor. Rountinized displays of affect distance workers from their own emotions or turn them into a resource for the industry. In the context of finance, Linda McDowell has described how masculinity in investment banks is marked by bodily labor as men shape themselves into service workers to interact with clients ("Body Work: Heterosexual Gender Performances in City Workplaces," in *Mapping Desire*, ed. D. Bell and G. Valentine (London: Routledge, 1995), 75–98. Although the focus on service work in these studies is not suited to an analysis of the labor of traders, the focus on emotion can extend to their context. I combine attention to displays of market affect with Goffman's attention to the presentation of self as located in particular times and spaces, and as dependent on specific social situations. At the same time, the idea that the market elicits the basic instincts of men who act within it forms the normative framework for these specific performances.

11. Max Weber, *The Protestant Ethic and the Spirit of Capitalism*, trans. T. Parsons (1930; repr., New York: Routledge, 1992).

12. Max Weber, *Max Weber on the Methodology of the Social Sciences*, ed. Edward Shils (Glencoe, IL: Free Press, 1949), 99.

13. Norbert Elias describes the historical development of "precepts of conduct regarded as 'civilized'" in *The Civilizing Process* (Oxford: Blackwell, 1978). He examines codes of behavior that make specific ways of controlling affect automatic as well as "regulation and restraint imposed on the expression of desires and impulses" (156). Traders' codes invert the codes of civilized behavior. The codes that govern "socially desirable behavior" on the trading floor emphasize the absence of any such

codes. The "matter of self-control" for traders involves stripping what is civilized from their behavior. Traders craft behavior that matches their ideals. They "make themselves over into living embodiments of their professional morality" (Loïc Wacquant, "The Prizefighter's Three Bodies," *Ethnos* 63, no. 3 [1998]: 22).

14. The maverick performances coupled with traders' risk-taking bravado critique and reject the constraints of bourgeois social life.

15. In his essay "The Mandatory Expression of Sentiments," Marcel Mauss describes how emotional language and excitement are determined by formal strictures and obligations (unpublished ms., trans. Loïc Wacquant, 1921). Mauss's observation of the nonspontaneity of feeling applies to feelings that are constructed to convey spontaneity and the individuality of action. It is a reminder to be particularly cautious when claims to the impulsive and the natural are made.

16. Pierre Bourdieu, *Practical Reason* (Cambridge: Polity Press, 1998).

17. Erving Goffman's approach to the theatrics of social life provides insight on this drama. The asocial performances of the pit and the trading floor are "front-stage," and the deep and useful networks of trust, reciprocity, and loyalty among traders are "back-stage" actions (see *The Presentation of Self in Everyday Life* [1959; repr., Harmondsworth: Penguin, 1990]). The front-stage performances of an economic self anchor the aesthetics of risk-taking. Trading pits and dealing floors are theaters of capitalism where the action has real consequences for markets around the world.

18. Theater and the marketplace have been always been entangled. Bakhtin's analysis of grotesque aesthetics is enacted in and contained by marketplaces, and historian Jean–Christophe Agnew has documented the tandem rise of capitalism and the Anglo-American theater (*Worlds Apart: The Market and the Theater in Anglo-American Thought, 1550–1750* [New York: Cambridge University Press, 1986]). Bakhtin's analysis of the grotesque is particularly useful for the trading floor. The defining principle of grotesque realism according to Bakhtin is degradation, "the lowering of all that is high, spiritual and abstract"; see Mikhail Bakhtin, *Rabelais and His World*, trans. H. Iswolsky (Bloomington: Indiana University Press, 1984), 19.

19. In Bakhtin's description, marketplace and carnival are linked in grotesque performances. The carnival takes place in the market that offers a space removed from "official culture." In turn, the grotesque performance defines the space. Similarly, the traders' maverick aesthetics define the time and space of the market (Bakhtin, *Rabelais*).

20. As Simmel says, "The brutality of a man purely motivated by monetary considerations and acting, to this extent, on the same axiom of greatest advantage and least sacrifice, often does not appear to him at all as a moral delinquency, since he is aware only of a rigorously logical behavior, which draws the objective consequences of the situation." (Simmel, "Domination," 110).

21. In the movie *The Full Monty* unemployed steel workers improvise a novel way of making money in the eviscerated economy of northern England. They transform themselves from hardened factory workers to male strippers. In the ladies club, their labor is reduced to parading sheer male flesh. It is all that they have left to sell. They are men whose bodies are the source of their labor and value—a statement of the power of economic forces to strip men to the raw. In the wasteland of northern English industry, capitalism literally strips men bare.

22. Echoing Weber's notion of modernity founded in the separation of life spheres, Bruno Latour asserts in *We Have Never Been Modern* (trans. C. Porter [Cambridge, MA: Harvard University Press, 1993]) that the belief in the ability to separate spheres is the foundation of modern action.

23. Michael Lewis, *Liar's Poker* (New York: Penguin, 1989), 119–20.

Chapter Six

1. Karin Knorr Cetina and Urs Bruegger, "The Market as an Object of Attachment: Exploring Post-Social Relations in Financial Markets," *Canadian Journal of Sociology* 25, no. 2 (2000): 141–68.

2. Futures are traded in auctions markets. According to Charles Smith's argument in *Auctions: The Social Construction of Value* (New York: Free Press, 1989), auctions thrive where the value of objects is ambiguous or uncertain. Futures contracts are just such objects. They represent an obligation to buy or sell a financial commodity weeks or months in the future. Traders constantly process events that affect national economies and new information about the future health or weakness of stock markets and adjust their assessment of a financial commodity's value accordingly. This evaluation is reflected in the changing price of the commodity.

3. For Foucault, the art of self-governance involves techniques for "training of oneself by oneself" (Herbert Dreyfus and Paul Rabinow, *Michel Foucault: Beyond Structuralism and Hermeneutics* [Chicago: University of Chicago Press, 1983], 246). Such techniques treat the self as an object to be formed in harmony with a specific end. Traders strive to eliminate nonmarket influences in order to create a person who can be absorbed completely in the rhythms of the market. They work to submit himself to the authority of the market, stripped of their own thoughts, analyses, and desires.

4. Michel Foucault has most famously employed the concept of discipline in *Discipline and Punish: The Birth of the Prison* (1977; repr., New York: Vintage, 1995). Discipline, in this sense, produces individuals, yet Foucault's concept of ethical work is more relevant to traders' practices of discipline. Paul Rabinow states that "[t]he task of ethical work for Foucault is to establish the right relationship between intellect and character in the context of practical affairs" (*Ethics: Subjectivity and Truth* [New York: New Press, 1997], 1: xxxiii). Traders forge this relationship of the self to the self in and for the practice of speculation. The process of Foucault's discipline is inverted. Trading as a performance of discipline sublimates the individual and his particular interiority to the larger market.

5. Traders may also try to reap a profit from the difference between the price bid and the price offered, called the "bid/ask spread." They buy at the lower price and sell at the higher price (or vice versa), taking advantage of the insider's "edge." The spread is the market-makers' premium, but it is not always easy or available to take.

6. Viviana Zelizer, in *The Social Meaning of Money* (Princeton, NJ: Princeton University Press, 1997), has shown that people create specific uses and meanings around money as they "cope with their multiple social relations." Her point, against the background of the classical theories of Weber and Simmel, is that people use money to maintain social ties, and these ties mark money. Money cannot simply create "sensualists without spirit" as Weber feared; rather, in Zelizer's analysis, money is subservient to logics of the family, charity, and gifts. Yet the ability of money to dis-

tance social ties must also be taken as an anthropological subject. If we begin with Zelizer's observation that social connections personalize money, the trader's techniques of separation are all the more surprising. On the trading floor money must be crafted into a technology of social distance; such distance is not a property that inheres in money per se. The trader's reimagining of dollars as ticks shows just how difficult it is to strip money of its power as a social connector.

7. The most profitable traders are the most willing to take losses quickly; see Peter R. Locke and Steven C. Mann, *Do Professional Traders Exhibit Loss Realization Aversion?* (Washington, DC: Commodity Futures Trading Commission, 1999). In the language of behavioral finance, this willingness to take risks with losses that may erode profits further is called "loss realization aversion," a term drawn from the "prospect theory" of Daniel Kahneman and Amos Tversky ("Prospect Theory: An Analysis of Decision under Risk," *Econometrica* 2 [1979]: 263–92). Locke and Mann claim that critics of behavioral finance will find satisfaction in the fact that the more successful traders demonstrate less loss aversion than those who draw fewer profits, proving that the gainful traders behave "rationally" according to the profit motive. However, the strict economic rationality that the critics laud is not simply a characteristic of successful traders that trumps the "irrational" weaknesses of the others. Both individually and collectively, traders consciously consider the problem of action under uncertainty. The norms and practices of discipline—the culture of the trading floor—encourage traders to reflect on and limit their inclination to gamble with losses. These techniques and models of disciplined behavior make traders appear more like the rational actors of orthodox finance than like the biased and irrational actors of behavioral finance. Culture works to produce traders whose actions confirm the models of rationality; it is not the agent of irrationality, as is so frequently assumed.

8. The bias for the present and the short time increments of market action are not shared by other financial actors. Financial strategists for investment banks or even mortgage brokers who are looking to hedge the risks of simple interest rates work with time frames that can look months into the future. Scalping is a form of speculation particular to the market makers who provide consistent liquidity for futures markets.

9. Richard Sennett has pointed out that "risk-taking . . . lacks the quality of a narrative, in which one event leads to the next"; see *Corrosion of Character: The Personal Consequences of Work in the New Capitalism* (New York: W. W. Norton, 1998), 83.

10. Robert Koppel, *The Tao of Trading: Discovering a Simpler Path to Success* (Chicago: Dearborn Trade, 1998).

11. Their terms hue closely to Csikszentmihalyi's description of optimal experiences; see Mihaly Csikszentmihalyi, *Flow: The Psychology of Optimal Experience* (New York: Harper & Row, 1990).

12. Henri Hubert and Marcel Mauss's work on sacrifice helps to illuminate the problem of actors engaging a divine presence: "Sacrifice is a religious act that can only be carried out in a religious atmosphere and by means of essentially religious agents. But, in general, before the ceremony neither sacrifier nor sacrificer, nor place, instruments or victim possess this to a suitable degree. The first phase of the sacrifice is intended to impart it to them. They are profane; and their condition must be changed. . . . All that touches upon the gods must be divine; the sacrifier is

obliged to become a god himself in order to be capable of acting upon them" (*Sacrifice: Its Nature and Function* [Chicago: University of Chicago Press, 1964], 19–20).

Chapter Seven

1. Nick Leeson, the currency trader who bankrupted the venerable Barings Bank in the trading pits of Singapore, is the most infamous of this breed. He has chronicled his exploits from a cell in a Singapore prison; see his *Rogue Trader* (London: Little, Brown, 1996).

2. Jonathan Crary, *Techniques of the Observer: On Vision and Modernity in the Nineteenth Century* (Cambridge, MA: MIT Press, 1990).

3. Karin Knorr Cetina and Urs Bruegger, "The Market as an Object of Attachment: Exploring Post-Social Relations in Financial Markets," *Canadian Journal of Sociology* 25, no. 2 (2000): 141–68.

4. The narrative of progressive rationalization is, of course, most familiar to us from the work of Max Weber. In "Science as a Vocation" (in Gerth and Mills, *From Max Weber*), he bluntly states, "The fate of our times is characterized by rationalization and intellectualization"(155), a position still consistent with the work of abstraction in futures. It is important to distinguish between the power of rationalization as an ideal in the financial industry that parallels Weber and Simmel's accounts of progressive rationalization and an anthropological analysis of rationalization that takes this ideal as a social fact.

5. The social context of financial interpretation is evident in the friendships and feverish affect of pit traders. Looking first at the face-to-face context of open outcry markets, where the density of social life is overwhelming, we can observe and become attuned to the social dimensions of online calculations. This sensitivity is especially important where self-conscious rationalization has actively sought to eliminate the social as an element of economic calculations. The problem is not one of a dualistic division between face-to-face and online transactions. Rather, the problem lies in how rationalized technological systems create a specific context for financial calculation.

6. Bruce G. Carruthers and Barry Cohen, "Knowledge of Failure or Failure of Knowledge? Bankruptcy, Credit, and Credit Reporting in the Nineteenth-Century United States," paper presented at the American Sociological Association meetings, Washington, D.C., August 2000.

7. Theodore Porter, *Trust in Numbers: The Pursuit of Objectivity in Science and Public Life* (Princeton, NJ: Princeton University Press, 1995); Michael Power, *The Audit Society: Rituals of Verification* (New York: Oxford University Press, 1997); and Mary Poovey, *A History of the Modern Fact: Problems of Knowledge in the Sciences of Wealth and Society* (Chicago: University of Chicago Press, 1998).

8. Chicago Board of Trade, *Action in the Marketplace* (Chicago: Board of Trade of the City of Chicago, 1997). The difference between the bid and ask is called the "spread." Ideally the trader can make money buying at the bid and selling at the offer, pocketing the difference, but this method is not always available. Bids and offers theoretically represent the totality of supply and demand for a product in a given moment. Market participants must be able to see all the bids and offers in the market to evaluate market conditions accurately.

9. See Paul Rabinow's "Representations Are Social Facts" (in *Essays in the Anthropology of Reason* [Princeton, NJ: Princeton University Press, 1996], 29–58) for a critique of this epistemology in the social sciences. In the case of financial markets, the epistemologies of financial designers become social facts as they direct the construction of technologies in search of "correct representations."

10. The CBOT created the pit structure to solve problems that arose as the market space became overcrowded with eager speculators. Originating in the agricultural trade of the Midwest, the CBOT was established by men trading certificates of grain ownership to be delivered several months down the line from farms in Nebraska, Iowa, or Illinois to the Chicago grain elevators; see William Cronon, *Nature's Metropolis: Chicago and the Great West* (New York: W. W. Norton, 1991). By 1869 trading at the CBOT had become so popular and crowded that the speculators could not see all the bids and offers available. Market reporters complained in the pages of their daily papers that traders in search of better sight lines were climbing onto their desks and obstructing the reporters' vision. After trying out several shapes for a raised structure that would provide better views of the traders in the market, the CBOT introduced the octagonal pits in 1869; see William D. Faloon, *Market Maker: A Sesquicentennial Look at the Chicago Board of Trade* (Chicago: Board of Trade of the City of Chicago, 1998).

11. In this sense Alan Lind and his fellow designers resemble Paul Rabinow's depiction of technicians of general ideas (*French Modern: Norms and Forms of the Social Environment* [Chicago: University of Chicago Press, 1995]): they put into practice normative ideas of economic action. They are self-conscious intellectuals gravitating to and instantiating ideals of rationalization and designing economic abstractions to facilitate practices more closely resembling perfect competition.

12. In *We Have Never Been Modern* (Cambridge, MA: Harvard University Press, 1993), Bruno Latour discusses "purification," the division of the social from the natural, as a hallmark of modernism. Here, the numerical representation helps to rid the financial arena of social influence. With numbers, the economic sphere is construed as a space of natural competition.

13. In *Plans and Situated Actions* (New York: Cambridge University Press, 1987), Lucy Suchman argues that purposeful action is "fundamentally concrete and embodied." Actions are "taken in the context of particular concrete circumstances." They are "situated" and not the outcome of a process of abstract planning.

14. I use *technological frame* to indicate how technology shapes the content it provides to the user. Wiebe Bijker has used the concept differently. Bijker uses *technological frame* to describe "the ways in which relevant social groups attribute various meanings to an artifact" (Wiebe Bijker, Thomas P. Hughes, and Trevor Pinch, *The Social Construction of Technological Systems: New Directions in the Sociology and History of Technology* [Cambridge, MA: MIT Press, 1989], 108).

15. Frank Knight in his classic work *Risk, Uncertainty and Profit* defines uncertainty as the condition of judgment and of entrepreneurial profit: "With uncertainty entirely absent, every individual being in possession of perfect knowledge of the situation, there would be no occasion for anything of the nature of responsible management or control of productive activity" (*Risk, Uncertainty and Profit* [Chicago: University of Chicago Press, 1971], 267). Knight's use of uncertainty highlights problems

of economic action where risks are not calculable. I prefer to use *ambiguity* rather than *uncertainty* to underscore the many possible interpretations of a present situation. Traders could be considered *informational entrepreneurs* because they create profit-seeking interpretations of market direction out of this ambiguity. This view follows Pat O'Malley's description of the *uncertain subjects* of neoliberalism rather than appealing to older formulations of entrepreneurship that fit a paradigm of rational modernization. See "Moral Uncertainties: Contract Law and Distinctions between Speculation, Gambling and Insurance," in *Risk and Morality,* ed. R. V. Ericson and A. Doyle, (Toronto: University of Toronto Press, 2003), 231–57.

16. John Murphy, *Technical Analysis of the Financial Markets* (New York: New York Institute of Finance, 1999), 64.

17. Differences in opinions and interpretation yield opposing views. These contrasting outlooks on the future direction of the market allow for every buyer to find a seller and every seller to find a buyer. At the same time, anticipating and acting on the presumed interpretations of other traders in the market is a common profit-making strategy that can create a self-fulfilling prophecy in price action.

18. Murphy, *Financial Markets,* 60.

19. Wayne Baker has shown how, in large pits, traders break up into trading areas within the pit, undermining the ideal of competitiveness. The noise of trading and the potential errors of trading with a physically distant partner encourage traders to focus their attention on the area closest to them; see Wayne E. Baker, "The Social Structure of a National Securities Market," *American Journal of Sociology* 89, no. 4 (1984): 775–811.

20. Chicago Board of Trade, *CBOT Handbook* (Chicago: Board of Trade of the City of Chicago, 1993).

21. Joshua D. Coval and Tyler Shumway, "Is Noise Just Sound?" CBOT Educational Research Foundation Paper, 1998.

22. See Burton Malkiel, *A Random Walk Down Wall Street* (New York: W. W. Norton, 1996), and Peter Bernstein, *Capital Ideas* (New York: Free Press, 1992) for a synopsis of the "random walk" in stock and commodities pricing and its implications for traders, investors, and financial theory. According to Malkiel, "A random walk is one in which future steps or directions cannot be predicted on the basis of past actions. In the stock market, it means that short-run changes in stock prices cannot be predicted" (Malkiel, *Random Walk,* 24).

23. The interface that traders use at Perkins Silver is not the only one available. Members of Eurex have access to the exchange's stock interface, which is also numerically based but visually more rigid than the E-trader model. Earlier interfaces, like those for the now defunct CBOT Project A trading system, tried to replicate the face-to-face environment of the pit by associating names and personal trade histories with each exchange. The precursor to the Eurex exchange, the DTB (Deustcheterminebourse), never operated with a pit system. Its electronic market has always relied strictly on numbers.

24. Paul Rabinow, *French Modern: Norms and Forms of the Social Environment* (Chicago: University of Chicago Press, 1995).

25. Porter, Theodore, *Trust in Numbers: The Pursuit of Objectivity in Science and Public Life* (Princeton, NJ: Princeton University Press, 1995).

26. The term *disintermediation* came into vogue in the 1980s as a way of describing the development of new instruments, such as mortgage-backed assets, that allowed companies to borrow directly from the market rather than going through a commercial lender. The techniques of disintermediation removed institutional ties and drew companies to the "core" processes of the market. The same rationality operates in the logic of reducing the market representation to numbers.

27. John S. Brown, and Paul Duguid, *The Social Life of Information* (Boston: Harvard Business School Press, 2000).

28. I was practicing a technique called "spreading" in ten, five, and two-year German treasury bond futures nicknamed the Bund, Bobl, and Shaz. Spreading is a technique that takes advantage of the difference in volatility between bonds of different durations. The price of a ten-year bond is more volatile than that of a two-year bond because the longer time frame introduces more opportunities for changing economic conditions and greater uncertainties. A spreader takes opposite positions in each of two instruments using the more stable instrument to limit the loss potential of a position in the more volatile contract.

29. This background communication is part of the "ecologies of evaluative principals" of the trading room; see Daniel Beunza and David Stark, "Tools of the Trade: The Socio-Technology of Arbitrage in a Wall Street Trading Room," *Industrial and Corporate Change* 13, no. 2 (2004): 369–400.

Conclusion

1. Max Weber, *Economy and Society* (Berkeley and Los Angeles: University of California Press, 1978), 1:636.

2. Donald MacKenzie and Yuval Millo, "Constructing a Market, Performing Theory: The Historical Sociology of a Financial Derivatives Exchange," *American Journal of Sociology* 109, no. 1 (2003): 107–45.

3. Economic sociologists Paul DiMaggio, Walter Powell, and Neil Fligstein have developed Bourdieu's language of "fields" to understand economic practice. Fields are defined primarily by the distribution of actors in social space. Tracing technological transformations reminds us that social space and the physical materials of connection are interdependent. See Paul DiMaggio and Walter Powell, "The Iron Cage Revisited: Institutional Isomorphism and Collective Rationality in Organizational Fields," *American Sociological Review* 48 (1983): 147–60; and Neil Fligstein, *The Architecture of Markets : An Economic Sociology of Twenty-first-Century Capitalist Societies* (Princeton, NJ: Princeton University Press, 2001).

4. Daniel Miller refers to this as "virtualism"; see "Conclusion: A Theory of Virtualism," in James G. Carrier and Daniel Miller, eds., *Virtualism: A New Political Economy* (New York: Berg, 1998), 187–217.

5. Michel Callon, "Introduction: The Embeddedness of Economic Markets in Economics," in *The Laws of the Markets*, ed. Michel Callon (Malden, MA: Blackwell, 1998), 1–57; Bill Maurer, *Mutual Life, Ltd: Islamic Banking, Alternative Currencies, Lateral Reason* (Princeton, NJ: Princeton University Press, 2005); Donald MacKenzie, "Social Connectivities in Global Financial Markets," *Environment and Planning D: Society and Space* 22 (2004): 83–101.

6. Paul Rabinow, in *French Modern: Norms and Forms of the Social Environment* (Chicago: University of Chicago Press, 1995) calls these translators "technicians of general ideas."

7. These are not the only materials used to rationalize markets. The standardization of contracts, for instance, is a crucial precondition for the operation of futures markets that I describe. However, the daily work of rationalization represents a different order of action, one that requires tweaking and adjustment rather than the construction of systems.

8. Bruce Carruthers, *City of Capital* (Princeton, NJ: Princeton University Press, 1996); David Kynaston, *The City of London* (London: Pimlico, 1988); Andrew Leyshon and Nigel Thrift, *Money/Space* (New York: Routledge, 1997).

9. William Cronon, *Nature's Metropolis: Chicago and the Great West* (New York: W. W. Norton, 1991); Donald L. Miller, *City of the Century: The Epic of Chicago and the Making of America* (New York: Touchstone, 1996).

10. Manuel Castells calls this sharing of connectivity without sharing of territory, "the space of flows"; see *The Rise of the Network Society* (New York: Blackwell, 1996).

11. Arjun Appadurai calls these "technoscapes" and "financescapes," adding the suffix *-scape* to denote the "fluid irregular shapes . . . that characterize international capital" (*Modernity at Large: Cultural Dimensions of Globalization* [Minneapolis: University of Minnesota Press, 1996], 33).

12. Castells, *Network Society*.

13. Saskia Sassen, *The Global City* (Princeton, NJ: Princeton University Press, 2001).

14. Peter J. Taylor, *World City Network: A Global Urban Analysis* (New York: Routledge, 2004).

15. Andrew Barry, *Political Machines: Governing a Technological Society* (London: Athlone Press, 2001); Wiebe Bijker, Thomas P. Hughes, and Trevor Pinch, *Social Construction of Technological Systems* (Cambridge, MA: MIT Press, 1989).

16. Barry, *Political Machines*.

17. Thomas F. Gieryn, "What Buildings Do," *Theory and Society* 31, no. 1 (2002): 41.

18. Castells, *Network Society*.

19. This parallels Simmel's classic argument that money functions to objectify value across both social and geographic distance. It also emphasizes Simmel's observation that the use of money entails trust in the institutions that produce it. For Simmel, this meant the state; futures contracts, however, require trust in the CBOT, its accounting practices, and its mechanisms for clearing trades; see Georg Simmel, *The Philosophy of Money* (1907; repr., New York: Routledge, 1990).

20. Karin Knorr Cetina and Urs Bruegger, "Global Microstructures: The Virtual Societies of Financial Markets," *American Journal of Sociology* 107, no. 4 (2002): 905–50.

21. Beunza, Daniel, and David Stark, "Tools of the Trade: The Socio-Technology of Arbitrage in a Wall Street Trading Room," *Industrial and Corporate Change* 13, no. 2 (2004): 369–400.

22. Niklas Luhmann, "Describing the Future," in *Observations on Modernity* (Stanford, CA: Stanford University Press, 1998), 69–70.

23. In this way, traders form an "epistemic community"; see Karin Knorr Cetina, *Epistemic Cultures: How the Sciences Make Knowledge* (Cambridge, MA: Harvard University Press, 1999).

24. George Lipsitz, *The Possessive Investment in Whiteness* (Philadelphia, PA: Temple University Press, 1998).

25. Mitchell Abolafia (*Making Markets: Opportunism and Restraint on Wall Street* [Cambridge, MA: Harvard University Press, 1996]); Wayne Baker ("The Social Structure of a National Securities Market," *American Journal of Sociology* 89, no. 4 [1984]: 775–811); and Donald MacKenzie, in "Social Connectivities," have shown that these "local aspects" of global connections can affect prices and other basic market operations.

26. Kris Olds and Nigel Thrift identify this location in the present with the management consultants and others who populate the "cultural circuit of capital," noting that it is "meant to produce a kind of dynamic equilibrium in which the brink (the 'edge of chaos') is the place to be" ("Cultures on the Brink: Reengineering the Soul of Capitalism—On a Global Scale," in *Global Assemblages: Technology, Politics, and Ethics as Anthropological Problems*, ed. A. Ong and S. J. Collier [New York: Blackwell, 2005], 274). The confluence of expert and practitioner knowledge is remarkable, and underscores the idea that traders' self-production signals the human possibilities and costs of working in a world that is permanently on the edge of the future.

27. In this way, the new representational modes of the trading screen extend the logic of the ticker tape, an information technology invented in 1867; see Alex Preda, "On Ticks and Tapes: Financial Knowledge, Communicative Practices, and Information Technologies on Nineteenth-Century Financial Markets," paper presented at New York Conference on the Social Studies of Finance, Columbia University, May 3–4, 2002.

28. Roy Smith and Walter Ingo, *Global Banking* (New York: Oxford University Press, 2003).

Abolafia, Mitchell. *Making Markets: Opportunism and Restraint on Wall Street.* Cambridge, MA: Harvard University Press, 1996.

Abu-Lughod, Janet. *New York, Chicago, Los Angeles: America's Global Cities.* Minneapolis: University of Minnesota Press, 1999.

Agnew, Jean-Christophe. *Worlds Apart: The Market and the Theater in Anglo-American Thought, 1550–1750.* New York: Cambridge University Press, 1986.

Amin, Ash, and Nigel Thrift. "Introduction." In *Cultural Economy Reader,* ed. A. Amin and N. Thrift, x–xxx. New York: Blackwell, 2004.

Andreas, A. T. *History of Chicago. From the Earliest Period to the Present Time.* Chicago: A. T. Andreas, 1884.

Appadurai, Arjun. *The Social Life of Things.* New York: Cambridge, 1986.

——— . *Modernity at Large: Cultural Dimensions of Globalization.* Minneapolis: University of Minnesota Press, 1996.

Baker, Tom, and Jonathan Simon. "Embracing Risk." In *Embracing Risk: The Changing Culture of Insurance and Responsibility,* ed. T. Baker and J. Simon, 1–25. Chicago: University of Chicago Press, 2002.

Baker, Wayne E. "The Social Structure of a National Securities Market." *American Journal of Sociology* 89, no. 4 (1984): 775–811.

Bakhtin, Mikhail. *Rabelais and His World.* Trans. H. Iswolsky. Bloomington: Indiana University Press, 1984.

Barry, Andrew. *Political Machines: Governing a Technological Society.* London: Athlone Press, 2001.

Barry, Andrew, Thomas Osborne, and Nikolas S. Rose. *Foucault and Political Reason: Liberalism, Neo-liberalism and Rationalities of Government.* Chicago: University of Chicago Press, 1996.

Bataille, Georges. *The Accursed Share.* Vol. 1. New York: Zone Books, 1989. Orig. pub. in 1967.

Beck, Ulrich. *Risk Society: Towards a New Modernity.* London: Sage, 1992.

Becker, Gary. "Nobel Lecture: The Economic Way of Looking at Behavior." *Journal of Political Economy* 101, no. 3 (1993): 385–409.

Bender, Thomas, and William R. Taylor. "Culture and Architecture: Some Aesthetic Tensions in the Shaping of Modern New York City." In *Visions of the Mod-*

ern City: Essays in History, Art, and Literature, ed. W. Sharpe and L. Wallock, 189–219. Baltimore, MD: Johns Hopkins University Press, 1987.

Bernstein, Peter L. *Capital Ideas: The Improbable Origins of Modern Wall Street.* New York: Free Press, 1992.

Beunza, Daniel, and David Stark. "Tools of the Trade: The Socio-technology of Arbitrage in a Wall Street Trading Room." *Industrial and Corporate Change* 13, no. 2 (2004): 369–400.

Bijker, Wiebe, Thomas P. Hughes, and Trevor Pinch. *Social Construction of Technological Systems.* Cambridge, MA: MIT Press, 1989.

Boholm, Asa. "The Cultural Nature of Risk: Can There Be an Anthropology of Uncertainty?" *Ethnos* 68, no. 2 (2003): 159–78.

Bourdieu, Pierre. "The Sense of Honor." In *Algeria 1960*, 93–123. New York: Cambridge University Press, 1979.

———. *Practical Reason.* Cambridge: Polity Press, 1998.

Bourdieu, Pierre, and Loïc J. D. Wacquant. *An Invitation to Reflexive Sociology.* Chicago: University of Chicago Press, 1992.

Brown, John S., and Paul Duguid. *The Social Life of Information.* Boston: Harvard Business School Press, 2000.

Buford, Bill. *Among the Thugs.* New York: Vintage, 1990.

Burawoy, Michael. *Manufacturing Consent: Changes in the Labor Process under Monopoly Capitalism.* Chicago: University of Chicago Press, 1979.

Burchell, Graham. "Liberal Government and Techniques of the Self." In Barry, Osborne, and Rose, *Foucault and Political Reason*, 19–36. Chicago: University of Chicago Press, 1996.

Burchell, Graham, Colin Gordon, and Peter Miller, eds. *The Foucault Effect: Studies in Governmentality.* Chicago: University of Chicago Press, 1991.

Callon, Michel. "Introduction: The Embeddedness of Economic Markets in Economics." In *The Laws of the Markets*, ed. Michel Callon, 1–57. Malden, MA: Blackwell, 1998.

Caplan, Pat. "Introduction: Risk Revisited." In *Risk Revisited*, ed. P. Caplan, 1–28. London: Pluto Press, 2000.

Carey, James W. "Technology and Ideology: The Case of the Telegraph." In *Communication as Culture: Essays on Media and Society*, 201–29. 1988. Reprint, New York: Routledge, 1992.

Carrier, James G. "Abstraction in Western Economic Practice." In Carrier and Miller, eds., *Virtualism.*

Carrier, James G., and Daniel Miller, eds. *Virtualism: A New Political Economy.* New York: Berg, 1998.

———. "From Private Virtue to Public Vice." In *Anthropological Theory Today*, ed. H. Moore, 24–47. Malden, MA: Polity, 1999.

Carruthers, Bruce. *City of Capital.* Princeton, NJ: Princeton University Press, 1996.

Carruthers, Bruce G., and Barry Cohen. "Knowledge of Failure or Failure of Knowledge? Bankruptcy, Credit, and Credit Reporting in the Nineteenth-Century United States." Paper presented at the American Sociological Association meetings, Washington, D.C., August 2000.

Carruthers, Bruce, and Arthur L. Stinchcombe. "The Social Structure of Liquidity: Flexibility, Markets, and States." *Theory and Society* 28 (1999): 353–82.

Castel, Robert. "From Dangerousness to Risk." In Burchell, Gordon, and Miller, *The Foucault Effect*, 281–98.

Castells, Manuel. *The Rise of the Network Society.* Malden, MA: Blackwell, 1996.

Chancellor, Edward. *Devil Take the Hindmost: A History of Financial Speculation.* New York: Plume, 1999.

Chicago Board of Trade. *CBOT Handbook.* Chicago: Board of Trade of the City of Chicago, 1993.

——. *Action in the Marketplace.* Chicago: Board of Trade of the City of Chicago, 1997.

Clifford, James. *Routes: Travel and Translation in the Late Twentieth Century.* Cambridge, MA: Harvard University Press, 1997.

Comaroff, Jean. "Occult Economies and the Violence of Abstraction: Notes from the South African Postcolony." *American Ethnologist* 26, no. 2 (1999): 279–303.

Comaroff, Jean, and John Comaroff. "Millennial Capitalism: First Thoughts on a Second Coming." *Public Culture* 12, no. 2 (2000): 291–343.

Commission on the Future of Multi-Ethnic Britain. *The Report.* London: Profile Books, 2000.

Connell, Robert W. *Masculinities.* Berkeley and Los Angeles: University of California Press, 1995.

Coval, Joshua D., and Tyler Shumway. "Is Noise Just Sound?" CBOT Educational Research Foundation Paper, 1998.

Cowing, Cedric B. *Populists, Plungers, and Progressives: A Social History of Stock and Commodity Speculation, 1890–1936.* Princeton, NJ: Princeton University Press, 1965.

Crary, Jonathan. *Techniques of the Observer: On Vision and Modernity in the Nineteenth Century.* Cambridge, MA: MIT Press, 1990.

Cronon, William. *Nature's Metropolis: Chicago and the Great West.* New York: W. W. Norton, 1991.

Csikszentmihalyi, Mihaly. *Flow: The Psychology of Optimal Experience.* New York: Harper & Row, 1990.

Davis, Mike. *City of Quartz: Excavating the Future in Los Angeles.* New York: Verso, 1990.

de Sola Pool, Ithiel, ed. *The Social Impact of the Telephone.* Cambridge, MA: MIT Press, 1977.

di Leonardo, Micaela. "White Ethnicities, Identity Politics and Baby Bear's Chair." *Social Text* 41 (1994): 165–89.

DiMaggio, Paul, and Walter Powell. "The Iron Cage Revisited: Institutional Isomorphism and Collective Rationality in Organizational Fields." *American Sociological Review* 48 (1983): 147–60.

Doran, James. "FBI Called as NYSE Merger Turns Ugly." *The Australian,* July, 28, 2005.

Douglas, Mary, and Aaron Wildavsky. *Risk and Culture.* Berkeley and Los Angeles: University of California Press, 1982.

Dreyfus, Herbert, and Paul Rabinow. *Michel Foucault: Beyond Structuralism and Hermeneutics*. Chicago: University of Chicago Press, 1983.

Elias, Norbert. *The Civilizing Process*. Oxford: Blackwell, 1978.

Espeland, Wendy, and Mitchell L. Stevens. "Commensuration as a Social Process." *Annual Review of Sociology* 24 (1998): 313–43.

Ewald, Francois. "Insurance and Risk." In Burchell, Gordon, and Miller, *The Foucault Effect*, 197–210.

Faloon, William D. *Market Maker: A Sesquicentennial Look at the Chicago Board of Trade*. Chicago: Board of Trade of the City of Chicago, 1998.

Faubion, James, ed. *Foucault: Aesthetics, Method, and Epistemology*. New York: New Press, 1998.

———. "Introduction." In Faubion, *Foucault*, xiii–xlii.

Ferris, William G. *The Grain Traders: The Story of the Chicago Board of Trade*. East Lansing: Michigan State University Press, 1988.

Fischer, Claude S. *America Calling: A Social History of the Telephone to 1940*. Berkeley and Los Angeles: University of California Press, 1992.

Fischer, Michael M. J. *Emergent Forms of Life and the Anthropological Voice*. Durham, NC: Duke University Press, 2003.

Fligstein, Neil. *The Architecture of Markets: An Economic Sociology of Twenty-first-Century Capitalist Societies*. Princeton, NJ: Princeton University Press, 2001.

Foucault, Michel. *The History of Sexuality*. Vol. 2. *The Use of Pleasure*. New York: Penguin, 1985.

———. *Discipline and Punish: The Birth of the Prison*. New York: Vintage, 1995. Orig. pub. in 1977.

———. "Polemics, Politics, and Problematizations: An Interview with Michel Foucault." In *Ethics: Subjectivity and Truth*, ed. Paul Rabinow, 111–19. New York: New Press, 1997. Orig. pub. in 1984.

———. "A Preface to Transgression." In Faubion, *Foucault*, 69–87.

———. "The Thought of the Outside." In Faubion, ed. *Foucault*, 147–69.

Galassi, Peter. *Andreas Gursky*. New York: Museum of Modern Art, 2001.

Garland, David. "Rise of Risk." In *Risk and Morality*, ed. R. Ericson and A. Doyle, 48–86. Toronto: University of Toronto Press, 2003.

Garsten, Christina, and Anna Hasselstrom. "Risky Business: Discourses of Risk and (Ir)responsibility in Globalizing Markets." *Ethnos* 68, no. 2 (2003): 249–70.

Geertz, Clifford. "Deep Play: Notes on the Balinese Cockfight." In *Interpretation of Cultures*, 412–53. New York: Basic Books, 1973.

———. "Suq: The Bazaar Economy in Sefrou." In *Meaning and Order in Moroccan Society*, ed. C. Geertz, H. Geertz, and L. Rosen, 123–313. New York: Cambridge University Press, 1979.

———. *Available Light: Anthropological Reflections on Philosophical Topics*. Princeton, NJ: Princeton University Press, 2000.

Gerth, H. H., and C. Wright Mills, eds. *From Max Weber*. New York: Oxford University Press, 1946.

Giddens, Anthony. *The Consequences of Modernity*. Stanford, CA: Stanford University Press, 1991.

——. *Modernity and Self-identity: Self and Society in the Late Modern Age.* Cambridge: Polity Press, 1991.

Gieryn, Thomas F. "What Buildings Do." *Theory and Society* 31, no. 1 (2002): 35–74.

Glick, Ira O. "A Social Psychological Study of Futures Trading." PhD diss., Department of Sociology, University of Chicago, 1957.

Goffman, Erving. "Where the Action Is." In *Interaction Ritual*, 149–270. New York: Pantheon, 1967.

——. *The Presentation of Self in Everyday Life.* Harmondsworth: Penguin, 1990. Orig. pub. in 1959.

Gordon, Colin. "Governmental Rationality: An Introduction." In Burchell, Gordon, and Miller, *The Foucault Effect*, 1–54.

Granovetter, Mark. "Economic Action and Social Structure: The Problem of Embeddedness." *American Journal of Sociology* 91, no. 3 (1985): 481–510.

Greising, David, and Laurie Morse. *Brokers, Bagmen, and Moles: Fraud and Corruption in the Chicago Futures Markets.* New York: John Wiley & Sons, 1991.

Gudeman, Stephen. *The Anthropology of Economy.* Malden, MA: Blackwell, 2001.

Harvey, David. *The Urban Experience.* Baltimore, MD: Johns Hopkins University Press, 1989.

——. *The Condition of Postmodernity.* Malden, MA: Blackwell, 1993.

Henwood, Doug. *Wall Street.* New York: Verso, 1997.

Hertz, Ellen. *The Trading Crowd: An Ethnography of the Shanghai Stock Market.* New York: Cambridge University Press, 1998.

Hirschman, Albert O. *The Passions and the Interests: Political Arguments for Capitalism before its Triumph.* Princeton, NJ: Princeton University Press, 1997. Orig. pub. in 1977.

Hochschild, Arlie Russell. *The Managed Heart: Commercialization of Human Feeling.* Berkeley and Los Angeles: University of California Press, 1983.

Holmes, Douglas R., and George E. Marcus. "Cultures of Expertise and the Management of Globalization: The Refunctioning of Ethnography." In *Global Assemblages: Technology, Politics, and Ethics as Anthropological Problems*, ed. A. Ong and S. Collier, 235–52. New York: Blackwell, 2005.

Holston, James. *The Modernist City: An Anthropological Critique of Brasília.* Chicago: University of Chicago Press, 1989.

Hounshell, David A. *From the American System to Mass Production, 1800–1932: The Development of Manufacturing Technology in the United States.* Baltimore, MD: Johns Hopkins University Press, 1984.

Hubert, Henri, and Marcel Mauss. *Sacrifice: Its Nature and Function.* Chicago: University of Chicago Press, 1964.

Hughes, Thomas P. *Networks of Power: Electrification in Western Society, 1880–1930.* Baltimore, MD: Johns Hopkins University Press, 1983.

——. "The Evolution of Large Technological Systems." In W. Bijker, T. P. Hughes, and T. Pinch, *Social Construction of Technological Systems*, 51–82.

Hutton, Will. *The State We're In.* London: Vintage, 1996.

Jameson, Frederic. "Culture and Finance Capital." *Critical Inquiry* 24 (1997): 246–65.

Kahneman, Daniel, and Amos Tversky. "Prospect Theory: An Analysis of Decision under Risk." *Econometrica* 2 (1979): 263–92.

Kamin, Blair. "A New Fortress for Financial Wars." *Chicago Tribune*, February 19, 1997.

Kindleberger, Charles. *Manias, Panics and Crashes: A History of Financial Crises.* New York: Basic Books, 1989.

Knight, Frank. *Risk, Uncertainty and Profit.* 1921. Reprint, Chicago: University of Chicago Press, 1971.

Knorr Cetina, Karin. *Epistemic Cultures: How the Sciences Make Knowledge.* Cambridge, MA: Harvard University Press, 1999.

Knorr Cetina, Karin, and Urs Bruegger. "The Market as an Object of Attachment: Exploring Post-Social Relations in Financial Markets." *Canadian Journal of Sociology* 25, no. 2 (2000): 141–68.

———. "Global Microstructures: The Virtual Societies of Financial Markets." *American Journal of Sociology* 107, no. 4 (2002): 905–50.

Koppel, Robert. *The Tao of Trading: Discovering a Simpler Path to Success.* Chicago: Dearborn Trade, 1998.

Kynaston, David. *The City of London.* London: Pimlico, 1988.

———. *LIFFE: A Market and Its Makers.* Cambridge: Granta Editions, 1997.

Lakoff, Andrew, and Stephen Collier. "Ethics and the Anthropology of Modern Reason." *Anthropological Theory* 4, no. 4 (2004): 419–34.

Latour, Bruno. *Science in Action: How to Follow Scientists and Engineers Through Society.* Cambridge, MA: Harvard University Press, 1987.

———. *We Have Never Been Modern.* Trans. C. Porter. Cambridge, MA: Harvard University Press, 1993.

Law, John. "Technology and Heterogeneous Engineering: The Case of Portuguese Expansion." In W. Bijker, T. P. Hughes, and T. Pinch, *Social Construction of Technological Systems,* 111–34.

———, ed. *A Sociology of Monsters: Essays on Power, Technology and Domination.* New York: Routledge, 1991.

———. *Aircraft Stories: Decentering the Object in Technoscience.* Durham, NC: Duke University Press, 2002.

Le Bon, Gustave. *The Crowd: A Study of the Popular Mind.* New York: Penguin Books, 1977.

Lee, Benjamin, and Edward LiPuma. "Cultures of Circulation: The Imaginations of Modernity." *Public Culture* 14, no. 1 (2002):191–213.

Leeson, Nick. *Rogue Trader.* London: Little, Brown, 1996.

Leidner, Robin. *Fast Food, Fast Talk: Service Work and the Routinization of Everyday Life.* Berkeley and Los Angeles: University of California Press, 1993.

Levy, Ron. "The Mutuality of Risk and Community: The Adjudication of Community Notification Statutes." *Economy and Society* 29, no. 4 (2000): 578–601.

Lewis, Michael. *Liar's Poker.* New York: Penguin, 1989.

Leyshon, Andrew, and Nigel Thrift. *Money/Space.* New York: Routledge, 1997.

Lipsitz, George. *The Possessive Investment in Whiteness.* Philadelphia, PA: Temple University Press, 1998.

Locke, Peter R., and Steven C. Mann. *Do Professional Traders Exhibit Loss Realization Aversion?* Washington, DC: Commodity Futures Trading Commission, 1999.

Luhmann, Niklas. *Risk, a Sociological Theory.* New York: A. de Gruyter, 1993.

———. "Describing the Future." In *Observations on Modernity,* 63–74. Stanford, CA: Stanford University Press, 1998.

Lupton, Deborah. 1995. "The Embodied Computer/User." *Body and Society* 1, nos. 3–4 (1995): 97–112.

———. *Risk.* New York: Routledge, 1999.

Lyng, Stephen. "Edgework: A Social Psychological Analysis of Voluntary Risk Taking." *American Journal of Sociology* 95, no. 4 (1990): 851–86.

Mackay, Charles. *Extraordinary Popular Delusions and the Madness of Crowds.* Boston: L. C. Page, 1974.

MacKenzie, Donald. "Physics and Finance: S-Terms and Modern Finance as a Topic for Science Studies." *Science, Technology and Human Values* 26, no. 2 (2001): 115–44.

———. "Social Connectivities in Global Financial Markets." *Environment and Planning: Society and Space* 22 (2004): 83–101.

MacKenzie, Donald, and Yuval Millo. "Constructing a Market, Performing Theory: The Historical Sociology of a Financial Derivatives Exchange." *American Journal of Sociology* 109, no. 1 (2003): 107–45.

Malinowski, Bronislaw. *Argonauts of the Western Pacific.* 1922. Reprint, Prospect Heights, IL: Waveland Press, 1984.

Malkiel, Burton Gordon. *A Random Walk Down Wall Street.* New York: W. W. Norton, 1996.

Maurer, Bill. "Complex Subjects: Offshore Finance, Complexity Theory, and the Dispersion of the Modern." *Socialist Review* 25, nos. 3–4 (1994): 113–45.

———. *Mutual Life, Ltd: Islamic Banking, Alternative Currencies, Lateral Reason.* Princeton, NJ: Princeton University Press, 2005.

Mauss, Marcel. "The Mandatory Expression of Sentiments." Unpublished manuscript. L. Wacquant, ed. and trans. 1921.

McDowell, Linda. "Body Work: Heterosexual Gender Performances in City Workplaces." In *Mapping Desire,* ed. D. Bell and G. Valentine, 75–98. London: Routledge, 1995.

———. *Capital Culture: Gender at Work in the City.* Malden, MA: Blackwell, 1997.

Miller, Daniel. 1998. "Conclusion: A Theory of Virtualism." In Carrier and Miller, *Virtualism,* 187–217.

Miller, Donald L. *City of the Century: The Epic of Chicago and the Making of America.* New York: Touchstone, 1996.

Mitchell, Richard G. *Mountain Experience: The Psychology and Sociology of Adventure.* Chicago: University of Chicago Press, 1983.

Miyazaki, Hirokazu. "The Temporalities of the Market." *American Anthropologist* 105, no. 2 (2003): 255–65.

Murphy, John. *Technical Analysis of the Financial Markets.* New York: New York Institute of Finance, 1999.

Noble, David F. *A World without Women: The Christian Clerical Culture of Western Science*. New York: Oxford University Press, 1993.

Norris, Frank. *The Pit: A Story of Chicago*. 1902. Reprint, New York: Doubleday Page, 1994.

Offner, Avner. "Between the Gift and the Market: The Economy of Regard." *Economic History Review* 50 (1997): 450–76.

Olds, Kris, and Nigel Thrift. "Cultures on the Brink: Reengineering the Soul of Capitalism—On a Global Scale." In *Global Assemblages: Technology, Politics, and Ethics as Anthropological Problems*, ed. A. Ong and S. J. Collier, 270–90. Malden, MA: Blackwell, 2005.

O'Malley, Pat. "Risk and Responsibility." In Barry, Osborne, and Rose, *Foucault and Political Reason*, 189–209.

———. "Uncertain Subjects: Risks, Liberalism, and Contract." *Economy and Society* 29 (2000): 460–84.

———. "Moral Uncertainties: Contract Law and Distinctions between Speculation, Gambling and Insurance." In *Risk and Morality*, ed. R. V. Ericson and A. Doyle, 231–257. Toronto: University of Toronto Press, 2003.

Ong, Aihwa. *Flexible Citizenship: The Cultural Logics of Transnationality*. Durham, NC: Duke University Press, 1999.

———. *Buddha Is Hiding: Refugees, Citizenship, the New America*. Berkeley and Los Angeles: University of California Press, 2003.

Palmer, Catherine. "'Shit Happens': The Selling of Risk in Extreme Sports." *Australian Journal of Anthropology* 13, no. 3 (2000): 323–36.

Pinch, Trevor, and Wiebe E. Bijker. "The Social Construction of Facts and Artifacts; or How the Sociology of Science and the Sociology of Technology Might Benefit Each Other." In W. Bijker, T. P. Hughes, and T. Pinch, *Social Construction of Technological Systems*, 17–49.

Poovey, Mary. *A History of the Modern Fact: Problems of Knowledge in the Sciences of Wealth and Society*. Chicago: University of Chicago Press, 1998.

———. "Residual Materialities." Unpublished manuscript. 2004.

Porter, Theodore. *Trust in Numbers: The Pursuit of Objectivity in Science and Public Life*. Princeton, NJ: Princeton University Press, 1995.

Power, Michael. *The Audit Society: Rituals of Verification*. New York: Oxford University Press, 1997.

Preda, Alex. "On Ticks and Tapes: Financial Knowledge, Communicative Practices, and Information Technologies on Nineteenth-Century Financial Markets." Paper presented at New York Conference on the Social Studies of Finance, Columbia University, May 3–4, 2002.

Pryke, M. "An International City Going 'Global': Spatial Change in the City of London." *Environment and Planning D: Society and Space* 9 (1991): 197–222.

Rabinow, Paul. *French Modern: Norms and Forms of the Social Environment*. Chicago: University of Chicago Press, 1995.

———. "Representations Are Social Facts." In *Essays in the Anthropology of Reason*, 29–58. Princeton, NJ: Princeton University Press, 1996.

———. *Ethics: Subjectivity and Truth*. Vol. 1. New York: New Press, 1997.

———. "Midst Anthropology's Problems." *Cultural Anthropology* 17, no. 2 (2002): 135–50.

———. *Anthropos Today: Reflections on Modern Equipment.* Princeton, NJ: Princeton University Press, 2003.

Riles, Annelise. "Property as Legal Knowledge: Means and Ends." *Journal of the Royal Anthropological Institute* 10, no. 4 (2004): 755–976.

Ross, Andrew. *No-Collar: The Humane Workplace and Its Hidden Costs.* New York: Basic Books, 2003.

Sahlins, Marshall. *Stone Age Economics.* Chicago: Aldine Atherton, 1972.

Salzinger, Leslie. *Genders in Production: Making Workers in Mexico's Global Factories.* Berkeley and Los Angeles: University of California Press, 2003.

Sassen, Saskia. *Losing Control? Sovereignty in an Age of Globalization.* New York: Columbia University Press, 1996.

———. *The Global City.* Princeton, NJ: Princeton University Press, 2001.

Schorske, Carl E. *Fin-de-siècle Vienna: Politics and Culture.* New York: Vintage Books, 1981. Orig. pub. 1961.

Schumpeter, Joseph. *Capitalism, Socialism and Democracy.* New York: Harper & Row, 1950. Orig. pub. 1942.

Sennett, Richard. *Flesh and Stone: The Body and the City in Western Civilization.* Boston: Faber and Faber, 1994.

———. *Corrosion of Character: The Personal Consequences of Work in the New Capitalism.* New York: W. W. Norton, 1998.

Shapin, Steven. *A Social History of Truth: Civility and Science in Seventeenth-Century England.* Chicago: University of Chicago Press, 1994.

Simmel, Georg. *The Philosophy of Money.* 1907. Reprint, New York: Routledge, 1990.

———. "Domination." In *Georg Simmel on Individuality and Social Forms,* ed. D. N. Levine. 1908. Reprint, Chicago: University of Chicago, 1971.

———. "The Stranger." In *Georg Simmel on Individuality and Social Forms,* ed. D. N. Levine, 143–49. 1908. Reprint, Chicago: University of Chicago Press, 1971.

Simon, Jonathan. "Taking Risks: Extreme Sports and the Embrace of Risk in Advanced Liberal Societies." In Baker and Simon, *Embracing Risk,* 177–207. Chicago: University of Chicago Press, 2002.

Simpson, Joe. *Touching the Void.* New York: HarperCollins, 1988.

Sinclair, Upton. *The Jungle.* 1906. Reprint, New York: Penguin, 1985.

Smith, Charles W. *Auctions: The Social Construction of Value.* New York: Free Press, 1989.

Smith, Roy, and Walter Ingo. *Global Banking.* New York: Oxford University Press, 2003.

Solman, Paul. "Chicago May Consider End to Open Outcry." *Financial Times,* June 20, 1998.

Strange, Susan. *Casino Capitalism.* New York: Manchester University Press, 1984.

Strathern, Marilyn. "Cutting the Network." *Journal of the Royal Anthropological Institute* 2, no. 3 (1996): 517–35.

Suchman, Lucy. *Plans and Situated Actions: The Problem of Human-Machine Communication.* New York: Cambridge University Press, 1987.

Suttles, Gerald. "Introduction." In Mitchell, *Mountain Experience,* viii–xii.

Taylor, Charles Henry. *History of the Board of Trade of the City of Chicago.* Chicago: Robert O. Law, 1917.

Taylor, Peter J. *World City Network: A Global Urban Analysis.* New York: Routledge, 2004.

Thrift, Nigel. *Knowing Capitalism.* London: Sage, 2005.

Tichi, Cecelia. *Shifting Gears: Technology, Literature, Culture in Modernist America.* Chapel Hill: University of North Carolina Press, 1987.

Useem, Michael. "Business and Politics in the United States and the United Kingdom." In *Structures of Capital,* ed. S. Zukin and P. DiMaggio, 263–91. New York: Cambridge University Press, 1989.

Urban, Greg. *Metaculture: How Culture Moves Through the World.* Minneapolis: University of Minnesota Press, 2001.

Wacquant, Loïc. 1998. "The Prizefighter's Three Bodies." *Ethnos* 63, no. 3 (1998): 325–52.

Wall Street Journal. "Really Big Board." April 22, 2005.

Weber, Max. "Science as a Vocation." In Gerth and Mills, *From Max Weber,* 129–58.

———. *Economy and Society.* Vol. 1. Berkeley and Los Angeles: University of California Press, 1978.

———. *The Protestant Ethic and the Spirit of Capitalism.* Trans. T. Parsons. New York: Routledge, 1992. Orig. pub. in 1930.

Weiner, Annette. "Inalienable Wealth." *American Ethnologist* 12, no. 2 (1985): 210–27.

White, Harrison. "Where Do Markets Come From?" *American Journal of Sociology* 87 (1981): 517–47.

Willis, Carol. *Form Follows Finance: Skyscrapers and Skylines in New York and Chicago.* New York: Princeton Architectural Press, 1995.

Willis, Paul E. *Learning to Labor: How Working-Class Kids Get Working-Class Jobs.* New York: Columbia University Press, 1981.

Woolgar, Steve. "Configuring the User: The Case of Usability Trials." In Law, *Sociology of Monsters,* 58–97.

Young, Michael, and Peter Willmott. *Family and Kinship in East London.* 1957. Reprint, Berkeley and Los Angeles: University of California Press, 1992.

Zelizer, Viviana. *The Social Meaning of Money.* Princeton, NJ: Princeton University Press, 1997.